T0339428

"Pope's *Sustainable Crowdfunding* is an excellent guide to understanding crowd-sourcing, seeking funding, and developing a fundable proposal. It provides useful cases and strategies for teaching crowdsourcing. *Sustainable Crowdfunding* uniquely supports winning campaigns after funding with strategies for bringing plans into reality."

—**Michael J. Salvo**, *Purdue University, USA*

"Accessible prose and intriguing case studies, this text fills a void in public rhetorics scholarship. Pope offers a novel framework for understanding crowdfunding as sustainable social justice-aligned coalitional action through concerted attention to UX and XA. Chapter-concluding discussion questions are an especially useful resource for tech comm educators."

—**Jessica Clements**, *Whitworth University, USA*

SUSTAINABLE CROWDFUNDING

This book analyzes the communication and writing strategies necessary to craft and maintain ongoing crowdfunding campaigns to support businesses, nonprofits, artists, and others.

Drawing on theory from technical communication and user experience, as well as mixed methods research, and text mining, this book takes an evidence-based approach to understanding the successes and failures of crowdfunding campaigns. It examines campaigns across a range of platforms, including Kickstarter, GoFundMe, IndieGoGo, and Patreon. The book breaks down successful exemplar campaigns that have proven long-term success to show what has worked and why, giving readers a solid foundation to research and create a campaign of their own.

Sustainable Crowdfunding serves as a supplemental text for courses in technical and professional communication, user experience, communication research methods, and digital marketing, and will be of interest to both communication scholars and advanced crowdfunding professionals. Online interactive tools for qualitative and quantitative analysis are available at https://rhetoricaldata.com. A stop word appendix for the book can be accessed at www.routledge.com/9781032312736

Adam R. Pope is Assistant Professor and Director of the Graduate Certificate in Technical Writing and Public Rhetorics at the University of Arkansas, USA.

ATTW Series in Technical and Professional Communication

Tharon Howard, Series Editor

For additional information on this series please, visit www.routledge.com/ATTW-Series-in-Technical-and-Professional-Communication/book-series/ATTW, and for information on other Routledge titles, visit www.routledge.com.

SUSTAINABLE CROWDFUNDING

Research-Based Analysis for Communication Campaigns

Adam R. Pope

Routledge
Taylor & Francis Group

NEW YORK AND LONDON

Designed cover image: Orbon Alija/© Getty Images

First published 2023
by Routledge
605 Third Avenue, New York, NY 10158

and by Routledge
4 Park Square, Milton Park, Abingdon, Oxon, OX14 4RN

Routledge is an imprint of the Taylor & Francis Group, an informa business

© 2023 Adam R. Pope

The right of Adam R. Pope to be identified as author of this work has
been asserted in accordance with sections 77 and 78 of the Copyright,
Designs and Patents Act 1988.

All rights reserved. No part of this book may be reprinted or reproduced
or utilised in any form or by any electronic, mechanical, or other
means, now known or hereafter invented, including photocopying and
recording, or in any information storage or retrieval system, without
permission in writing from the publishers.

Trademark notice: Product or corporate names may be trademarks or
registered trademarks, and are used only for identification and explanation
without intent to infringe.

Library of Congress Cataloging-in-Publication Data
Names: Pope, Adam R., author.
Title: Sustainable crowdfunding: research-based analysis for communication
    campaigns / Adam R. Pope.
Description: New York, NY: Routledge, 2023. | Series: ATTW series
    in technical and professional communication, 2639-3085 | Includes
    bibliographical references and index.
Identifiers: LCCN 2022061083 (print) | LCCN 2022061084 (ebook) |
    ISBN 9781032312811 (hbk) | ISBN 9781032312736 (pbk) | ISBN
    9781003308966 (ebk)
Subjects: LCSH: Business communication. | Business writing. | Crowd
    funding.
Classification: LCC HF5718 .P668 2023 (print) | LCC HF5718 (ebook) |
    DDC 658.4/5—dc23/eng/20230407
LC record available at https://lccn.loc.gov/2022061083
LC ebook record available at https://lccn.loc.gov/2022061084

ISBN: 9781032312811 (hbk)
ISBN: 9781032312736 (pbk)
ISBN: 9781003308966 (ebk)

DOI: 10.4324/9781003308966

Typeset in Bembo
by Apex CoVantage, LLC

Access the Support Material: www.routledge.com/9781032312736

For Granny Mac, Mom and Dad, Emily, Miles,
Amelia, and Noah

CONTENTS

INTRODUCTION

This is a book about sustainable crowdfunding, a coalitional fundraising approach that provides an alternative to traditional financial institutions and their attendant gatekeeping on project and entrepreneurial success. As you navigate this text, we'll move from defining crowdfunding as a site for potential coalitional action for technical communicators to framing the work of technical writing in crowdfunding as experience architecture (XA).

As we go through the book, we'll take time to coordinate our investigations into the history of crowdfunding, the theories behind crowdfunding, and case studies of successful serial crowdfunding campaigns with discussions on the practical technical writing work needed to bring these campaigns into the world. For example, we'll work in our first two chapters to frame the history and scholarship of crowdfunding before shifting to framing the genre in terms of the creation and curation of XAs.

Crowdfunding is no simple sight of inquiry, and one of the overarching goals of this study is to provide technical communicators and technical communication scholars with a broad-reaching framework to understand these campaigns and their successes. As XAs, any given campaign exists as a nexus of multiple communication channels and sites that work together to attract and then recruit a coalition of like-minded backers to provide the funding needed to make a given crowdfunding project a reality.

Crowdfunding, however, has evolved over the past decade plus to move beyond the simplistic model of "give us money to do this project," and this text aims to provide a window into the expanding scope and duration of crowdfunding in the realm of subscription-based campaigns that don't scope or limit funding to a set period but instead frame crowdfunding as an ongoing two-way relationship between a given organization or creator and the backing coalition that provides them with support.

Why a Book on Crowdfunding?

As an academic project, this text began in some ways during 2012 and 2013, the last years of my time as a Ph.D. student. As I navigated the academic job market in my final year of graduate study, a series of crowdfunding campaigns caught my eye that promised to resurrect a series of long-dead video game series and genres that held a special place in my heart. *DoubleFine Adventure, Torment: Tides of Numenera, Torment: Tides of Numenera,* and still other campaigns caught my attention as they raised, at times, millions of dollars in funding with the promise of returning classic genres of computer and video games to the market after years of neglect.

As a technical communication scholar and practitioner, these campaigns caught my eye outside of their nostalgic draw because of the potential of the crowdfunding genre to serve as a home for technical writing and communication. I realized that these companies (and many others like them in the years to come) were effectively leveraging a new genre of technical communicator, albeit one that looked and acted at times suspiciously like older existing genres like grants and proposals. Despite these differences, these new genres were different in that they publicized the project *and* crucially the process of funding and then fulfilling these projects.

Over the intervening years, I slowly began to collect data and started to theorize on what crowdfunding as a genre looked like to technical communicators. As my inbox regularly filled up with monthly updates on various gaming projects, I realized that at their core, these projects were functioning as ongoing technical communication endeavors that documented (after the initial funding was over) the process of taking the promised project and making it a reality. There were discussions of game systems; there were entire updates centered on music production and art direction, and even discussions on mundane bits like engine choice and asset creation workflows. All of it, I realized, was technical writing at the core.

Once I had a moment to breathe, professionally, I started putting my findings into the publication process, first tackling these campaigns as fundamentally affectively focused through an analysis of the gaming Kickstarter *Bloodstained* (2017) and then as a complex genre that required documentation and mapping (2018). With these two initial projects under my belt, I realized that to really get a handle on crowdfunding as a genre, I needed to expand my scope and set my sights on a book-length project.

In the process of building this book, my thinking continued to evolve as I realized that crowdfunding was more than a simple genre of technical communication that was evolving out of grant and proposal writing. Crowdfunding existed as a nexus, with campaigns preceded by extensive recruitment and coalition building and then maintained across the fulfillment process with extensive technical writing and communication within a given platform like Kickstarter with concurrent work continuing at the same sites that helped build the initial coalitional interest. These weren't simple genres, but XAs.

As I worked through the book proposal process, I also came to realize the powerful potential of crowdfunding to serve as a site of coalitional action and social justice, with crowdfunding platforms often serving as alternative routes to publication and production for historically marginalized groups that can encounter gatekeeping and prejudice in the traditional funding process.

During all of this, I remained fundamentally convinced that at its core, crowdfunding is and will continue to be a genre that fundamentally exists through and because of technical communication. This book, then, is an attempt to map out the scope, scale, and theory of that work for future technical communication scholars and practitioners.

In carrying out this work, I have been particularly aware of my own positionality and privilege. As a white, neurodivergent, cisgender man in the American South, I write from a position of relative privilege. I have attempted to leverage my position in this book to share these narratives of crowdfunding, especially crowdfunding that promotes social justice among historically marginalized and multiply marginalized communities. I have also attempted to capture how historically marginalized creators have leveraged crowdfunding to bypass traditional funding gatekeepers, including those marginalized by their race, culture, and neurodiversity.

Chapter Overview

In Chapter 1, we'll define what exactly crowdfunding is, map a brief history of the genre and its historical antecedents, and lay out the extant scholarship on the genre in technical communication (with some additional analysis of scholarship outside of tech comm).

In Chapter 2, we'll move on from a general definition of crowdfunding and frame the genre as fundamentally existing as sustained XAs while providing researchers and practitioners with a framework for analyzing successful crowdfunding exemplars to plan their own forays into the genre.

Chapter 3 focuses on the political and practical implications of the various crowdfunding platforms available to creators, framing these discussions through theories of technical communication while providing teams looking to build their own campaign with an analytic framework for their choices.

Chapter 4 plots out the theories and practical processes needed to build and then implement a crowdfunding campaign, beginning not with the crafting of a given campaign and its deliverables but instead with a broad-reaching analysis of how a given campaign builds the engagement and coalition needed to launch a successful project.

Chapter 5 then turns to provide us with two competing visions of what the start of a series of successful discrete campaigns can look like in the crowdfunding space through the lens of two case studies: Lady Tarot Cards and The STEAM Chasers, both Kickstarter campaigns that would spawn multiple successful follow-up projects for their creators.

Chapter 6 shifts our focus to nonprofit crowdfunding and provides an analysis of how interconnected crowdfunding campaigns can succeed by juggling social media production, subscription crowdfunding, and traditional discrete campaigns through the lens of the work of Rancho Relaxo, a nonprofit animal rescue and charity.

Chapter 7 brings our discussion to a close with a look at the work of sustaining crowdfunding across multiple campaigns, tying together the strands of thought in the preceding chapters with a discussion on how the different aspects and avenues of crowdfunding can coalesce into what is fundamentally at its core a technical writing project.

Each chapter ends with a brief summary and some suggestions for future discussions.

A Note on Sources

In several chapters, as I trace the evolution of crowdfunding over time as well as the antecedent examples of crowdfunding, I rely on tech magazine and blog reporting to track events as they have unfolded over the past few years. This research work in the tech press and other online references has been necessary to track the evolution of crowdfunding over time, as the genre has developed at a blistering pace that many times academic publications simply can't keep up with. When possible, I've tried to rely on academic sources and summaries of happenings in crowdfunding, but at times, these secondary sources play an important role in forming our understanding of how these genres have shifted over time and been presented to the public in the popular and tech sector press.

In addition to these sources, I also rely heavily on the content produced and curated by the crowdfunding platforms and adjacent crowdfunding services and blogs. Often, these platforms are some of the only sources of information on their inner workings and policies, content often supplemented by case studies and post-mortems from creators on their own experiences and strategies on these same platforms.

Content Warning

Some of the content, as well as some of the sources, referenced in this book contain subject matter that may be upsetting or problematic for some audiences. The text includes references to child exploitation as well as the exploitation of sex workers, as well as descriptions of animal abuse (these are limited primarily to the case study narrative from Chapter 6).

1
DEFINING CROWDFUNDING

In this first chapter, we'll sketch out the definition, history, and origins of crowdfunding as a method of funding, focusing on the potential of crowdfunding to serve as a basis for coalitional action that can provide alternative routes to traditional funding sources, sources that often reject novel and unusual projects and that have a history of rejecting projects from historically marginalized and multiply marginalized individuals. This presentation of crowdfunding as an alternative to traditional gatekeepers in the business world in particular has become important to the ethos and argumentation of many campaigns, and even to the platforms themselves that support and define crowdfunding.

What Is Crowdfunding?

What exactly is crowdfunding? What does it do, how does it differ from existing methods of startup funding, and how is it even different from, say, a local National Public Radio station's annual fall fundraising drive? Before we go any further, I want to answer these questions and define the boundaries of what we mean when we say "crowdfunding" or talk about crowdfunding campaigns. In doing so, I'll rely primarily on some of the definitional work done by Ethan Mollick, an early researcher of crowdfunding known for his collaboration with Kickstarter for their Fulfillment Report.

Defining Crowdfunding and Its Scope

I begin with Ethan Mollick's (2014) definition from his influential early research on Kickstarter. Mollick's work began the formal scholarly definition of crowdfunding and what success looked like in a quantitative sense at a point where

DOI: 10.4324/9781003308966-1

little formal academic knowledge had been generated on the subject (p. 1). Mollick defines crowdfunding as "efforts by entrepreneurial individuals and groups—cultural, social, and for-profit—to fund their ventures by drawing on relatively small contributions from a relatively large number of individuals using the internet, without standard financial intermediaries" (p. 2). Situating crowdfunding firmly within an entrepreneurial tradition, Mollick's definition relies on a contrast between crowdfunding and more traditional mechanisms for funding projects such as angel investors or friends and family funding. In Mollick's framing, crowdfunding serves, at least in part, as a rejection of the traditional funding mechanisms for entrepreneurial enterprises through a turn to distributed funding. Read differently, crowdfunding can be seen as a way around the gatekeeping traditional fundraising avenues bring with them. Though I'll come back to this later in the chapter, it is worth noting that the gatekeeping function of traditional financial intermediaries is significant in the unequal success that many multiply marginalized creators and their organizations face (Jones, 2017).

For Mollick, crowdfunding is influenced by, but separate and distinct from, crowdsourcing and micro-financing (p. 2). Though I agree with Mollick on the difference between the crowdsourcing and crowdfunding, I believe there is some overlap in the ways that crowdfunding is talked about in certain entrepreneurial circles that rhetorically situates it closely with the quasi-magical thinking put forward in pop business texts like *Wikinomics* (Tapscott & Williams, 2006) that are worth discussing. In texts like *Wikinomics*, crowdsourcing is pitched as a low-effort and high-reward approach to leveraging online contributors for business success. Crowdfunding can at times be pitched in the same way in some circles, but nothing could be further from the truth. Crowdfunding isn't a magical panacea, and it isn't a shortcut to success for projects in need of funding. It is a complex, multifaceted technical writing project that builds and then sustains a compelling user experience across multiple channels over multiple months and even years. And, outside of outliers, research shows that crowdfunding campaigns usually either succeed by slim margins or fail with a massive funding shortfall (Mollick, 2014, p. 2). With that said, serial crowdfunding campaigns, that is campaigns that follow successful campaigns, show markedly better success rates (Butticè et al., 2017), with Kickstarter's early figures showing that the success rate of follow-up campaigns as high as 73%, the success rates continuing to rise with each subsequent campaign up to a staggering 91% in a sixth campaign (Gallagher & Salfen, 2015). This phenomenon of serial success reflects an important aspect of crowdfunding, one this text is built upon: crowdfunding as a sustainable income stream that relies on the social capital and sustained user experience serial campaigns provide.

While crowdfunding can be used to start a novel venture, Mollick notes that creators often come to campaigns with a variety of objectives in mind (p. 3). For example, a creator might use a crowdfunding campaign to prove the worth of an idea to a group of potential investors in the traditional startup world, especially when that idea has been rejected by those same authorities. In fact, some campaigns build their entire rhetorical appeal around that sense of industry/ gatekeeper rejection (Igarashi, n.d.). Crowdfunding can also be used by creators to test an idea quickly with minimal buy-in from the creator. In fact, the concept of testing the market for a product via crowdfunding has been used by some of the largest companies out there, including General Electric with their crowd-funding campaign for their Opal Icemaker on Indiegogo, a campaign that was explicitly tied to a desire to test the market viability of the product before committing to manufacture (General Electric, 2015). For smaller organizations and individual creators, crowdfunding can also help mitigate financial risk in certain types of product genres. For example, web comic artists often leverage crowd-funding campaigns for print runs of their comics, removing the risk of traditional publishing models where a full run of comics is ordered and then must be sold via online and convention sales to break even or make a profit (Guigar et al., 2008). Finally, crowdfunding campaigns can be leveraged as a marketing tool (Mollick, 2014, p. 3), allowing creators to build excitement for nascent projects and create a community around them before launch in a process that shares many similarities with the open development model that has been popularized in video game development (Thominet, 2020).

Beyond defining crowdfunding and the goals of founders, Mollick (2014) and other scholars (Burkett, 2011) typify campaigns by their goal/focus. For our purposes, I use Mollick's four-part breakdown for crowdfunding campaigns: reward-based crowdfunding, patronage crowdfunding, lending crowdfunding, and investment crowdfunding (p. 2). Reward-based crowdfunding is exemplified by industry leader Kickstarter, where campaigns are tied to a tiered reward system. Patronage-based crowdfunding is closer to the GoFundMe, Patreon, OnlyFans, Buy Me a Coffee, and other similar platforms where donations aren't explicitly tied to a reward of some type, though Patreon offers tiers of donation and access that can mirror reward structures. Investment-based crowdfunding focuses on investment in the vein of traditional startup funding and is more tightly regulated and controlled in the United States. Fig.co, an early offshoot of video game crowdfunding on Kickstarter, is an example of the approach (though Fig is now part of Republic). Lending crowdfunding is an offshoot of micro-financial lending and falls outside the scope of this book project. Of all the models, the most common by far are reward-based and patronage crowdfunding, with the remaining two serving more niche roles in the wider crowdfunding industry.

When looking at typologies of crowdfunding, an important aspect of reward-based and patronage-based crowdfunding (the focus of this book and much of the industry) is the relationship these types of crowdfunding create between the creator of a project and their constituency. Rhetorically, the two blend together by providing either a sense of ownership in the creation of a project or in terms of motivating donors/backers through the promise of a reward of some type. Both patronage and reward-based sites offer different tiers of access to content, for example, based on the level of donation, and sites that are primarily rewards-based such as Kickstarter often offer non-reward donation tiers for projects. In addition, research shows that many backers of even reward-based crowdfunding campaigns have patronage as a primary goal of their activities (Edelstein, 2016). Both types of crowdfunding can provide backers with the ability to cultivate the types of projects and ventures they want to see in the world as activists (Greenberg & Mollick, 2017) or patrons in the more traditional sense of the term. In addition, both types can provide content or rewards that are tied to levels of funding, even if that reward is tied to simply giving a donation. Even GoFundMe provides potential donors with guidance on how to thank backers, with suggestions not limited to providing handmade physical gifts in return for donations made (GoFundMe Team, 2016).

One other important aspect of crowdfunding that can't be overlooked before going further is the role that intermediaries play in crowdfunding. Though Mollick (2014) explicitly decouples crowdfunding from traditional financial intermediaries, that isn't to say that intermediaries don't exist. Intermediaries are often essential to successful crowdfunding (Burkett, 2011), though the occasional success can be found outside of platform-based crowdfunding if an organization has a large enough infrastructure and reach, such as in the case of Wikipedia (p. 68). Crowdfunding platforms, as I will lay out later in Chapter 3, serve an essential role in curating and shaping the space available for the compelling user experiences that motivate backers and keep backers engaged enough to create sustained success on crowdfunding platforms. For example, even organizations with established donor and charity programs and massive endowments such as Yale or Harvard leverage crowdfunding platforms like GiveCampus to facilitate campaigns for their schools (GiveCampus, n.d.).

A Working Definition of Crowdfunding

Having sketched out the variations of crowdfunding and the role that intermediaries play across the various types of funding available, we can settle on our own working definition that we can leverage moving forward. Borrowing from Mollick (2014) and Burkett (2011), I define crowdfunding as it will be referenced during the rest of this book as follows:

> Crowdfunding is a funding approach that replaces traditional financial intermediaries with a many-to-one model of funding usually carried out on crowdfunding—specific platforms where specific projects and causes are funded by a number of individual donors providing donations in exchange for a user experience that consists of a combination of information, services, or physical deliverables that are distributed to donors via the services provided by the project's crowdfunding platform or another intermediary.

This definition underscores the essential nature of the exchange of information that comes with a crowdfunding pledge. Even in situations where donors are not signing up for actual rewards, their status as donors makes them privy to extra information and updates on the progress of the campaign they have backed or the organization/individual they're supporting via patronage on a service like Only-Fans or Patreon. Even in cases that fall toward the edges of this definition, such as online charity leader GoFundMe, campaigns to provide medical support or financial support are built around a system of updates by those hosting the campaign, as we'll see in Chapter 6's case study of the Rancho Relaxo animal rescue. Information exchange is an inherent part of the genre and how these platforms present it.

In addition to information exchange, the definition highlights the unavoidable impact that platforms have on crowdfunding enterprises. When I discuss platforms, I rely on Tarleton Gillespie's (2010) explication of platforms as online locations/services that can be read as interacting on computational, figurative, architectural, and political levels (p. 352). As I will elaborate on in Chapter 3, the platform that hosts a given crowdfunding campaign is essential in defining what the campaign consists of, how it self-presents, and the user experience it offers to backers while also mediating the visibility or relative invisibility of a given campaign on the platform.

A third important facet of the aforementioned definition is the linking of crowdfunding to funding a specific project or cause. Crowdfunding campaigns are tied to content creation: they result in the creation of a good, service, or completion of a project or artistic work. Charity fundraising platforms like GoFundMe tie campaigns to projects, fiscal support, or medical support. Indiegogo and Kickstarter link their campaigns to specific products or services. Finally, subscription-based services like Patreon, Buy Me a Coffee, or OnlyFans tie their platforms to supporting "creators" and their creations (though as we'll see in Chapter 6, non-profits also use these services). Regardless of focus, there is a specificity of focus in crowdfunding that is often guided by the given platform and the exceptions the platforms set and control.

Are Nonprofit Funding Drives Crowdfunding?

Having defined what crowdfunding is, I would like to take a moment to identify what crowdfunding *isn't* before we go any further in our discussions. Some immediate similarities come to mind between crowdfunding as an approach and the approach taken by public fundraising drives by many nonprofits, including local National Public Radio stations in the United States, as well as international charities like the United Way and various instantiations of the Red Cross/Red Crescent. Many of these organizations hold public calls for donations, supporting themselves via the aggregated impact of many individual donors. These campaigns and their long histories beg the question: are these also crowdfunding?

By our definition, the answer is generally no. While charity drives share a great deal in common with crowdfunding, they do not normally rely on a platform-driven model for collecting funds, but they tend to be general rather than venture or project-based, and they often are not directly linked to the exchange of information. So, the normal public crowdfunding drives in communities by local and national organizations are often *not* crowdfunding per se, though they rely on crowds of donors.

Having noted this difference, I would point out that just because these drives aren't crowdfunding doesn't mean that can't be crowdfunding. In many cases, as I hope will become evident through this book, crowdfunding can offer real and important advantages to nonprofits that rely on traditional giving models and the associated rhetoric and genres that come with them. Yes, traditional fundraising can be powerful—the infamous Sarah McLachlan ad for the American Society for the Prevention of Cruelty to Animals raised over $30 million in its first run (Strom, 2008)—but as this book will show, sustainable relationships, coalitions, and user experiences created by crowdfunding represent compelling additions to nonprofit approaches for funding as well as new ways of going about doing the work of an organization that can build and sustain a compelling user experience for donors that keeps them engaged and eager to contribute.

Crowdfunding History

Having sketched out a general definition of crowdfunding as well as our own working definition, I'd like to move on to tracing the history of the genre and its platforms, followed by a survey of the early research findings, before moving on to our eventual end goal: situating crowdfunding as a coalitional model of fundraising. The history of crowdfunding can be divided into three phases: pre-online crowdfunding projects, early online crowdfunding (before and during the advent of online platforms), and the modern crowdfunding platform period (which has lately started to lean heavily into patronage-style crowdfunding that was less common in the early days). Each of these phases can be seen as addressing and shaping the idea of crowdfunding, though I would hesitate to say that there is any real lineage that can be traced across the entire history of crowdfunding.

Though much of the modern understanding of crowdfunding revolves around the advent of Internet-based funding platforms that began to arise around the turn of the century, crowdfunding as a social phenomenon can be traced at least as far back as the late 1800s. Whether we go that far back depends on the scope of our discussion and understanding of crowdfunding as a digitally native genre of funding or we view crowdfunding as a broader approach to seeking resources for a project. If only to underscore the role that platforms play in modern crowdfunding, I've opted to include a regularly cited pre-cursor to online crowdfunding in our discussion of history.

Pre-online Crowdfunding

In the United States, the first major crowdfunding campaign is arguably the campaign to fund the pedestal for the Statue of Liberty in New York City (Zhao et al., 2019). Started in 1885 by Joseph Pulitzer in his newspaper *New York World*, the campaign covered a shortfall in funding for the statue's base and allowed the statue to remain in New York via the contributions of individual donors ("The Statue of Liberty and America's Crowdfunding Pioneer," 2013). Instead of an online platform, the campaign was carried out via newspapers and other analog methods of campaigning.

The statue had been gifted by France and was to be installed in the United States, but the gift of the statue did not include a corresponding base for the statue to be displayed upon. The statue sat in crates for over a year without an actual pedestal or location to be installed (National Park Service, 2015b). The American Committee for the Statue of Liberty was tasked with providing this funding but was unable to meet their funding goal (National Park Service, 2015a). As it appeared that New York would be unable to provide for the statue (the state governor at the time, Grover Cleveland, refused to allow the city of New York to pay) and because Congress was unable to provide a funding package, other cities including Baltimore, Boston, San Francisco, and Philadelphia began to offer to relocate the gifted statue and pay for a pedestal ("The Statue of Liberty and America's Crowdfunding Pioneer," 2013). Pulitzer made a public entreaty via his newspaper, connecting the campaign and statue rhetorically to the people of France and the people of America, as opposed to the millionaires and the rich:

> We must raise the money! The World is the people's paper, and now it appeals to the people to come forward and raise the money. The $250,000 that the making of the Statue cost was paid in by the masses of the French people- by the working men, the tradesmen, the shop girls, the artisans- by all, irrespective of class or condition. Let us respond in like manner. Let us not wait for the millionaires to give us this money. It is not a gift from the millionaires of France to the millionaires of America, but a gift of the whole people of France to the whole people of America.

While the display of the statue itself might seem to be the reward, Pulitzer went so far as to pledge to print the name of each individual donor on the front page of his paper, providing public recognition and a reward of sorts to backers. In addition, during the campaign, the paper would run human interest stories that were small narratives of individual donors such as children (National Park Service, 2015b). The eventual swell of small donations matches the modern crowdfunding approach quite well. Between the explicit reward in the case of the front-page mention and the ongoing updates via the human interest stories, the campaign, and its unified platform (*The New York World*), this early crowdfunding campaign mirrored the eventual genre's development into the modern platform-centered model we see today.

Before we move on, I also want to note the explicitly coalitional framing of the narrative in the pitch from Pulitzer. The statue, in his words, came not from the rich of France but instead from the common people, and the campaign for the statue in Pulitzer's framing is the same—a project by the people for the people without the intervention of the millionaires of the day. As we'll see toward the end of the chapter, this coalitional framing and language is an important precursor to the coalitional potential of modern crowdfunding projects.

Early Online Crowdfunding

Moving beyond the historical antecedent in the campaign for the Statue of Liberty, most modern crowdfunding narratives start between 1997 and 2000 and focus on the music industry (Gamble et al., 2017; Strähle & Bulling, 2018; Zhao et al., 2019) as the impetus for the earliest online crowdfunding campaigns. The earliest music campaign by some accounts is the informal one for the British band Marillion that raised over $60,000 to finance a reunion tour in 1997 (Bradley & Luong, 2014, pp. 96–97). After that initial success, the band would go on to fully finance the recording of a studio album released in 2001 by selling copies of the album to fans before the actual recording and release. The album was sold for £15, and around 12,000 fans bought the preorder to fund the album (*Marillion Fans to the Rescue*, 2001).

In the same year that Marillion's crowdfunded album experiment was released, the first commercial crowdfunding site, artistShare, was launched to provide a platform for musicians to release projects backed by fans (About Us, n.d.). Since 2003, the site has supported 33 Grammy-nominated projects and 11 Grammy-winning projects. In the site's current format, the language used to self-describe the platform foregrounds the experiential angle of crowdfunding and the ability to both contribute to the creation of new artistic projects while concurrently getting to experience that creation through curated updates.

The Big 3: Indiegogo, Kickstarter, GoFundMe

Some seven years later in 2008, Indiegogo was launched, with Kickstarter following in 2009 (Zhao et al., 2019) and GoFundMe in 2010 (Mac, n.d.). Though several other smaller crowdfunding ventures were founded and operated in the space between the first Marillion campaign and the founding of Indiegogo, Kickstarter, and GoFundMe, these three platforms in many ways have come to define the modern crowdfunding space, with other platforms operating in contrast or opposition to these three. So, we'll cover each platform's history in a bit more depth.

Indiegogo was founded in 2008 by Danae Ringelmann, Eric Schell, and Slava Rubin (though some accounts cite 2007 as the original date, I am using the date provided by Indiegogo's own site). Each founder came into the project with some frustrations around venture capital and fundraising. Ringelmann attempted to produce a play but was unable to raise enough funding. Schell had been frustrated fundraising for a Chicago theater company, and Rubin had been raising money to cure multiple myeloma, a disease that took his father's life (*Learn About Indiegogo | Indiegogo*, n.d.). Indiegogo's focus from the start was on perk or reward-based crowdfunding that provided backers with incentives for funding the success of a given campaign (Townsend, 2016).

During its early years, Indiegogo was also prominently featured by the Obama White House in various initiatives. Shortly after its founding, Indiegogo featured prominently in President Obama's 2011 Startup America campaign to generate entrepreneurial activity and job growth during the protracted recovery from the Great Recession (Ringelmann, 2011). As late as 2014, the company was cited in Obama's speeches and taking part in the White House Maker Faire (AJ, 2014).

Launched in 2009, Kickstarter was also founded by a trio of founders: Perry Chenn, Yancey Strickler, and Charles Adler. The initial concept was brainstormed by Chenn in 2002 when he had attempted to raise money for a Kruder & Dorfmeister concert in New Orleans but wasn't able to raise enough funding to make it happen. At the time, Chenn imagined being able to raise money on the Internet, but only charging credit cards if the full $20,000 he'd needed was pledged. Chenn met Yancey in 2005, and shortly thereafter the duo added Adler to the team (Alderson, 2015). From 2005, the project was in development, but it took four years of work till the final launch in 2009. By 2015, Kickstarter was funding more projects annually than the US's National Endowment for the Arts.

GoFundMe was formally launched in 2010. Andrew Ballester and Brad Damphousse collaborated to create the service, and the initial development of the company was funded through its 5% fee on contributions (Tan & MacMillan, 2015). Differing from the other major players in crowdfunding, GoFundMe focused on charitable giving rather than creative projects. Within five years, the founders sold a majority of their stake to a consortium of investment groups (Mac, n.d.).

Subscription Crowdfunding

Whereas traditional crowdfunding platforms in the popular conception focus primarily on the model of donation or backing for rewards, subscription-based crowdfunding arose to provide an alternative to campaign-oriented approaches to crowdfunding. Traditional crowdfunding successes like Kickstarter and GoFundMe focus on causes and projects, and those causes and projects are filtered through a campaign model that focuses attention and donations in brief windows (though GoFundMe and Indiegogo both allow for donations after the initial period of giving in some cases). The contrast with subscription services is that donations aren't oriented around campaigns, but instead ongoing subscriptions with an expectation of content delivery (or that provide access to past content). As I have written this book, these platforms have continued to grow and represent a growing alternative to the campaign-oriented model.

Patreon for many is synonymous with the concept of subscription-based crowdfunding. The service was founded in 2013 by Jack Conte, an independent artist who was frustrated by the amount of revenue his projects earned on major tech platforms like YouTube. In particular, Conte credits the creation of the service to his music video *Pedals*, which cost him around $10,000 to create and only earned a few hundred dollars on YouTube despite a viewership in the millions (Beaumont, n.d.). Instead of focusing on singular projects and fundraising toward that goal, the original pitch for Patreon was that fans would provide an ongoing revenue stream to their favorite creators to fund the creators' passion projects (with fans of course getting an inside look into all of this, with the scope and access depending on the particular creator's tiers of subscription). Patreon received attention early on for their open policy regarding nudity, creating an economy of users who sold access to nude photos and other sexualized content on the platform (Plaugic, 2017). Over time, those policies have evolved to include specific prohibitions on certain types of erotic and sexualized content (*Benefit Guidelines | Patreon*, n.d.).

OnlyFans was founded by Tim Stokely three years after Patreon, in 2016, and the site quickly developed a reputation for catering to or serving as a hub of adults-only content. By 2020, the site had grown to over 30 million users, with numbers spiking during the early lockdowns of COVID-19. At that time, the site boasted around 420,000 creators, with around half of the material being estimated as pornographic in nature (@steadmanEveryoneMakingPorn). The influx of amateur accounts during the pandemic created some backlash among professional sex workers who leveraged the platform for income (Dickson, 2020). Later in 2020, Bella Thorne famously joined the platform promising to provide adult content, tallying up over $1 million of earnings in a single day and creating further controversy among sex workers who saw the platform as providing a safe haven for their trade free from industry exploitation and middlemen (Noor, 2020). By early 2021, the platform had over 120 million users and 1 million creators. The popularity of the platform spiked when Beyoncé included the song in a remix. In the wake of the site's growth during the pandemic, numerous celebrities joined the site, including Cardi B and Rebecca Minkoff (Ifeanyi, 2021).

In the summer of 2021, OnlyFans created a wave of backlash from creators and subscribers when it announced suddenly that it was banning sexually explicit content in October of 2021 (Lyons, 2021). The ban was reported as being precipitated by nervousness from banks and investment groups that did not want to be associated with pornography (Primack, 2021), though the chief executive officer (CEO) Tim Stokely later directly reported the cause was the company's banking partners (*OnlyFans CEO on Why It Banned Adult Content: 'The Short Answer Is Banks'—The Verge*, n.d.). Within a week, the platform reversed course and announced the ban would not take place in the face of a platform exodus (Lawler, 2021).

Founded in 2017, Buy Me a Coffee represents another turn in the crowdfunding space, the advent of virtual tipping platforms. Founded by Jijo Sunny and Joseph Sunny, the platform was designed to make supporting creators less transactional-feeling and more casual, with a self-professed goal of allowing creators to make money outside of algorithmic systems and advertising (The BMC Team, n.d.). The platform also offers subscription-based support, but in 2019 the founders suggested around 50% came from one-time donations, which the platform terms "tips" (Miller, n.d.). The result is a platform that foregrounds the ability to drop off a one-time tip or donation to creators on the platform as a token of appreciation disconnected from any subscription model.

By 2020, virtual tip jars like Buy Me a Coffee had spread to platforms as varied as Twitter, YouTube, TikTok, Twitch, and Facebook/Instagram with varying levels of percentages taken by the platforms themselves (*How Do Social Media's Virtual Tip Jar Features Compare?*, 2021). These tip jars as well as subscription-based platforms all self-promote as allowing "creators" to move away from attempting to gain fame and funding through the blackbox algorithmic systems of Facebook, YouTube, and other algorithm-driven platforms by focusing on direct fan relationships for funding.

Much as crowdfunding itself was originally cast as a rejection of the venture capital world and the funding mechanisms historically leveraged by startups, such as subscription and tip-jar crowdfunding, reject the dominant online monetization paradigm of successfully navigating algorithms to achieve viral fame or advertising-based revenue success. Advertising payouts have plummeted from their peaks in the early days of online content creation, and much as Conte noted in his pitch for Patreon, they fail to reward creators in a sustainable way, even with millions of views. Finally, platform algorithms remain blackboxed, though the EU's Digital Services Act promises to change that paradigm (Vincent, 2022).

Some in the creative space credit Kevin Kelly's "1000 True Fans" blog post as inspiration for the move to fan-oriented creators. Kelley's central thesis is that creators and artists don't need millions of fans, but simply 1,000 "true fans" that spend around $100 annually supporting the creator, generating an annual incoming of $100,000 (Kelly, n.d.). In Kelly's model, with a critical mass of "true" fans, a creator can comfortably subsidize their creative endeavors while focusing on fan relationships.

In practical terms, the heady promises of subscription-based crowdfunding should be viewed realistically as one of several potential revenue streams that fall short on their own of serving as a catch-all panacea. Some have gone so far as to cast the creator economy as a new form of the gig-economy, complete with precarious workers who rely on the platforms that host their content (and their ever-evolving policies that may or may not result in sudden deplatforming) (Chayka, 2021). Regardless, these platforms represent the current cutting edge of online crowdfunding and the next step in a genre and industry that continues to evolve by the year.

The Ethical Challenges of Crowdfunding

Before looking at the research on crowdfunding, I want to take a moment to focus on the ethical challenges that crowdfunding poses to technical communicators as well as to backers and founders of campaigns. While crowdfunding has the potential to support coalitional change and social justice, it also has ample potential and history of ethical breaches and exploitation that cannot go unexplored. The same magical thinking that inhabits much of the discussions around big tech also follows crowdfunding, as well as issues with financially precarious workers and their rights, ethical violations by platforms, and of course the potential of campaigns to fail or serve as a vehicle for theft.

Much of big tech and technology in general, with the mainstreaming of Silicon Valley startup culture, suffer from problems with magical thinking, the sense that technology or startups in general will suddenly transform the world for the better. Journalists and opinion piece writers have tackled the subject for years, looking at instances of magical thinking regarding AI (Naughton, 2018), education technology (Strauss, 2013), and general technology speculation (Knapp, 2011). The issue with these approaches is that they lean into the positive potential of technology without looking at the practical and ethical issues involved.

The modern approach to magical thinking in social media and online technology can be seen as extending from the pitch of the early 2000s pop-business text *Wikinomics* (Tapscott & Williams, 2006), an approach to the online crowd that views crowdsourcing as a means to leverage expertise and effort without having to provide any real form of compensation or benefits. Though the creator-centered language of the current online ecosystem obscures the relationship in modern discussions, even platforms like MySpace and YouTube were presented as examples of Wikinomics (p. 11) because these platforms (indeed almost all social online platforms) make their money because of the user-generated content they provide and receive for free. Yes, some platforms do have payment models to compensate creators on certain levels (like YouTube), but as mentioned previously in the discussion of the founding of Patreon, the monetization does not align with the effort put in by many creators. Additionally, some of the most popular platforms such as Instagram have no monetization payment system, instead relying on merchandise sales (which the platform gets a healthy cut from) or tip-jar-style donations.

In crowdfunding, the Wikinomics approach simply views the crowd and by extension crowdfunding as a way to simply make a project happen without real planning and engagement in the process. For technical writers in particular, this can be a danger when an organization you are a part of or that wishes to hire you for a freelance project wants a crowdfunding campaign without understanding the risks, work necessary, and timeline needed to make the project become a reality. The need to provide a detailed campaign structure, pitch, and timely update schedule during fulfillment can run headlong into the idea that the campaign will simply succeed by virtue of existing. As we'll see in Chapters 5 and 6, crowdfunding campaigns are complex and long-term commitments, not low-effort panaceas.

A second issue with crowdfunding, and in some ways an extension of the cynical *Wikinomics* approach to technology, is the precariousness that platform-based work creates for workers, particularly subscription-based crowdfunding, something that subscription-based crowdfunding shares with the broader gig economy. According to data from the US Federal Reserve, gig economy workers tend to be more financially fragile, though that fragility is not uniform (Board of Governors of the Federal Reserve System, 2019). In addition, black, indigenous, and people of color (BIPOC) gig workers are more likely to be killed on the job than their white counterparts (Hoque, 2022). Within the specifics of subscription-based crowdfunding, as seen in the case of Patreon and then OnlyFans moving to suddenly deplatform pornographic creators, creators' income streams are subject to the whims of platforms and their policies (Dickson, 2020). OnlyFans deserves a special mention for allegedly going even further in their mistreatment and attacks on adult performers: in 2022, the platform was accused in a class-action lawsuit to have bribed Meta employees to place adult performers that didn't operate on the OnlyFans platform on a "terrorist blacklist" (Belanger, 2022).

In addition to the first two ethical issues around the general crowdfunding views in business and their impact on workers who leverage those tools for their primary means of making a living, crowdfunding platforms themselves can and have had ethical issues related to their policies and self-governance. For example, the BBC found that OnlyFans had an ad-hoc compliance manual that was used that allowed for up to three strikes before banning sexual content that violated the laws in a given country, with the number of strikes allowed scaling with the level of popularity of the account, with a separate team entirely dealing with the site's most popular accounts (Titheradge, 2021). For OnlyFans, this represents a pattern as the BBC previously had uncovered that the site's age-verification process was lax at best, with content creators as young as 14 selling sexually explicit content on the site (Titheradge & Croxford, 2021).

Beyond policies that allow or even condone illegal behavior, crowdfunding platforms can and do present themselves as transformational while simultaneously running their own organizations with policies that appear to run counter to their stated goals. Kickstarter, famously, announced that it had become a Public Benefit Corporation in order to move away from the need to focus on profit above all else (Chenn, 2018). However, the company also aggressively fought efforts to unionize, a move that seemingly runs counter to the ethos put forward in Public Benefit Corporation messaging (Covert, 2020).

Finally, in addition to the issues noted earlier, crowdfunding campaigns can and do simply fail or serve as a means for grifting or theft. There are countless examples of campaigns that fail after receiving funding due to inept management of supply chains and planning. For example, the long-time second-highest campaign of all time on Kickstarter, the Coolest Cooler, ran into constant issues with sourcing affordable parts to meet their pledged orders, eventually going so far as to settle with the Oregon Department of Justice over unfulfilled orders (Carman, 2019). One of the early board game successes on Kickstarter, *The Doom That Came to Atlantic City* resulted in action by the Federal Trade Commission as the creator allegedly took the funds raised and used them for rent, transportation, and eventually a move (Mullin, 2015). On Indiegogo, the $3.5 million campaign for the Onagofly F115 similarly ended in legal action, with backers claiming that the received product was inoperable and did not align with pitch videos. The Onagofly project paralleled a similar $3.4 million failure of the Zano drone on Kickstarter (Farivar, 2015). Successful funding, even in the millions of dollars, in no way guarantees the success of a campaign.

Crowdfunding as a whole is vulnerable to a myriad of ethical challenges that technical communicators must be aware of and plan for in their work with the platforms. The platforms themselves can and do allow and facilitate ethically problematic content; the creators of campaigns can have unrealistic expectations of success, or manage a successful campaign's funds poorly, or simply disappear with the money raised. Yes, crowdfunding has transformative potential, but like any technical communication or business genre, it comes with the need to maintain a healthy awareness of the ethical risks and implications of activity within the genre. We'll come back to these ethical risks and look at them more closely in Chapter 4 when we cover drafting and running a campaign.

Crowdfunding Research

Having looked at the definition and history of crowdfunding, I would like to now turn to academic research on the subject before tackling ethical concerns and wrapping up the chapter with a vision of crowdfunding as a space for coalitional action. I'll first look at the crowdfunding research within technical communication before looking at the notable work carried outside of the field.

Technical Communication Approaches

While crowdfunding research has grown over the past several years across a number of fields, scholarship on the subject of technical communication and professional writing is still relatively rare. From 2014 through 2022, a number of pieces across the discipline broach the subject of crowdfunding, with various authors offering up their own approach to unpacking the rhetorical work of crowdfunding. However, over that span, no one approach has become the definitive approach in the literature.

The first coverage of crowdfunding in technical communication is by Ilyra Tirdtatov (Tirdatov, 2014), who looks at a sample of 13 campaigns on Kickstarter and leverages the classic rhetorical lens of *ethos, pathos,* and *logos.* Each of Tirdatov's 13 campaigns is taken from the top-earning categories available at the time. The analysis framework leverages a multifaceted typology of appeals and tracks the appeals across the space of the 13 projects, looking at the project description text.

Kyle P. Vealey and Jeffrey M. Gerding's (2016) work on teaching crowdfunding appears next, as the two look at teaching crowdfunding projects as civic engagement within the framework of entrepreneurial writing for business students. In their pedagogy, Vealey and Gerding focus on storytelling about public problems as a means of persuasion (p. 420). Gerding and Vealey continue in a discussion of the +POOL crowdfunding campaign (2017) to tackle pollution issues in New York City. In analyzing the +POOL campaign, they frame the work as civic entrepreneurship and provide an analysis of how the approach can be leveraged to tackle "wicked" problems that resist simple solutions.

Ashley Rose Mehlenbacher (2017) tackles crowdfunding in science in particular via genre move analysis. Mehlenbacher's work situates crowdfunding in direct conversation with the traditional scientific genre of proposal writing, and looks for parallel structures between the two genres and ways that knowledge from traditional science writing processes can be modified or adapted to the genre of crowdfunding. Mehlenbacher goes on to expand this approach by situating this discussion in a broader book-length work on science communication online (2019).

Adam R. Pope (2017) analyzes crowdfunding via the lenses of affect and publics, looking at the ways that crowdfunding campaigns motivate backers to identify with and follow campaigns. That work continues via a discussion of the writing demands of the genre using the same lens (Pope, 2018).

Kari Campeau and Yee Thao (2022) analyze crowdfunding for medical reasons on the GoFundMe platform, leveraging a mixed methodology to analyze the ways that crowdfunding creators told their story and appealed for funding. Campeau and Thao's work underscores the essential nature of medical crowdfunding in the modern era in the United States and how the genre can serve as citizen-generated tech comm while underscoring the ways this crowdfunding maintains unjust social systems (p. 15).

Stephen Carradini and Carolin Fleischmann (2022) survey a large corpus of crowdfunding campaigns (327,586) to analyze the impact of visualizations on the final crowdfunding success, finding that while images, videos, and links were associated with more successful campaigns, gifs and galleries did not have the same association. Carradini and Fleischmann's work underscores the ways that multimodal online texts change the way that crowdfunding works versus more traditional pitch genres.

Though there isn't a single approach to the research, nor is there an approach that appears to progress beyond the literature of a single author in the four branches of research on crowdfunding, I would argue if anything this speaks to the breadth of the genre and the variety of approaches that crowdfunding presents to technical and professional writers. Vealey and Gerding (2016) and Gerding and Vealey (2017) tackle from civic entrepreneurship; Mehlenbacher (2017, 2019) from the direction of science communication; Campeau and Thao (2022) from the perspective of user-created tech comm; and Tirdatov (2014) Pope (2017, 2018), and Carradini and Fleischmann (2022) from the direction of crowdfunding as a stand-alone genre for study. Each strand of research shows how crowdfunding can and does support markedly different research approaches and use cases.

In this text, I hope to expand on the work done previous in the field, while bringing into the conversation user experience design/user experience architecture as well as social justice-aligned coalitional action to provide an in-depth look at how crowdfunding as a genre operates from pitch through fulfillment into subsequent campaigns. In doing so, I also hope to rely on some touch points in the broader discussions of crowdfunding across the larger research world, though primarily focusing on business-aligned research.

Mollick et al.

While going outside of one's own discipline can be a difficult challenge (as Janice Lauer, 1984 famously notes in her discussion of Composition as a "dappled discipline"), technical communication stands at a crossroads between any number of potential homes and disciplines within and without our institutions of higher learning (Sullivan & Porter, 1993). In approaching crowdfunding research for this project, I look briefly to research outside of technical communication and professional writing, looking primarily at the most-cited and foundational work on the subject by Ethan Mollick. While there are entire discourses around crowdfunding across entrepreneurial, music business, art, and other journals and fields, attempting to look at all research ever on crowdfunding would be counterproductive at best in a text that aims to provide a technical communication-based approach to the subject for practitioners and researchers alike. As such, I primarily look to Mollick for this narrative because his contributions have had an outsized impact on the discourse across fields of study. His (2014) dynamics piece alone has over 1,135 citations tracked by Web of Science, with Google Scholar providing an even more bullish 4,498 citations at the time of this chapter's writing.

Mollick's work has an added advantage in being rather broad in focus, with Mollick contributing to work on crowdfunding that looks at the activist choice and female founders (Greenberg & Mollick, 2017), evidence on the democratization of startup funding via crowdfunding (Mollick & Robb, 2016), delivery rates on Kickstarter (@KickstarterFulfillmentReport), and comparing crowdfunding versus expert evaluations (Mollick & Nanda, 2016). Though this work is not central to my own premise and approach, it informs the conversation and provides an important window into other ways of viewing crowdfunding and its discourse in other disciplines.

Taken together, Mollick's body of work casts crowdfunding as a novel approach to entrepreneurial funding that provides alternatives to traditional gatekeeping while delivering on promises fairly consistently. In addition, Mollick finds that crowdfunding assessments of quality align fairly closely to expert choices and potentially offer underrepresented founders a chance to overcome traditional barriers to funding from support within their own community via activist funders.

Mollick's (2014) exploratory dynamics piece looks at the rise of crowdfunding as a viable alternative to traditional startup funding, creating a definition and typology of crowdfunding along the way. Mollick sketches out rationales for the motivations of founders and funders, looks over the extant literature at the time, and then carries out a study of crowdfunding projects to provide some insights into factors associated with successful crowdfunding campaigns. The project's definition and mapping work on crowdfunding has continued to show up across fields in lit reviews, and the work remains an important milestone in crowdfunding.

Mollick's collaboration with Kickstarter for their Fulfillment Report (*Kickstarter Fulfillment Report*, n.d.) covers the rate of fulfillment with Kickstarter projects as well as the satisfaction of backers, painting a fairly positive picture of outcomes on the platform across categories. Overall the report finds around 9% of campaigns that succeeded in funding failed to grant rewards, with no major differences in this rate across all of the platforms categories for campaigns. Additionally, projects that raised less than $1,000 were more likely than others to fail to fulfill their promises. Finally, 15–20% of backers of failed projects felt the failure was handled well. Taken in total, the report pushes back against any claims that crowdfunding and Kickstarter in particular are riddled with fraudsters and failed projects.

Mollick and Nanda (2016) examine the capabilities of crowdfunding audiences to assess project quality when compared with professional assessors of value in the art world. Mollick and Nanda note that historically entrepreneurial individuals' successes have been filtered through a relatively small group of experts that can prevent potentially successful ideas from every getting funded (p. 1533). Looking specifically at theater, Mollick and Nanda find that experts and crowdfunding audiences' preferences aligned quite closely (p. 1549) while noting that expert critiques might be more likely to back "artistically challenging" projects. From the project, Mollick and Nanda note that crowdfunding doesn't encourage risky or poor project choice, and in fact may actually democratize the funding landscape by lowering barriers to entry (p. 1551). In particular, they note that crowdfunding may well be easier and less intimidating for some creators compared to the relatively complex process of applying for and receiving National Endowment for the Arts grants (p. 1549).

Finally, Greenberg and Mollick (2017) articulate the role of activist choice homophily in crowdfunding. More broadly, homophily represents individuals' tendency to support those that they identify with (p. 341). Greenberg and Mollick define this particular type of homophily as one where "the basis of homophilic support is not merely dyadic similarity but rather perceptions of shared structural barriers stemming from a common group-level social identity and an underlying desire to help overcome them" (p. 342). In their discussion, Greenberg and Mollick seek to examine why female founders of crowdfunding campaigns outperform their male counterparts, settling on a potential explanation that female founders benefit from activist choices from other women who seek to support their campaigns as a way of jointly resisting and overcoming barriers placed against women in venture capital and technology in general (p. 367). As I close, I want to highlight the role of activist-choice homophily in our understanding of crowdfunding, as I believe the concept provides an avenue for understanding crowdfunding as a potentially transformative approach to startup funding and nonprofit funding that can promote social justice and inclusion in technical communication and beyond through coalitional action.

Crowdfunding as Coalitional Action

Having looked at crowdfunding's definition, history, and the findings of early research on the subject, I would like to close this chapter by looking at how crowdfunding can serve as a coalitional approach to startup funding that can and should support increased diversity, equity, and inclusion in the nonprofit and business communities. Crowdfunding provides business and nonprofit founders with coalitional avenues to achieve funding that bypass traditional gatekeeping structures that have maintained gendered and racial barriers in startup success.

When discussing coalitional action, I use the definition by Walton et al. (2019) that coalitions are groups of individuals who are brought together by a shared interest in an issue rather than by a shared worldview on a given subject. As Walton, Moore, and Jones point out, coalitions don't require everyone to be on the exact same page with the same beliefs: they simply require a group of people willing to work on a common issue together (p. 55).

I argue that crowdfunding and coalitional action are a natural fit, though crowdfunding is in no way fundamentally just or biased toward coalitional action (as noted in the section on the ethical challenges of the genre). Crowdfunding, however, offers an ideal vehicle for supporting coalitional responses because of the genre's focus on finite campaigns and projects offers coalitions a platform to mobilize around a given issue that they care about that then can support continued dialog and updates and energy as the campaign develops and then continues into future work (or ongoing support as in the case of Patreon).

With that said, the question could be posed, do all campaigns have to be about and center on social justice? The simple answer is yes! As Walton et al. (2019) explain, "Technical communicators make decisions every day that will either contribute to systems of oppression or resist and reject them" (p. 139). Crowdfunding campaigns, like other technical writing, can maintain barriers to social justice as easily as they can dismantle them. Any crowdfunding campaign must assess its own positionality and relationship to its audience and their goals to prevent further injustice or the maintenance of existing injustices.

Building off of findings from Greenberg and Mollick (2017) about activist choice homophily, crowdfunding provides a fertile ground for activist choices in supporting projects, organizations, and causes that a given backer aligns with, something that we see in numerous crowdfunding platforms (and even in traditional shopping venues increasingly). For example, Kickstarter's discovery page presents users with the "LGBTQIA+" category for campaigns, GoFundMe's discover lists a category dedicated to "Celebrate Black Joy," and Indiegogo has categories for human rights, the environment, and local businesses to name a few. Though a deeper discussion of how platforms position themselves and support different types of campaigns and founders will have to wait for Chapter 3, the platform-level embedding of activist choice is an important facet of crowdfunding's potential for coalitional action.

Activist choice homophily, however, places limits on our understanding of coalitional action in unhelpful ways that are worth addressing. As Walton et al. (2019) note, it is a mistake to suggest that groups of individuals who share identity markers like race or gender inherently hold the same worldview or perspectives (p. 55). Greenberg and Mollick's presentation seemingly limits activist choice to a simple homophily category exactly like the one Walton et al. critique. Instead of focusing on the homophily as leveraged by Greenberg and Mollick, I suggest that we focus on the shared dedication to issues and causes and simplify the discussion to simply activist choice in crowdfunding.

As we've noted throughout the chapter, social justice can be seen as inherently part of the development of crowdfunding as an alternative to traditional startup funding avenues. We know, for example, that entire industries such as big tech are systematically hostile to women (Mundy, 2017), and that women and BIPOC historically run into barriers when seeking funding for startup ventures (Mollick, 2014; Mollick & Nanda, 2016; Mollick & Robb, 2016). Crowdfunding positions itself as an alternative to traditional gatekeepers, providing direct access to those who might be interested in your campaign or issue without the need for vetting by the same start-up infrastructure that has maintained unequal success for generations.

Working within technical communication, Natasha N. Jones (2017) reminds us that black-owned businesses are outnumbered by white-owned businesses by roughly 3 to 1, with black entrepreneurship lagging behind white entrepreneurship consistently due to a myriad of systemic factors (p. 320). Systemic gaps in wealth contribute to unequal access to loans and other traditional funding sources for black entrepreneurs (p. 322). Despite these obstacles, Jones finds that black entrepreneurs have had success and continue to succeed, often with an ethic of empowerment, looking to explicitly help other entrepreneurs like themselves succeed against their shared barriers, contributing to cultural empowerment (p. 331).

Jones defines cultural empowerment thus:

> Cultural empowerment, as a process and outcome, relates specifically to how a group achieves goals that are generally important to and valued by the entire group. Central to the definition of cultural empowerment that I present is a recognition that cultural empowerment must account for a group's values, beliefs, and ideals.
>
> *(p. 326)*

In looking at Jones' definition, I want to highlight the need for this empowerment to account for values, beliefs, and ideals in the substance of crowdfunding and the user experiences it creates, as we will see in the case study (in Chapter 5) on the STEAM Chasers book series by Dr. Doresa Jennings.

As we'll see, crowdfunding campaigns often succeed specifically because they highlight a set of values, ideals, and goals that resonate within the audience of backers, allowing the backers to see their actions as backers as generative and in support of the ideals they themselves hold and see in a given campaign. Unlike the traditional business startup process that is often highly white and male and promotes and tolerates only particular ways of being and existing while excluding others such as BIPOC workers with natural hair (@alexiafernandezcampbellDreadlocksLawsuitBlack2018; @alexiafernandezcampbellCaliforniaCrownAct2019), crowdfunding emphasizes telling and presenting authentic stories and ideals to backers who are drawn to those exact values, ideals, and goals and are interested in using campaigns for cultural empowerment.

For a brief example of culturally empowering and groundbreaking crowdfunding campaigns, we can look to the serial success of *Coyote & Crow the Role Playing Game* on Kickstarter and Backerkit. *Coyote & Crow the Role Playing Game* is a sci-fi fantasy tabletop role-playing game created by Connor Alexander (and team) that is set in a version of the near future where the Americas have never been colonized. The project team is composed almost entirely of Natives, an important facet of the presentation of the project and game system. The project was available for funding on Kickstarter from March 2, 2021, till April 1, 2021, raising $1,073,453 in funding from 16,269 backers, dwarfing the campaign's goal of $18,000. The project was a success, and was even nominated for a Nebula (Hall, 2022). The project would go on to a second success on a new platform, Backerkit, raising a total of $172,960 from 2,417 backers for an expansion of the existing *Coyote & Crow* setting that provided additional material for role-playing games set in the system.

With its explicit focus on a game based on Native culture and created by a primarily Native team, *Coyote & Crow* is just one of many potential examples of the ways that crowdfunding campaigns and platforms have been used to empower cultures and groups that have been historically marginalized in traditional industries and publication systems.

Wrapping Up

In this chapter, we've laid out a definition of crowdfunding, traced the history and evolution of the genre, reviewed the scholarship on crowdfunding within technical communication and the wider academic world, and laid out a case for viewing crowdfunding as inherently open to and ideal for social justice and coalitional action. In the next chapter, we'll frame crowdfunding campaigns through the lens of XA, providing a methodology for technical communicators carrying out these campaigns in addition to providing us with a way to systematically survey and analyze existing campaigns to inform our own future projects.

Discussion Questions

1. What is your own experience with crowdfunding? When do you first remember seeing crowdfunding projects? How would you characterize your historic interactions with them?
2. What types of coalitional action do you think would align well with crowdfunding in your own local circumstance? How would the subject translate into a given crowdfunding campaign? What platform type do you think would make the most sense for this work?

References

About Us. (n.d.). *ArtistShare.* Retrieved April 18, 2022, from www.artistshare.com/about

AJ. (2014, June 19). President Obama Lauds Indiegogo, maker community. *The Indiegogo Review.* https://go.indiegogo.com/blog/2014/06/president-obama-lauds-indiegogo-maker-community.html

Alderson, R. (2015, June 2). How Kickstarter changed the world: Founder Yancey strickler on the origins of the platform. *It's Nice That.* www.itsnicethat.com/features/how-kickstarter-changed-the-world-founder-yancey-strickler-on-the-origins-of-the-platform

Beaumont, C. (n.d.). Patreon and drip: An analysis of subscription-based crowdfunding platforms. *Canada Media Fund.* Retrieved April 21, 2022, from https://cmf-fmc.ca/now-next/articles/patreon-and-drip-an-analysis-of-subscription-based-crowdfunding-platforms/

Belanger, A. (2022, August 11). Lawsuits: OnlyFans bribed Instagram to put creators on "terrorist blacklist" [Updated]. *Ars Technica.* https://arstechnica.com/tech-policy/2022/08/lawsuits-onlyfans-bribed-instagram-to-put-creators-on-terrorist-blacklist/

Benefit Guidelines | Patreon. (n.d.). Retrieved April 25, 2022, from https://patreon.com/ policy/benefits

Board of Governors of the Federal Reserve System. (2019). *Report on the economic well-being of U.S. households in 2018.* https://www.federalreserve.gov/publications/files/2018-report-economic-well-being-us-households-201905.pdf

Bradley, D. B., & Luong, C. (2014). Crowdfunding: A new opportunity for small business and entrepreneurship. *The Entrepreneurial Executive, 19,* 95–104.

Burkett, E. (2011). A crowdfunding exemption? Online investment crowdfunding and U.S. securities regulation. *Transactions: The Tennessee Journal of Business Law, 13,* 63–106.

Butticè, V., Colombo, M. G., & Wright, M. (2017). Serial crowdfunding, social capital, and project success. *Entrepreneurship Theory and Practice, 41*(2), 183–207. https://doi. org/10.1111/etap.12271

Campeau, K., & Thao, Y. (2022). "It makes everything just another story": A mixed methods study of medical storytelling on GoFundMe. *Technical Communication Quarterly, 32*(1), 33–49. https://doi.org/10.1080/10572252.2022.2047792

Carman, A. (2019, December 9). Crowdfunding disaster coolest cooler is shutting down and blaming tariffs for its downfall. *The Verge.* www.theverge.com/2019/12/9/21003445/ coolest-cooler-update-business-tariffs-kickstarter

Carradini, S., & Fleischmann, C. (2022). The effects of multimodal elements on success in Kickstarter crowdfunding campaigns. *Journal of Business and Technical Communication, 37*(1), 1–27. https://doi.org/10.1177/10506519221121699

Chayka, K. (2021, July 17). What the "creator economy" promises—and what it actually does. *The New Yorker.* www.newyorker.com/culture/infinite-scroll/what-the-creator-economy-promises-and-what-it-actually-does

Chenn, P. (2018, November 28). Kickstarter is a PBC. Here's what that means and why it matters. *Kickstarter Magazine.* https://medium.com/kickstarter/kickstarter-is-a-pbc-heres-what-that-means-and-why-it-matters-d90b2389ea6c

Covert, B. (2020, May 27). How Kickstarter employees formed a union. *Wired.com.* www. wired.com/story/how-kickstarter-employees-formed-union/

Dickson, E. J. (2020, May 18). Sex workers built OnlyFans. Now they say they're getting kicked off. *Rolling Stone.* www.rollingstone.com/culture/culture-features/onlyfans-sex-workers-porn-creators-999881/

Edelstein, J. (2016, April 26). Meet the superbackers. They might not wear capes as they soar . . . | by Kickstarter | Kickstarter Magazine | Medium. *Medium.com.* https:// medium.com/kickstarter/meet-the-superbackers-962bf714fc2e

Farivar, C. (2015, November 24). Kickstarter has no clue how drone startup raised $3.4M then imploded. *Ars Technica.* https://arstechnica.com/information-technology/2015/11/ kickstarter-learned-of-zano-collapse-through-a-bare-bones-project-update/

Gallagher, D., & Salfen, J. (2015, March 24). By the numbers: When creators return to Kickstarter. *Kickstarter News Archive.* www.kickstarter.com/blog/by-the-numbers-when-creators-return-to-kickstarter

Gamble, J. R., Brennan, M., & McAdam, R. (2017). A rewarding experience? Exploring how crowdfunding is affecting music industry business models. *Journal of Business Research, 70,* 25–36. https://doi.org/10.1016/j.jbusres.2016.07.009

General Electric. (2015, August 3). Consumers Crave Opal™ nugget ice maker | GE News. *GE.com.* www.ge.com/news/press-releases/consumers-crave-opal™-nugget-ice-maker

Gerding, J. M., & Vealey, K. P. (2017). When is a solution not a solution? Wicked problems, hybrid solutions, and the rhetoric of civic entrepreneurship. *Journal of Business and Technical Communication, 31*(3), 290–318. https://doi.org/10. 1177/1050651917695538

Gillespie, T. (2010). The politics of 'platforms.' *New Media & Society, 12*(3), 347–364.

GiveCampus. (n.d.). Educational fundraising technology | raise money with GiveCampus. *GiveCampus.* Retrieved March 31, 2022, from https://go.givecampus.com/

GoFundMe Team. (2016, November 4). Twenty affordable ways to say thank you to donors. *GoFundMe.* www.gofundme.com/c/blog/thank-you-to-donors

Greenberg, J., & Mollick, E. (2017). Activist choice homophily and the crowdfunding of female founders. *Administrative Science Quarterly, 62*(2), 341–374. https://doi.org/10.1177/0001839216678847

Guigar, B., Kellet, D., Kurtz, S., & Straub, K. (2008). *How to make webcomics.* Image Comics.

Hall, C. (2022, September 15). Indigenous RPG Coyote & Crow is a hit, and a new anthology of adventures is on the way. *Polygon.* www.polygon.com/tabletop-games/23353743/coyote-and-crow-indigenous-tabletop-rpg-anthology

Hoque, U. (2022, April 12). BIPOC gig workers are more likely to be killed on the job, new report says. *Prism.* http://prismreports.org/2022/04/12/bipoc-gig-workers-are-more-likely-to-be-killed-on-the-job-new-report-says/

How do social media's virtual tip jar features compare? (2021, August 5). *The Daily Dot.* www.dailydot.com/unclick/tools-review-creator-economy-virtual-tip-jars/

Ifeanyi, K. C. (2021, March 26). The NSFW future of OnlyFans, where celebs, influencers, and sex workers post side by side. *Fast Company.* www.fastcompany.com/90611207/the-nsfw-future-of-onlyfans-where-celebs-influencers-and-sex-workers-post-side-by-side

Igarashi, K. (n.d.). Bloodstained: Ritual of the night. *Kickstarter.* Retrieved August 3, 2021, from www.kickstarter.com/projects/iga/bloodstained-ritual-of-the-night

Jones, N. (2017). Rhetorical narratives of Black entrepreneurs: The business of race, agency, and cultural empowerment. *Journal of Business and Technical Communication, 31*(3), 319–349. https://journals.sagepub.com/doi/full/10.1177/1050651917695540

Kelly, K. (n.d.). 1,000 true fans. *The Technium.* Retrieved April 25, 2022, from https://kk.org/thetechnium/1000-true-fans/

Kickstarter Fulfillment Report. (n.d.). Retrieved April 18, 2022, from www.kickstarter.com/fulfillment

Knapp, A. (2011, March 23). When tech speculation becomes magical thinking. *Forbes.* www.forbes.com/sites/alexknapp/2011/03/23/when-tech-speculation-becomes-magical-thinking/

Lauer, J. M. (1984). Composition studies: Dappled discipline. *Rhetoric Review, 3*(1), 20–29.

Lawler, R. (2021, August 25). OnlyFans says never mind, it actually won't ban porn on October 1st. *The Verge.* www.theverge.com/2021/8/25/22640988/onlyfans-no-ban-porn-sexually-explicit-content-creators

Learn About Indiegogo | Indiegogo. (n.d.). *Indiegogo.* Retrieved April 21, 2022, from www.indiegogo.com/about/our-story

Lyons, K. (2021, August 19). OnlyFans to prohibit sexually explicit content beginning in October. *The Verge.* www.theverge.com/2021/8/19/22632797/onlyfans-prohibit-sexually-explicit-content-porn-creators

Mac, R. (n.d.). How anti-Kickstarter GoFundMe became the crowdfunding king with causes not projects. *Forbes.* Retrieved April 18, 2022, from www.forbes.com/sites/ryanmac/2015/09/24/gofundme-largest-crowdfunding-platform-1-billion-donations/

Marillion Fans to the Rescue. (2001, May 11). http://news.bbc.co.uk/2/hi/entertainment/1325340.stm

Mehlenbacher, A. R. (2017). Crowdfunding science: Exigencies and strategies in an emerging genre of science communication. *Technical Communication Quarterly, 26*(2), 127–144. https://doi.org/10.1080/10572252.2017.1287361

Mehlenbacher, A. R. (2019). *Science communication online: Engaging experts and publics on the internet.* The Ohio State University Press. https://ohiostatepress.org/books/titles/9780814213988.html

Miller, T. (n.d.). This startup wants to make it much easier for creators to get paid. *Forbes.* Retrieved April 25, 2022, from www.forbes.com/sites/theodorecasey/2019/11/01/this-startup-wants-to-make-it-much-easier-for-creators-to-get-paid/

Mollick, E. (2014). The dynamics of crowdfunding: An exploratory study. *Journal of Business Venturing, 29*(1), 1–16. https://doi.org/10.1016/j.jbusvent.2013.06.005

Mollick, E., & Nanda, R. (2016). Wisdom or madness? Comparing crowds with expert evaluation in funding the arts. *Management Science, 62*(6), 1533–1553. https://doi.org/10.1287/mnsc.2015.2207

Mollick, E., & Robb, A. (2016). Democratizing innovation and capital access: The role of crowdfunding. *California Management Review, 58*(2), 72–87. https://doi.org/10.1525/cmr.2016.58.2.72

Mullin, J. (2015, June 11). Feds take first action against a failed Kickstarter with $112K judgment. *Ars Technica.* https://arstechnica.com/tech-policy/2015/06/feds-take-first-action-against-a-failed-kickstarter-with-112k-judgment/

Mundy, L. (2017, March 14). Why is silicon valley so awful to women? *The Atlantic.* www.theatlantic.com/magazine/archive/2017/04/why-is-silicon-valley-so-awful-to-women/517788/

National Park Service. (2015a, February 26). *Joseph Pulitzer—Statue of Liberty National Monument (U.S. National Park Service).* www.nps.gov/stli/learn/historyculture/joseph-pulitzer.htm

National Park Service. (2015b, February 26). *Pulitzer-in depth—Statue of Liberty National Monument (U.S. National Park Service).* www.nps.gov/stli/learn/historyculture/pulitzer-in-depth.htm

Naughton, J. (2018, August 5). Magical thinking about machine learning won't bring the reality of AI any closer. *The Guardian.* www.theguardian.com/commentisfree/2018/aug/05/magical-thinking-about-machine-learning-will-not-bring-artificial-intelligence-any-closer

Noor, P. (2020, August 31). A Thorne in the site: The Bella Thorne and OnlyFans controversy explained. *The Guardian.* www.theguardian.com/media/2020/aug/31/bella-thorne-onlyfans-what-happened-explained

OnlyFans CEO on why it banned adult content: 'The short answer is banks'—The Verge. (n.d.). Retrieved April 25, 2022, from www.theverge.com/2021/8/24/22639356/onlyfans-ceo-tim-stokely-sexually-explicit-content-ban-banks

Plaugic, L. (2017, August 2). The women who sell nudes on Patreon. *The Verge.* www.theverge.com/2017/8/2/16074892/patreon-erotic-modeling-nsfw-content-nudes

Pope, A. R. (2017). Bloodstained, unpacking the affect of a Kickstarter success—present tense. *Present Tense: A Journal of Rhetoric in Society, 2*(6). www.presenttensejournal.org/volume-6/bloodstained-unpacking-the-affect-of-a-kickstarter-success/

Pope, A. R. (2018). Understanding the writing demands of crowdfunding campaigns with the genre-mapping report. *Business and Professional Communication Quarterly, 81*(4), 485–505. https://doi.org/10.1177/2329490618795935

Primack, D. (2021, August 19). OnlyFans has tons of users, but can't find investors. *Axios.* www.axios.com/onlyfans-investors-struggle-9cc92523-6607-40ad-9893-4175e7966b52.html

Ringelmann, D. (2011, April 20). President Obama's Startup America selects IndieGoGo as crowdfunding partner along side AMEX, Facebook, Google, HP, LinkedIn and Cisco.

The Indiegogo Review. https://go.indiegogo.com/blog/2011/04/president-obamas-startup-america-selects-indiegogo-as-crowdfunding-partner-along-side-amex-facebook.html

Strähle, J., & Bulling, L. (2018). Case study: Marillion. In J. Strähle (Ed.), *Fashion & music* (pp. 245–264). Springer. https://doi.org/10.1007/978-981-10-5637-6_13

Strauss, V. (2013, March 21). Magical thinking about technology in education. *Washington Post.* www.washingtonpost.com/news/answer-sheet/wp/2013/03/21/magical-thinking-about-technology-in-education/

Strom, S. (2008, December 26). Ad featuring singer proves Bonanza for the A.S.P.C.A. *The New York Times.* www.nytimes.com/2008/12/26/us/26charity.html

Sullivan, P. A., & Porter, J. E. (1993). Remapping curricular geography: Professional writing in/and English. *Journal of Business and Technical Communication, 7*(4), 389–422.

Tan, D. M., & MacMillan, D. (2015, June 24). GoFundMe founders to reap a fortune in buyout. *Wall Street Journal.* www.wsj.com/articles/BL-DGB-42425

Tapscott, D., & Williams, A. D. (2006). *Wikinomics: How mass collaboration changes everything.* Portfolio.

The BMC Team. (n.d.). About. *Buy Me a Coffee.* Retrieved April 25, 2022, from www.buymeacoffee.com/about

The Statue of Liberty and America's Crowdfunding Pioneer. (2013, April 24). *BBC News.* www.bbc.com/news/magazine-21932675

Thominet, L. (2020). Open video game development and participatory design. *Technical Communication Quarterly, 30*(4), 359–374. https://doi.org/10.1080/10572252.2020.1866679

Tirdatov, I. (2014). Web-based crowd funding: Rhetoric of success. *Technical Communication, 61*(1), 3–24.

Titheradge, N. (2021, August 19). OnlyFans: How it handles illegal sex videos—BBC investigation. *BBC News.* www.bbc.com/news/uk-58255865

Titheradge, N., & Croxford, R. (2021, May 26). The children selling explicit videos on OnlyFans. *BBC News.* www.bbc.com/news/uk-57255983

Townsend, T. (2016, March 30). Inside Danae Ringelmann's quest to make Indiegogo democratize startup funding. *Inc.com.* www.inc.com/magazine/201604/tess-townsend/indiegogo-danae-ringelmann-crowdfunding.html

Vealey, K. P., & Gerding, J. M. (2016). Rhetorical work in crowd-based entrepreneurship: Lessons learned from teaching crowdfunding as an emerging site of professional and technical communication. *IEEE Transactions on Professional Communication, 59*(4), 407–427. https://doi.org/10.1109/TPC.2016.2614742

Vincent, J. (2022, March 23). Google, meta, and others will have to explain their algorithms under new EU legislation. *The Verge.* www.theverge.com/2022/4/23/23036976/eu-digital-services-act-finalized-algorithms-targeted-advertising

Walton, R., Moore, K. R., & Jones, N. N. (2019). *Technical communication after the social justice turn: Building coalitions for action.* Routledge.

Zhao, Y., Harris, P., & Lam, W. (2019). Crowdfunding industry—history, development, policies, and potential issues. *Journal of Public Affairs, 19*(1), e1921. https://doi.org/10.1002/pa.1921

2

CROWDFUNDING AS EXPERIENCE ARCHITECTURE

In this chapter, I would like to define sustainable crowdfunding in quantifiable terms from scholarship in tech comm for those looking to study or generate such campaigns as technical writers and communicators. In Chapter 1, we looked at a broad definition of crowdfunding, and the concept of sustainable crowdfunding takes that definition and goes further, laying out a vision for a particular type of coalitional crowdfunding campaign that looks to leverage the genre for sustainable and community-driven financial support. Sustainable crowdfunding campaigns are those that are created with the end goal of becoming the first in a series of crowdfunding campaigns offered by the same organization over a period of months or years. These campaigns are envisioned as curated user experiences for coalitions of backers, providing additional value for campaign contributors beyond simply putting money toward a specific campaign deliverable. Sustainable crowdfunding, then, sees the crowdfunding genre as not only a supplement for the traditional channels for start-up funding but also an ongoing source of funding that continues beyond the traditional start-up phase of an organization's history. Whereas seed funding from various avenues, even crowdfunding, is often the first step of a funding process (Tomczak & Brem, 2013), one that ideally is not revisited, sustainable crowdfunding shifts that model by centering funding around a continual relationship with a core group of backers through discrete crowdfunding campaigns and ongoing patronage-style campaigns.

A coalitional backer community is central to sustainable crowdfunding and building and curating a compelling user experience is essential to carry out sustainable crowdfunding. Sustainable crowdfunding works, as I'll detail in this chapter, because creators respect and respond to the needs, desires, and goals of their backer coalitions. There is an ethic of social justice in sustainable crowdfunding as an approach to the genre. In situations where a campaign is actively responding

DOI: 10.4324/9781003308966-2

to an injustice, the 4Rs heuristic from Walton et al. (2019) can focus on the structure of a campaign and its content. In other situation, remaining mindful of the positionality, power, and privilege of a campaign and its backer coalition can help create a more equitable and just project that doesn't contribute to or worsen social injustices.

While this sustainable model of crowdfunding is a relatively new phenomenon, I argue that there are ample evidence that it has already shown a potential to stand alongside grant funding, start-up funding, and other methods of project sustainability in the few short years since crowdfunding came of age during the Obama administration as part of the financial reforms after the Great Recession (Ringelmann, 2011). Sites like GoFundMe, Indiegogo, and Kickstarter have entered the common vocabulary and have become almost default options for providing support to individuals and organizations in online spaces, and patronage-style crowdfunding like Patreon and OnlyFans have followed closely on their heels. These platforms have even become regular targets for political controversies (Monroe, 2019; Williams, 2015) and activism as even sovereign nations create campaign sites (*United24—The Initiative of the President of Ukraine*, n.d.). Numerous businesses and nonprofits have shown in the past decade that creating a sustained stream of crowdfunding campaigns is not only possible, but in some instances, it also may lead to greater successes and greater acclaim than projects tied to traditional funding gatekeepers that often cater to a specific and highly privileged class of creators.

I argue that these sustainable crowdfunding campaigns are at their heart rhetorical user experiences that are curated across the duration of a project and beyond, many times into the next project that a given organization may wish to carry out, even if that campaign may be dramatically different from previous offerings. The goals of a given campaign may be different from past campaigns, but the core relationship between the organization and the backers allows a smooth transition from one project to another, in a sustainable crowdfunding relationship. These relationships are built by the writers working on these campaigns as comprehensive user experiences that provide an ongoing value to those associated with the campaigns and organizations while respecting the positionality and voices of the backer coalition.

To illustrate how sustainable crowdfunding can shift paradigms, I would point to in order to illustrate how fluid and far-reaching these campaigns can be would be the Belgian game developer Larian Studios. In 2013, Larian launched their first campaign on the Kickstarter platform, Divinity: Original Sin (Larian Studios, LLC, 2013). The studio eventually produced the game, released it to widespread acclaim, and then followed up with a sequel, Divinity: Original Sin 2 in August 2015, drawing on their existing backers (via the original campaign) and capitalizing on their success from the first game (Larian Studios, LLC, 2015). This second game would go to even more critical acclaim than the first. In 2019, the studio followed up this series of successes with yet another Kickstarter campaign success, this time branching out from video games to a totally new project for a board game with the launch of the Divinity: Original Sin Board Game campaign (Larian Studios, LLC, 2019). Each of these campaigns from 2013 through 2019 targeted the same general backers and fans of Larian, connecting and linking to each other to bring existing backers into the new campaigns. Importantly, this success also propelled Larian to even greater potential successes outside of the crowdfunding realm as the studio was tapped in 2019 to create a sequel to perhaps the most acclaimed computer role-playing game of all time, Baldur's Gate 2 (Purchese, 2019). In the case of Larian, the ability to take over the legendary Baldur's Gate series was directly related to the successes that their Kickstarter campaigns afforded (Brown, 2019), allowing a small-scale Belgium studio to take over a game series from legendary North American developer BioWare.

Sustainable Crowdfunding as Experience Architecture

The larger world of a crowdfunding campaign is best viewed through the lens of user experience architecture, defined by Liza Potts and Michael J. Salvo (2017) as

> the architecture of media systems, resulting in a design capability for using those systems to communicate . . . a systems approach to the reciprocal process of analyzing and constructing social experiences in a variety of networked digital environments as well as a number of physical spaces.
>
> *(p. 3)*

In the words of Potts and Salvo, the work of XA moves practitioners of technical communication beyond singular touch points, documents that exist within a precise moment for a particular audience or set of users, and instead pushes practitioners into looking at the projects and work they create as taking part in a larger system whose orchestration becomes a task as important as the precision work of carefully creating, testing, editing, and publishing a singular deliverable.

The expanse of scope that XA allows is necessary for projects like serial crowdfunding campaigns, as these evolving projects can stretch over multiple years and countless deliverables. These campaigns don't fit traditional models of development and deployment that center around constant document cycling, but instead rely on a rapid-paced delivery that reacts to and maintains a relationship with users over time across multiple channels.

To illustrate the dynamic nature of crowdfunding and the natural match of the genre with the XA framework, we can turn to Larian's example from the original Divinity Campaign. That campaign hosted 75 updates during its duration, the second continued with an additional 52 updates, and before the board game project had even finished, the primary funding cycle over 12 updates had already been published. These updates were not simple snippets: they represented a great deal of content being created on a regular basis.

Word Count of All Divinity Updates

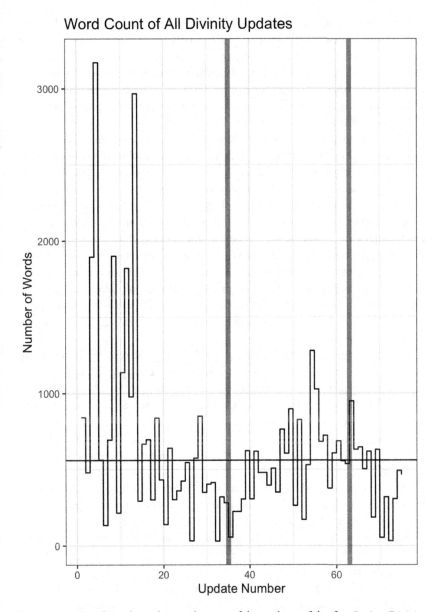

FIGURE 2.1   Graph tracking the word count of the updates of the first Larian *Divinity* campaign

Using the example of Divinity Original Sin, the 75 updates averaged a count of around 560 words, with some updates ranging over 3,000 words, as seen in Figure 2.1. The end of the initial campaign and the launch of the product are shown via two large gray vertical bars.

If we take the normal estimation of a double-spaced page being 250 words, some of these updates were over 12 single-spaced pages of text, with an average length of just over two single-spaced pages of text. This count doesn't even begin to incorporate the images and other multimedia content embedded in many updates. Note that the campaign's initial burst of content before backing had several large texts, followed by a slow building of length as the project go closer to the final launch.

This constant stream of content within the Larian campaign underscores Potts and Salvo's assertion that the XA requires that "we understand ecosystems of activity, rather than simply considering single task scenarios" (p. 4). In a campaign like Larian's, each update serves simultaneously as a continuation of a running conversation with backers, a single deliverable in a stream of ongoing content, and as a renewal of the commitment the campaign made with its backers. Complex rhetorical work is coordinated between each of these updates and the campaign itself, necessitating the move from the singular focus to the world of content ecosystems where texts don't exist in a vacuum, but instead, slowly form a living corpus that shapes the user experience. Simply taking into account the word count alone, a good deal of writing and organization is necessary, simply to maintain a sense of where the conversation is and where it has been going in these update streams.

The Divinity campaign illustrates how fluid a given writing situation can be, with engagement (tracked by comment count) and update length varying independently as the project progressed toward completion. As seen in Figure 2.2, the Divinity: Original Sin Campaign initially had a comment count that appeared to react to update length, but over time, the average comment count (shown in both regularized and literal line plots) increased independently of the update lengths in Figure 2.1, peaking as the project released (shown as a vertical grey line).

With situations like the Divinity campaign, there isn't a simple 1:1 correlation between update length and comment counts, but instead a slow growth over time. Interestingly, each time the comments drop to near zero, the following update managed to bring back backer engagement. This steady growth aligns with the examples we'll see in Chapter 6 from Rancho Relaxo's social media and subscription crowdfunding content.

Instead of looking to a stock formula for a given crowdfunding campaign, sustainable crowdfunding relies on technical writers who can maintain an XA that generates a high amount of output across a long period of time and multiple modalities while reacting to and eliciting user engagement. As seen in Figure 2.2, the Divinity team managed to increase the amount of user engagement with updates after the campaign was successfully funded, maintaining—and perhaps even increasing—the bond backers had with the campaign as it moved from funded to delivered.

Average Comment Count for Divinity Rises Over Time

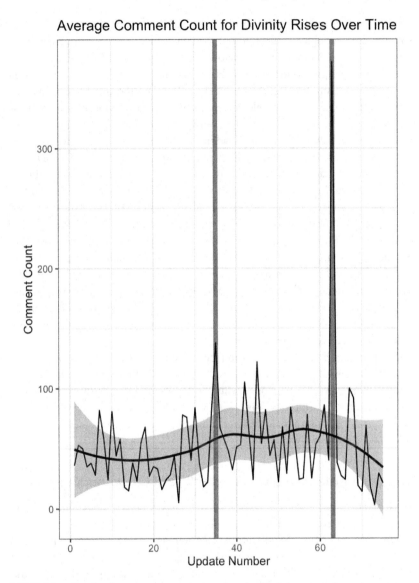

FIGURE 2.2   Graph of comment count over time in Divinity campaign

Experience Architecture and Crowdfunding

XA, as Potts and Salvo articulate it, provides the scope of practice needed to meaningfully create sustainable crowdfunding campaigns that coordinate across social media channels, crowdfunding platforms, email lists, press releases, and at times even face-to-face events. These campaigns work in evolving circumstances, documenting situations and deliverables in real time. Being tied to a single genre or medium or workflow isn't enough. We need to shift our thinking to a web of documents and deliverables that run according to a rhetorically aware process to build an experience that engages a unique coalition of backers that have been brought together by a given campaign or organization. Crowdfunding campaigns are too big, too fast, and too reactive to try to box into a simple document cycling or composition framework.

Using the game industry (one of the dominant early crowdfunding industries), we can see just how quickly the crowdfunding space evolves and reacts to feedback from users. Starting with the high-profile launch and success of the Double Fine Adventure campaign on Kickstarter in 2012 (Double Fine and 2 Player Productions, 2012) that raised $3,336,371 from 87,142 backers, the world of video game campaigns on the Kickstarter platform alone quickly ballooned into one of the site's most lucrative sectors, with big-name revivals of classic gaming series appearing quickly on the heels of the initial success by Double Fine. Within a month, the similarly successful Wasteland 2 would launch, raising a similarly impressive $2,933,252 from 61,290 backers (inXile Entertainment, 2012) and a veritable onslaught of classic game series reboots and spin-offs following in the year to come. Throughout this breakneck pace, these campaigns both created a new genre of funding in real-time but also reacted to the evolving conversation around that genre as they went (Pope, 2017).

The pace and breadth of these campaigns and their rhetorical situation necessitate the framework of Potts and Salvo's XA, with XA offering us a coherent way to view campaigns that in more traditional lenses might seem too unwieldy to unpack or too rapid and responsive to allow the type of studious deliberation that is often prized in a more traditional technical writing process. We need to go big, and we need to have a plan.

Planning for the Experience Architecture of Crowdfunding

To carry out a successful campaign, we need to scope our work properly and frame it well. Crowdfunding campaigns are not simply the pitch and a few updates along the way. That definition is entirely too narrow. As Potts and Salvo (2017) note in their framing of XA, we run the risk of missing critical context in our planning and implementation of complex projects when we start with too limited of a scope (p. 7). We need to frame the project not as a single deliverable or product, but instead as a series of interlocking interactive systems that have to be planned, managed, and evolved throughout the process of a given campaign.

To comprehensively research the writing situation and systems of crowdfunding XA, I focus on three central research moves to plan and implement a successful crowdfunding campaign that can branch off into sustainable success:

1. Listen—without filtering—to the coalition of backers.
2. Quantify the causes of audience engagement.
3. Define campaign expectations.

Using these three research moves, we can quantify the benchmarks of successful campaigns, giving us an understanding of the various systems of engagement we'll be working with and coordinating as we craft a coherent XA. Much of this research focuses on mapping the successes of existing campaigns, allowing us to build on existing best practices rather than attempting to create XA from nothing but our own intuition. Any new campaign must respectfully and mindfully assess their own positionality and that of their potential backers, and an important part of that picture is the expectations and pitfalls created by campaigns that have come before our own.

In the following sections, I sketch out the theoretical basis for each of these processes before explaining how they interweave to provide a model for planning future crowdfunding campaigns' XA.

Listening Without Filtering

First and foremost, an XA requires that writers and organizations listen while taking pains to avoid the simple conflation of their internal values and ideas with those of the target audience. Instead of creating the campaign we want or the campaign we think the audience wants, we must listen without filtering to potential backers, centering their values and goals in our own process. Drawing a parallel to the proposal and grant writing, crowdfunding teams must avoid the impulse to default to an internal mindset or even boilerplate text (Johnson-Sheehan, 2008) when a nuanced and audience-specific deliverable is needed. No one is ever fooled by boilerplate text outside of the author.

Listening without filtering aligns our work in crowdfunding with the approach advocated for by Walton et al. (2019). As the authors remind us, we must address inequities and unjust systems in our daily work to prevent "our daily, mundane practices" from contributing to "the marginalization, exploitation, and powerlessness of others" (p. 139). Crowdfunding exists in a space that inherently moves to recognize and reject traditional funding mechanisms. Going direct to backers bypasses the traditional structures of gatekeeping in startup funding and publication, but doesn't prevent us from recreating those structures and abuses in our alternatives (as seen in the case of adult content creators on OnlyFans and Patreon). To do better, we can't simply reject the existing status quo—we have to mindfully listen to those we're working with to provide an alternative that avoids creating new injustices.

As Walton et al. explain, the replacement of existing injustices "requires the consultation of others, the humbling of one's own idea about what should happen and how a problem should be addressed in light of what others say" (p. 143). We can't simply create the campaign that we think should exist—we have to go to our potential audiences and backer coalition members and listen to what they want and need. In doing so, we have to be willing to put our own desires and goals up for potential replacement or alteration. We can't simply listen to the things that align with what we want to hear.

One way to understand our backers is to look at what they have told us. In the case of crowdfunding, the most readily available source of data for the audience's values and preferences is the body of successful serial campaigns that have demonstrated their ability to capture and then maintain an audience's interest and passion. Crowdfunding campaigns do not function as zero-sum games—when one campaign gets cash, it doesn't prevent or discourage other campaigns from succeeding. Instead, crowdfunding portals have been shown to curate their own group of aficionados, sometimes called Superbackers, that regularly give to campaigns across a given subject area.

"Superbackers" as a term entered the crowdfunding vocabulary via the Kickstarter Blog in 2016 (Edelstein, 2016). Originally noted as a phenomenon in the Games section of the site, the term would later become adopted by Kickstarter's platform (@WhatSuperbacker) to highlight users that are frequent contributors to campaigns across the entire platform. Specifically, Kickstarter defines a Superbacker as "a user who has supported more than 25 Kickstarter projects with pledges of at least $10 in the past year." Currently, the platform provides such backers with perks that include a special newsletter, a badge, and access to dialogues with creators.

The Superbacker represents someone who doesn't simply support a campaign because they find it interesting—these backers instead see themselves in some ways as stewards and patrons of their particular interests and use the backing of campaigns to help support and curate their passions via crowdfunding. This crossover between campaigns and even platforms in pursuit of the stewardship of an area of interest helps explain the rhetorical potential of analyzing campaigns that mirror a project a technical writer may be researching for launch. Looking at the types of campaigns like our own future project can give us real-world examples of what backers feel and say and are excited about via backer totals, funding numbers, and comments on projects.

While each campaign's appeals may be set to attract users with a particular set of interests, the Superbacker phenomenon shows that the same backers can and do show up as backers in multiple projects that represent a broad category of interest for them. Successful campaigns close to our own provide us with a finite starting point in our attempts to listen without filtering our audiences and their desires.

Quantifying the Causes of Engagement

Having framed the importance of listening to our audience without filtering, the next step is to quantify the causes of engagement that we'll craft and plan an engaging campaign around. While in-depth interviews and community feedback events can be useful in this process, the practical value of simply looking at existing campaigns shouldn't be overlooked when we start initial planning and research for a project. We should carefully look at the projects that align with our own, paying attention to how they've excited backers and how they've disappointed them. This too is a form of listening.

To provide a framework for quantifying how backers are excited and disappointed, I first turn to Roger Grice (2017) who highlights the need to emotionally move the user in our XA work. Grice grounds his discussion on XA by first defining what he sees as the evolution of the design process and the approach that companies have followed to design over the past few decades. For Grice, design evolves as a product/organization/company matures from primarily being concerned with logos, "you can trust us and our product"; to focusing on ethos, "we are the type of company you want to buy products from"; to finally shifting to pathos, "you want to purchase our device" (pp. 48–49). This evolution from a focus on the product and the producer to a focus on the affect of the product provides us with guideposts for researching our users' values and desires. We know what the audience values (in the form of existing successes), but we also need to know what within that realm can be shared with them as part of our curated experience. In short, we need to know what types of deliverables provide value to our potential backer coalition.

Vital to Grice's approach is the notion that effective experiences are systematically developed as a part of XA (p. 42). In outlining the types of moves we should make, Grice provides the following parameters:

- "Build the user experience around people rather than around the product or process that those people will be using."
- "Actively engage people in their experience."
- "Shift our rhetorical strategy from logos, presenting in the seemingly most logical way, and ethos, relying on an organization's reputation, to pathos, presenting in the way that most appeals to people and engages their senses."

(p. 42)

For some technical communicators and writers, the aforementioned context may at first glance seem a bit uncomfortable as it seemingly moves us from providing technical information to creating an emotional resonance in the audience. The idea that technical communication can be rhetorical and persuasive can strike some in the field as uncomfortable or wrongheaded, but we, as Frost and Eble (2015) explain, can and should be aware of how persuasion works in technical communication, especially specialized persuasion. Persuasion and tech comm don't have to be separate. If anything, some of the best technical communication emotionally resonates with the user on some level. The work done in the Divinity campaign, for example, is emotional work (though emotional work in managing communities is often overlooked or devalued (deWinter et al., 2017). Updates during the funding and fulfillment phase are designed to get people excited about this project and to maintain that excitement for the long term.

Interestingly for technical communicators, the deliverables that create backers' XA during a campaign and fulfillment are for the most part simply a documentation of stages of development and the sharing of those phases with backers. It's technical writing that engages and excites these backer coalitions, more often than not, because of what that writing represents. Sustainable crowdfunding campaigns like Divinity manage to make the mundane emotional by crafting the experience in such a way as to connect what is happening in the daily fulfillment of a campaign with the same emotional message that originally brought backers to the table with their checkbooks at the ready. This mundane documentation lets our coalitions of backers see the things they value coming into existence, and that is powerful. XA provides us with a comprehensive approach to such mundane data to create these emotional connections.

Before moving further, I first want to note that none of this is new: companies and fandoms have been fervently clinging to any and all information around their favorite subjects forever. For example, the film, music, and video game industries have long catered to fans that crave even the smallest minutiae related to their passions. Fans of Bob Dylan, for example, can purchase a box set that has an entire disc made up of alternative takes and masters across a growing body of his work (*Springtime in New York to Be Released September 17 | The Official Bob Dylan Site*, n.d.), and Dylan's work is far from unusual in this regard. *Star Wars* fans, in the same way, have quarreled for decades over what is considered the "correct" versions of the original Star Wars Trilogy. Things can get silly fast when fandoms obsess. *The Lord of the Rings* films by Peter Jackson, as another example, are offered in a box set released at $800 that included 30 discs covering the films, extended cuts, bonus material, director commentaries and other notes, and various making-of documentaries (Gartenberg, 2016). Fan culture takes these fairly mundane aspects of film or music production and transforms them from the mundane into the mesmerizing. For example, One Tree Hill fans now can relive each episode with commentary on a podcast by some of the lead actresses on the show (Bria, 2022).

Jeff Rice (2016) in his work on the social and rhetorical world of crafting brewing explains this further. Rice makes the case that those who are truly obsessed move beyond surrounding themselves with their passion but are moved further to sharing that passion with others. As Rice notes talking about craft beer fans,

> Obsessed individuals don't want to keep their stories to themselves. They want to organize and share their experiences and beer achievements. Otherwise, excitement—no matter how mundane—is an individual experience and, as such, has limited meaning in the long term regarding the building of relationships . . . Sharing is central to the craft experience, whether in beer or elsewhere in the experience of consuming food. The obsessed individual, like me, needs to tap into that narrative of sharing.
>
> *(p. 13)*

This obsession with minutiae, as portrayed by Rice, becomes an obvious starting point for campaigns that draw on the existing passions of a targeted set of backers. Rice helps us recognize the power of campaigns to provide coalitions of backers a place to grow into full-fledged communities, discuss their passions, and see their projects come to life. We will eventually see this in Chapter 6's example of the growing community around Rancho Relaxo's social media presence, as well as in the serial successes of Chapter 5.

While the music and film industries have catered to this passion for minutiae, I argue that the video game industry, and especially the tabletop gaming industry, has been turning these tiny bits of the mundane into an experience for users for decades, perhaps partially explaining why platforms like Kickstarter now gain more than one-third of their entire revenue from video and board game-related projects and campaigns (Hall, 2020), with board games currently leading by a healthy margin. Both industries excelled at turning the mundane into marketable content, with videos hitting their stride in the 1990s and board games experiencing the start of a widely acknowledged golden age in the 2010s (Duffy, 2014). Each industry has demonstrated an aptness at adapting to changing media environments to boost sales and create experiences for potential users, and this experience has translated to success in the crowdfunding realm.

For an example of technical details and information-based updates that have created and sustained connections with audiences to create compelling user experiences, we need to look no further than Nintendo's first heyday in the 1990s during which the publisher/console manufacturer boosted sales and built excitement through multi-channel campaigns. The launch of *Super Metroid* in the summer of 1994 is one such example. *Super Metroid* is a notable example not only because of its use of multiple channels to market to potential users but also for its long-term impact on the discipline of game development (Baker, 2016). Not only did the game resonate with developers but it was also the spiritual antecedent to famous crowdfunding campaigns such as those for *Shovel Knight* (Yacht Club Games, 2013) and *Bloodstained* (Igarashi, 2015). During the lead-up to the game, Nintendo made use of a multi-pronged approach to orchestrate an experience that provided potential buyers with prelaunch user experience via constant snippets about the game, its features, and its larger world. In the Nintendo-published periodical *Nintendo Power*, the company started a *Metroid*-themed comic roll-out that started in February 1994, a full four months before the game's launch ("Super Metroid: Chapter 1: Red Alarm!," 1994) and that would run beyond that launch date as a story arc. (This matches a similar pattern of comic tie-ins with the SNES title *Star Fox* that launched in the same year). In addition, Nintendo leveraged magazine interviews ("Everything You Always Wanted To Know About Samus But Were Afraid to Ask," 1994) to create a steady drip of content for user experiences. They even went as far as to write and market a player's guide via their gaming magazine that integrated the lore of the game alongside concept art and gameplay tips and tricks, a pattern that the publisher used in several of their tent-pole games and that became part of the 1990s' gaming culture (Gach, 2022).

The Nintendo campaign around *Super Metroid* (and other 90s hits) demonstrates the lengths to which the gaming industry would go to create sustained user experiences that primarily revolved around information and the mundane. An interview preview of a game might only feature a few shots of an area in the game and some discussions of enemy mechanics, all fairly mundane bits of information, but for the passionate fans, simply sharing these mundane artifacts can be compelling, as Rice (2016) reminds us. The multimodal approach taken by Nintendo created TV shows, clothing, comics, and magazines that all revolved around and promoted deeper fandom and excitement for their games.

Another example that I believe we can learn from is the tabletop gaming industry, also a break-out success on crowdfunding platforms. Like video games, tabletop gaming companies excelled at creating and sharing steady streams of technical information and texts that spanned modalities to create compelling user experiences for fans. One example is the world building and avenues for experiences created around the game Dungeons and Dragons, known more commonly as D&D. D&D is a tabletop role-playing game where players control characters that go on various adventures, often in pre-existing worlds called campaign settings. One such campaign setting, the *Forgotten Realms*, is emblematic of the larger way that these settings create and orchestrate experiences for players and build emotional connections. The campaign setting, created by Ed Greenwood, was first shared with players in one of the official D&D magazines, *Dragon*, in 1979. This would be followed by the realms becoming officially adopted and used for numerous modules throughout the following years ("Forgotten Realms," 2021). The setting would eventually branch out into comic series as well as novel series and video games, several of which became revered as pinnacles of their genre. This combination of interactive play in a setting alongside officially scripted adventures that players could discuss, ad hoc campaigns created in the setting by players, as well as official storylines and characters detailed in books and comics created a shared experience for *D&D* players and an emotional attachment to the *Forgotten Realms*. Every new comic, campaign, or magazine article provides fans with more information (sometimes quite mundane, such as the hit dice and other combat information for a creature in an adventure) to fuel their passion. Even in the 2020s, the campaign setting is thriving with new books and games, building on a legacy that spans almost 40 years and that has a special place in many players' hearts.

While a discussion on the 1990s' video games and *Dungeons and Dragons* may seem out of place in a book about crowdfunding, I believe these examples serve as early exemplars of XA that create the type of emotional resonance that Grice (2017) calls for via the simple sharing of information and minutiae that Rice (2016) calls to our attention that holds such a dear place in fans' hearts.

A video game or tabletop board gaming campaign may not create a 1:1 pattern for how we should create campaigns in crowdfunding, but they do demonstrate effectively how to translate emotional investment that already exists and how to channel that into new and engaging experiences that can often simply revolve around documenting the process and project itself. For technical writers working with established organizations that are looking into branching into crowdfunding, the examples of these types of campaigns and the ways that they rely on nostalgia, emotion, and the mundane minutiae of a project to generate buy-in and excitement can be valuable starting points for crafting a compelling campaign's XA.

To craft a language and method for capturing the minutiae and details and language that compels our coalition of users, I turn to Christian Lundberg's (2009) concept of tropological economies that drive the discourse of a given public. Lundberg, relying on a definition of tropes that leans heavily on Jacques Lacan, explains that any given group's tropes exist in "an economy of exchange and articulation generative of all signs and their meanings" (p. 389). In this formulation, a trope doesn't exist to simply decorate a text: tropes exist in what Lundberg describes as an affective economy, serving as "sites of investment" for a particular public. Lundberg's use of public follows from the concept of public as defined by Michael Warner (2002) that terms a public a self-organizing group that exists through the process of being addressed in some way (p. 67), a model of audience that isn't entirely dissimilar to the concept of a coalition.

Warner's public is a useful model for the crowdfunding backers that a particular project attracts—the backer coalition comes into existence concurrent with the project, cocreating each other. During this cocreation, the tropological economy (Lundberg, 2009) comes into play, serving as the currency of the group's communications, demonstrating "readable regularities in the exchange of tropes, governed by patterns and practices of investment that lend themselves to repetition and reiteration across time" (p. 408). In short, the tropological economy provides a window into what our backers care about and are passionate about, providing a window into a community that has the potential to coalesce around a given crowdfunding campaign.

Successful crowdfunding campaigns mobilize the affective economy of a given community, creating an affective and rhetorical bridge between the campaign and the backers (Pope, 2017). The identification and use of terms that carry value within the economy of a given public provide us with a concrete way to listen to a community without filtering. Understanding the tropes and language of a given coalition allows us to demonstrate our alignment with the values, goals, and ideas of a given community. Lundberg offers up the example in his work of Mel Gibson's *The Passion of the Christ*, citing the film's marketing approach and its use of persecution as a mobilization of the tropes of the Evangelical community in the United States. For a crowdfunding campaign, the same holds true— successful campaigns are able to create goodwill and generate support with a public because they provide the public with a way of making visible their own values and goals. In providing these communities with the ability to reject systems that don't recognize their values and simultaneously back the creation of those that do, the crowdfunding campaign provides an almost intoxicating allure (Pope, 2017).

Since we know that backers (and Superbackers) often traffic in multiple campaigns that align with their existing passions and activist goals, it makes sense to mine successful campaigns as a starting point to identifying the associated coalitions and their tropological economies. These extant campaigns can be incredibly valuable because they provide a window into potential backer coalitions that may be similar to our own. As Walton et al. (2019) remind us, coalitions are not built on a shared worldview, but instead on a shared interest on "an issue of mutual importance" (p. 55). By looking at the coalitions other campaigns have built and the language and ideas they value, we can gain a better understanding of types of users our own project might attract and how to attract them by showing that they've been listened to.

By focusing on the finite materials creating during and after a campaign, the scope of text and media to be reviewed is manageable enough to carry out multiple investigations, allowing multiple data points to be carved out to help triangulate successes and successful tropes in a particular type of crowdfunding campaigns. In essence, this work allows for a rough calibration of the community's goals, desires, and passions and gives us a way to decenter our own goals and preconceptions. Yes, further audience research for a brand-new campaign is needed, but that work is always local and specific to a given setting. Quantifying the minutiae that bring passion to a campaign and the tropological economy that accompanies it allows us to understand how best to generate content that respects our coalition and attracts backers to our cause.

Defining Campaign Expectations

Having listened to users and quantified engagement, the final step in researching a campaign's XA is the simplest: we need to define the expectations set by peer campaigns and the platforms that house them. Without that basic understanding, even a well-researched campaign on other fronts can fail to create a compelling experience. If we don't provide the expected experience, our backers may feel we haven't listened to them, don't care about them, or simply don't respect them. Much as there is a difference between knowing what you are talking about and sounding like you know what you're talking about, there is a difference between a campaign that sounds like a campaign invested in its backers and their passions and a campaign that sounds or looks like an exploitative money grab. We can't, to echo Potts and Salvo (2017), set our scope too narrow or seem to be providing a low-effort and disrespectful campaign.

To articulate how we should think about benchmarking, I rely on the concept of genre ecology. As defined by Clay Spinuzzi and Mark Zachry (2000), a genre ecology "includes an interrelated group of genres (artifact types and the interpretive habits that have developed around them) used to jointly mediate the activities that allow people to accomplish complex objectives" (p. 172). Spinuzzi and Zachry argue that an ecological approach is necessary to understand the dynamic and interconnected way genres function (p. 173). Genre ecologies as a concept help us map the ways that crowdfunding campaigns don't simply exist in a vacuum.

Campaigns exist in a world where they have competitors and peers and often share backers with multiple other campaigns with the same stated goals, as evidenced by the Superbackers and others like them. Each campaign pushes an individual message, but that campaign is at the same time defined by the actions of those that have come before it and those that exist alongside it concurrently. The genre ecology framework helps articulate how individual campaigns emerge in response to both a specific need (the project being pitched) and the communal history preceding it that the publics aligned to a certain niche will be aware of via their ongoing interest in the conversation. This is another way we demonstrate respect for our coalition and their interests. Instead of a simple boilerplate campaign or a campaign in a vacuum, we tailor our work to the audience and the platform (as will be discussed in Chapter 3). Indiegogo campaigns need to look and feel like Indiegogo campaigns while also putting forward a message that resonates with viewers; the same can be said for GoFundMe, Kickstarter, Patreon, or any other platform that supports crowdfunding.

Strings of successful campaigns tend to align with approaches that have previously succeeded, creating a new branch of the genre ecology that may well support a variety of new projects living in the rhetorical space created by a particularly resonant success story. Once a campaign of a particular niche succeeds, the success not only energizes the coalition that funded the project but also demonstrates to them and other potential campaigns that success is possible. To illustrate this effect, we can look back to the bellwether video game campaigns that rocketed to success in the early days of Kickstarter. The blockbuster gaming Kickstarter procession began with DoubleFine's Adventure (Double Fine and 2 Player Productions, 2012), a game with a slightly goofy and personal pitch by studio lead Tim Shaffer. At the core of the message was the idea that fans could bring back a genre that had been allowed to die out in the gaming world. Later, that same year, the platform would see the Wasteland 2 (inXile Entertainment, 2012) campaign that shared the same general pitch (bring back a game), but with a healthy dose of cynicism about the state of corporate-run gaming studios and their ability to see the value in classic genres. Later on, the Bloodstained campaign (Igarashi, 2015) would take this one step further with the main developer, IGA, angrily throwing down a wine glass exclaiming that publishers no longer believed in the classic genre of his games, but he knew they were wrong. In just a short period of time in the shared platform of Kickstarter, this stream of games managed to evolve around the same general concept (games needed reviving by fans) while transforming in tone from one that was slightly goofy to cynical to outright angry (and campy) (Pope, 2017, 2018).

When looking to craft a successful campaign, the genre ecology can at times be daunting, but approaching research on standards set by peer campaigns can be simplified by applying a quantitative lens to the issue. To assess how much content is going to need to be produced during a campaign and its fulfillment, technical writers can survey adjacent campaigns that have run their course for data. Looking at a campaign's history and determining the total number of updates, the frequency of those updates, and the types of content found in those updates (images, text, videos, etc.) can be a useful marker for determining what a reasonable outlay of material for your own campaign may look like. If peer campaigns are putting out a certain level of content and may well share backers with your own campaign, there is pressure if not incentive to put out as much or more content of the same type and frequency.

Bringing It Together

To carry out a successful campaign, we need to scope our work properly and frame it well. Crowdfunding campaigns are not simply the pitch and a few updates along the way. That definition is entirely too narrow. As Potts and Salvo (2017) note in their framing of XA, we run the risk of missing critical context in our planning and implementation of complex projects when we start with too limited of a scope (p. 7). We need to frame the project not as a single deliverable or product, but instead as a collection of coordinated content systems that have to be planned, managed, and evolved throughout the process of a given campaign.

Having gone through the rationale for our three research moves, listening, quantifying, and defining, we need to see what the data from these research dives shows us and how we can leverage that data to understand the scope and contents of successful campaigns architectures that center our coalitions of backers. Our end goal in researching campaigns is to have enough data in place to craft a nuanced, situated, and reactive XA that engages our audience because it has been created through listening to them and providing an experience and goals that resonate with their own priorities. Ideally, the process of building a successful campaign then shifts into an ongoing relationship between the campaign and backers that continues to advance the goals of the coalition that has formed around a given project.

Case Study Methodology

Having discussed our three research moves: listening, quantifying, and defining as well as mapping out the case studies to be analyzed, I now want to map out the specific research methodologies that we'll use to gather data for analysis via the theories discussed in this chapter. My research aims to provide a pattern for mining the texts of case studies to provide us with a window into the values of a coalition of backers via listening to their voices without filtering; quantifying the mundane details, minutiae, and tropes that the campaigns share and document to create engagement; and finally defining the scope and breadth of the XA workload during and after a campaign's launch window.

I have chosen to leverage an explanatory sequential mixed methods analysis as defined by John W. and J. David Creswell (2017). The approach relies on a two-pass approach to analysis that begins with a quantitative analysis that is used to generate initial findings that are then tested and expanded via a qualitative analysis. As Creswell and Creswell explain, "The intent of this design is to have the qualitative data help explain in more detail the initial quantitative results, thus it is important to connect the quantitative results to the qualitative data collection" (p. 222). To achieve this connection, I will be using text mining to perform the quantitative analysis before shifting to qualitative analysis via a close reading and coding process that will be seeded by the findings of the quantitative review. Traditional coding processes with qualitative research are time intensive, and with the scope and scale of crowdfunding campaigns and their associated deliverables and feedback, there is a non-trivial chance that certain patterns and insights may simply be overlooked due to the overwhelming number of deliverables in larger and more active campaigns that need to be worked through. While the front-loading of the quantitative reading necessarily changes our point of view and introduces some biases into the reading, we all already bring any number of points of view and biases to our discussions, with even the questions we ask framing what we find in our research as Bruno Latour (2007) and countless others have noted. To create as transparent a data set as possible, I will be using bespoke stop words lists in my quantitative analysis that are unique to each project and published as an online appendix to this text.

By using quantitative review first, I hope to avoid overlooking patterns in the text that may not be as visible when each piece of the corpus is read individually via coding. As Talea Anderson (2021) notes in work on the Disability March, quantitative approaches allow us to capture more patterns and connections than we might find simply through a close reading. Anderson leverages Douglas Eyman's (2015) argument that contrasting methods often buttress each other with one providing insights into a space the other cannot access. If anything, the quantitative methods provide an even more direct approach to methods such as the grounded theory analysis, as seen in the work carried out by Wolff (2015) on Springsteen's tweets, as the tools can be leveraged to simply report the frequency of terms and patterns in use without the need to read each text and make detailed notes (though that step is the second phase of my method). With that said, we must keep in mind that any software tool or library brings within it an embedded logic that skews results and carries its own biases (such as built-in stop words collections that shape the final results). As ample research shows us, algorithmic data tools are anything but innocent (Gruwell, 2018; Hocutt, 2018; West & Pope, 2021), though most of the usages in this text will be simple numeric counts and frequency plots rather than more advanced topic-modeling and interpretive algorithms. With that said, in order to provide as much transparency and replicability as possible, each of the individual *R* tools that I use will be provided as leveraged via an interactive online interface, providing access to the exact tools and datasets used in this book for those looking to expand on my casework or start their own projects.

In Figure 2.3, I sketch out my overall research process with a focus on providing a technology process map similar to the work of Palmeri and McCorkle (2017). Texts are first collected via web scraping with the *Node.js* library *Puppeteer* or simple copy/paste work in niche cases. Next, the relevant data from the page HTML is located and converted into a table via the *rvest* packing in the *R Tidyverse* (*Tidyverse*, n.d.). Once in the table, the data is formatted in the tidy format (pioneered by Hadley Wickham, 2014) with each row representing a single observation. Basic date and word count review is done before the data is loaded into the *quanteda* (Benoit et al., 2018) package for the bulk of the analysis with some supplemental analysis being carried out via the *TidyText* (@queirozTidytextTextMining2022) package. When that analysis is done, the terms and concepts that present themselves across a given case study are used to seed the codebook for the qualitative reading of the text. The coding returns to the quantitative data as needed to provide a top-level view of where and how terms are used. By the end of the qualitative phase, the key tropes, types of minutiae and mundane information shared, and genres of the updates as well as the engagement data for these items and the benchmark data for each campaign are collected for use in planning future crowdfunding writing in similar spaces.

Figure 2.3 maps my own process, though your own actual practice will likely differ based on the needs of a particular team and their time constraints and tool choices. The goal of this two-channel approach is to provide the widest possible scope and understanding of what existing XAs in crowdfunding look like before moving into planning a future campaign.

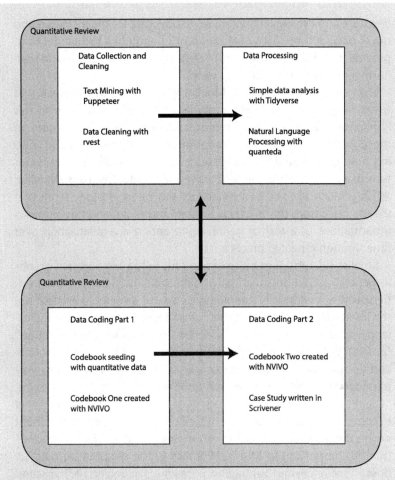

Data Processing Overview

FIGURE 2.3   Technology process map for book case studies

Quantitative Text Analysis

Though not as widespread as rhetorical readings of texts, quantitative research has a history in rhetorical research as well as technical and professional writing. Most of the scholarship draws on existing threads in the digital humanities, with a focus on data visualization being common.

Derek N. Mueller has defined a great deal of space on the subject through his work on nephological modeling (2012) and chart-based distance reading (Mueller, 2012b). Mueller builds on models from literature and the digital humanities to advocate for the increased and novel perspectives that visualization of quantitative textual data can provide for scholars and writers as they attempt to move beyond their normal grounding and point of view.

Nephological modeling, as Mueller defines it, is an approach that treats texts as accessible via a "horizon-mindful" viewpoint. In this horizontal approach, Mueller compares texts across the history of the Conference on College Composition and Communication, noting how over time these addresses merge into a discourse and culture that creates a sort of "discursive inertia" for speakers (Mueller, 2012a). Much like the benchmarking and genre ecology work previously discussed, this inertia is created and maintained by previous instantiations of a text or genre, representing a regularization over time through repeated practice.

Mueller (2012b) goes on to expand his scope arguing that graphs in general, based on quantitative data sets, "help us see with fresh perspective continually unfolding tensions among specialization, the interdisciplinary reach of rhetoric and composition, and the challenges these present to newcomers to the scholarly conversation" (p. 196). With the changing breadth and depth of the field of Rhetoric and Composition, Mueller argues this approach provides a new way to understand where the field has gone and is going. As he explains, "Graphing provides a partial readout of the field's pulse with respect to compactness and diffuseness, which complicates speculation about where the field stands at any given moment and where it is headed" (p. 198). Important in Mueller's phrasing, the quantitative data set doesn't move beyond our traditional readings or universally transcend them in importance or weight, but instead supplements them by providing the vital signs of a given field's conversations and subject matter a given point.

Mueller's articulation of the value of quantitative textual analysis merges neatly with the task facing technical and professional writers looking to gauge the conversation and experiences of crowdfunding campaigns, as these campaigns and their deliverables and user feedback on those deliverables can grow so large as to challenge our ability to get the full picture. While a qualitative close reading of these texts can be useful, even the most dedicated coder may well miss connections that are formed across such broad bodies of work. The ability to get a general sense of term frequency, textual relationships, and textual sentiment can allow us to work smarter in that close reading, and supplement our traditional point of view with a broader, perhaps even nephological perspective.

Mueller's (2012b) phrasing that these approaches provide a "partial" readout (p. 198) also resonates with important critiques of distant reading in the broader world of the digital humanities. Mueller, and these critiques, notes and respects the limits of a distant or quantitative analysis in providing definitive answers to textual questions. Without the situated context of a rhetorical reading of a body of texts, these quantitative revelations provide only a narrow window into the situation of a text, a window that may well be deceptive in its framing of the overall situation.

Word Clouds

Word clouds are a visually oriented approach to sharing term frequency in a given text. As Mueller (2012a) notes, word clouds show how texts "drift *across* one another." The word cloud gives a general overview of the terms in a group of texts or single text by illustrating from the center out the frequency of terms based on color and size. In the following word cloud example, you'll see the most common terms from a sample case study, *Divinity: Original Sin*. Interestingly, "now" and "can" are prominently centered, as seen in Figure 2.4.

Without even going into the context of the *Divinity* backer campaign, we can see a general shape of topics based on the terms shown

FIGURE 2.4   A word cloud of the Larian Divinity project's updates

earlier. As this is an example case study, I won't be doing any in-depth analysis. The word cloud in Figure 2.4 was created with *quanteda* (Benoit et al., 2018) and represents the top 150 words across all *Divinity* updates, after the removal of symbols, numbers, punctuation, and stop words. The stop words are terms that have been categorized as generally not contributing to the overall meaning of a sentence or text. For this example case study, I rely on the standardized *quanteda* English stop words list instead of a bespoke one.

In the major case studies, I'll primarily use comparative word clouds to interrogate the terms and usage patterns that show up distinctly in each phase of a given campaign. These comparative word clouds differ from standard word clouds in that term frequency across the whole corpus of documents is compared with frequency in each category, providing a crucial insight into what is unique in each campaign segment when usage is compared to other segments of the same corpus.

Lexical Dispersion Plots

Beyond the KWIC search and word clouds, I'll also use lexical dispersion plots, these plots are simply a way of visualizing term frequency across a text, and are common in natural language processing solutions such as the *Natural Language Toolkit* package for *Python* (Bird et al., 2009). For quantitative review, this plot allows the reader to view the general sense of where in a text a term occurs. Analysis can be universal across a body of texts, or it can be broken down by specific texts. This type of analysis allows researchers to see if a term is used across a text evenly, or if the term is used in a particular portion of a text or texts. Searching multiple terms can even allow insight into how terms are used together (or not). Dispersion plots also supplement qualitative readings by visualizing where codebook content appears with very little effort. Figure 2.5 displays a lexical dispersion plot for the Divinity project, and Figure 2.6 displays this same plot broken down by update number.

As seen in Figure 2.6, the use of "can" is weighted fairly heavily toward the start of the project, with later clusters occurring along the way. Note that not every update actually uses the term, and those that do not use the term are simply omitted from the plot. For example, Update 2 is not listed in the aforementioned plot, nor is Update 6.

Lexical dispersion plot, document: divinity

FIGURE 2.5   A lexical dispersion plot tracking the usage of the word "can" across all Divinity updates

Relative Frequency Analysis

In addition to mapping terms, relative frequency analysis can be calculated on updates. The analysis plot uses statistical analysis of the terms in a target reference text, and then compares them against the rest of

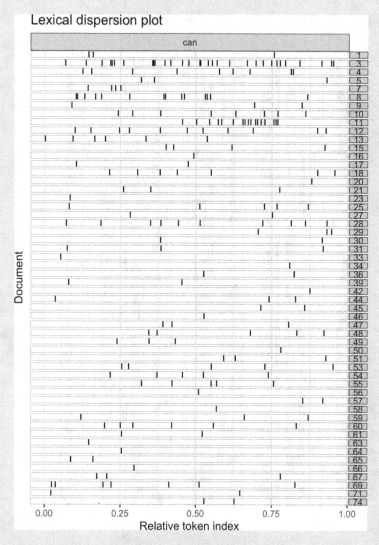

FIGURE 2.6 A lexical dispersion plot tracking the usage of the word "can" across all Divinity updates individually

the documents. Per *quanteda*, the keyness is a "signed two-by-two association originally implemented in *WordSmith* to identify frequent words in documents in a target and reference group" (*Relative Frequency Analysis (Keyness): Tutorials for Quanteda*, n.d.). A natural pattern for this would be a campaign's launch text versus the campaign's updates, or a campaign's updates before and after campaign success. There are numerous approaches to calculating values on the relative term frequency, but in this research, I use the default test in *quanteda* (Benoit et al., 2018), Pearson's chi-squared test, with Yates corrections applied. The subject of statistical methodologies to use when carrying out these tests is beyond the scope of this text, and secondary to my goals. Since I am using the quantitative analysis as a guidepost for qualitative analysis, the comparison is a useful tool to understand potential relationships between the texts. Figure 2.7 demonstrates a comparison of pre- and post-campaign backing updates for the *Divinity* sample study.

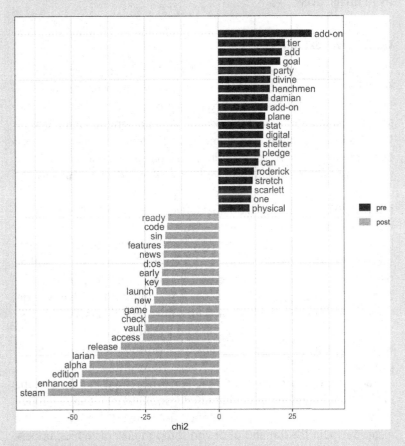

FIGURE 2.7 A relative frequency analysis of the terms used in the pre-funding and post-funding Divinity updates

At a glance, the *Divinity* data shows that the terms found more often before the campaign was backed focus on features within the proposed game and aspects of the campaign. In the post-success period, we see a shift to data on the testing and delivery of the campaign, such as an alpha test and the steam platform. Again, while this data should not be treated as a definitive treatment of these texts, as it ignores the overall context, something that critiques of digital humanities works of this type have highlighted as fundamental flaws in quantitative-only studies (Bode, 2017). But, since we're going to take these findings and leverage them for qualitative review, the content provides us with a robust starting point for thinking about these documents and coding them qualitatively.

Qualitative text analysis

Once the quantitative data is complete, we use that information to seed a qualitative reading of the texts, allowing the quantitative data to map the experience written large and provide waypoints as we navigate individual texts and their deliverables. The end goal in this is to listen to users, quantify engagement, and define the benchmarks for our own future campaign planning. For qualitative review, I focus on the main campaign and subsequent campaign updates of the selected case studies, relying on open coding approaches articulated by Sarah J. Tracy (2013). In approaching qualitative review, I reflect Tracy's assertion that "the researcher *is* the qualitative research instrument" (p. 11) by purposefully seeding my coding process and investigation of each site with a broad overview of the documents involved via quantitative analysis. My end goal is a complete "phronetic" or "practical wisdom" (p. 4) research project that builds contextualized knowledge while modeling such an approach for future researchers and writers. Such a project does not attempt to find a definitive answer, so much as an understanding of how to think through and use a given studied process.

Tracy's phronetic research has two key connections in the literature of technical communication that I build on, Michael J. Salvo's (2001) work with dialogic ethics, and Robert Johnson's (1998) work with *metis*. Salvo, in the framing of design through dialogic ethics, underscores the lack of quantification possible in design scenarios. Design is contextual, building on the locality being served and the users there;

good design is contextual, not universally applicable (p. 287). In the same way, phronetic research, and this larger project, attempts not to create the definitive solution for researchers and writers of crowdfunding, but instead attempts to create a durable, though not definitive, method for writing into a particular campaign's context. This process is akin to the building of *metis* or cunning intelligence discussed by Johnson in his work on user-centered design, where he illustrates the concept with a mechanic who has worked in a cold climate long enough to recognize a particular type of issue and its likely solution. The mechanics' knowledge is tied to their locality and is earned through experience and through a learned heuristic process. For Tracy, Johnson, and Salvo, the value of research and knowledge comes from localized interpretations, not universal guides.

My coding will consist of two cycles of coding, following Tracy's (2013) model. Each campaign is read in a first pass to create a series of first-level codes that will be used to create and maintain a codebook (pp. 189). In my case, the code book will already contain seed data from the quantitative analysis for verification purposes. The goal of this first phase of coding is to identify key phrases, ideas, and concepts, what Tracy refers to as the "essence" of a text (p. 189). This coding focuses on *what* is happening in the text, but not on *why* things are happening. There may be a regular centering of the coalition of a given project, or foregrounding of a given project's purpose, but these codes don't tell us the purpose of these moves, just that they exist. This process will be cyclical as codes will be regularized to prevent fragmentary coding where three or four terms may describe virtually the same phenomenon (p. 190). After the content has been mapped and described using the first level coding, coding will transition into a second-cycle set of coding creating second-level codes to interpret data points, as modeled by Tracy (p. 194). During the second round of coding, the first-round coding will be synthesized into a new codebook that moves from describing what to describing why, providing an interpretive framework for the data.

After the paired analyses, the final results will be articulated through the listening, quantifying, and defining framework to provide us with a window into a particular coalition and project's structure and relationship. With that said, coalitions are not worldviews as Walton et al. (2019) remind us. Our findings are not universal, but relate to the subject matter and timing of the studied campaigns.

Researching the Scale and Scope of Crowdfunding XA

To help set the scope properly of our crowdfunding XA work, I tackle a range of crowdfunding campaigns through two chapters of case studies. In Chapter 5, I focus on two discrete crowdfunding campaigns, that is, crowdfunding one campaign at a time. In Chapter 6, I focus on two interconnected crowdfunding approaches that feature ongoing subscription-based funding that is punctuated by the offering of objective-based campaigns on traditional crowdfunding platforms. Case studies are drawn from crowdfunding campaigns that have been identified as serial successes. To qualify, a campaign must be successful and be followed by another campaign that was also successful. The studies have been chosen to highlight the potential of crowdfunding to support social justice causes and nonprofit organizations.

The selected case studies provide a window into how crowdfunding can work in each of the major categories and helps build our larger-scale understanding of the XAs created by crowdfunding campaigns. Building off Grice's (2017) admonition to find and document exemplars, these case studies provide a window into what has worked for numerous successful campaigns, with a focus on diverse creators. The goal here is not to create unchanging recommendations for potential future campaigns, but to look into how to research successful campaigns and to sketch out in broad strokes the types of rhetorical moves that have been made by those campaigns as they build and maintain success in crowdfunding and create their own place in the crowdfunding genre ecology.

Discrete Campaigns

For discrete campaigns, I have chosen Lady Tarot Cards and STEAM Chasers from Kickstarter, both campaigns center on expanding the diversity in a given genre/area while providing contrasting visions for what success looks like in discrete crowdfunding. Lady Tarot Cards began with a campaign under the same name to create an "LGBT+ and POC friendly tarot card deck" (Lady Tarot Cards, 2020). STEAM Chasers (*The STEAM Chasers*, n.d.) is the first in three campaigns supporting the launch of a middle-grade book series teaching students about STEAM and Black American innovators. In the spirit of the 4Rs of Walton et al. (2019), each campaign is explicitly built around recognizing gaps in inclusivity and operates to provide an alternative/replacement that is more inclusive. The campaigns are discussed as a part of a string of serial successes, but qualitative and quantitative analysis is limited to the first campaign since these initial efforts are launched for the project's serial successes and provide us with a window into how to start the process of a serial crowdfunding success built on discrete campaigns.

Interconnected Campaigns

For interconnected campaigns, I focus on Rancho Relaxo (Caitlin Cimini, n.d.), a nonprofit animal rescue, across two interlinked GoFundMe Campaigns and a Patreon campaign that began during the second GoFundMe. The initial campaign to expand the animal rescue from 2016 met funding goals, but the project was unable to secure financing, preventing the project from meeting its central goal of expanding the animal rescue. The second campaign follows shortly on the first and provides a window into what sustainable crowdfunding looks like when a first campaign doesn't go as planned on a platform that supports open-ended funding. This narrative is supplemented with an analysis of the presentation of the Patreon presence for the rescue and an analysis of the frequency of content and types represented in a sample (based on public snippets, as Patreon is subscription-protected). We'll also look briefly at the social media content created by the charity in order to understand the content that on boards followers to Patreon (since Patreon is only mentioned directly by name in a single update). Since charities fundraise on a continual basis, the extended focus across multiple sites of fundraising for Rancho Relaxo provides us with a slightly different window into sustainable crowdfunding, one that also aligns with independent content creators (as we'll briefly discuss in Chapter 7).

Wrapping Up

Crowdfunding has demonstrated its value as a revenue source for businesses and nonprofits. Sustainable crowdfunding represents an approach that builds and then maintains an audience of dedicated backers in order to allow an organization to maintain an ongoing revenue stream that can supplement or replace traditional funding sources. Serial crowdfunding campaigns succeed because they build a relationship with backers that is then reinforced during a campaign before being transferred to a new campaign. In order to tackle the challenge in writing these campaigns and maintaining them, we rely on XA as a framework, recognizing that these campaigns are interconnected processes and workflows rather than a simple single-deliverable encounter. To plan a successful XA, we need to know what has worked and why things have worked, and so we turn to qualitative and quantitative reviews of existing successful campaigns, being mindful to listen without filtering to the coalitions of backers that have given campaigns life. By focusing on the key benchmarks set, the key tropes, key data, and key genres of successful campaigns, we're able to quantify what success looks like, contextually, in a given segment of crowdfunding that we wish to enter.

Discussion Questions

1. What crowdfunding platforms do you associate with different types of projects?
2. Research three failed crowdfunding campaigns. What are the key tropes and concepts used to discuss these campaigns? What is the diagnosis for their failure?

References

Anderson, T. (2021). *Identity and representation in the 2017 disability March.* https://kairos.technorhetoric.net/25.2/topoi/anderson/index.html

Baker, C. (2016, August 29). How "super metroid" inspired a generation of game makers—rolling stone. *Wired.com.* www.rollingstone.com/culture/culture-news/how-super-metroid-defined-an-era-and-inspired-a-generation-of-game-makers-250630/

Benoit, K., Watanabe, K., Wang, H., Nulty, P., Obeng, A., Müller, S., & Matsuo, A. (2018). Quanteda: An R package for the quantitative analysis of textual data. *Journal of Open Source Software, 3*(30), 774. https://doi.org/10.21105/joss.00774

Bird, S., Loper, E., & Klein, E. (2009). *Natural language processing with Python.* O'Relly Media Inc.

Bode, K. (2017). The equivalence of "close" and "distant" reading; or, toward a new object for data-rich literary history. *Modern Language Quarterly, 78*(1), 77–106. https://doi.org/10.1215/00267929-3699787

Bria, O. (2022, April 20). How Sophia Bush is "reclaiming" one tree hill on the drama queens podcast—exclusive. *TheList.com.* www.thelist.com/838476/how-sophia-bush-is-reclaiming-one-tree-hill-on-the-drama-queens-podcast-exclusive/

Brown, F. (2019, June 6). Larian was shot down the first time it wanted to make Baldur's Gate 3. *PC Gamer.* www.pcgamer.com/larian-was-shot-down-the-first-time-it-wanted-to-make-baldurs-gate-3/

Caitlin Cimini. (n.d.). *Our story—Rancho Relaxo.* Retrieved May 20, 2022, from www.ranchorelaxonj.org/our-story/

Creswell, J. W., & Crewell, J. D. (2017). *Research design: Qualitative, quantitative, and mixed methods approaches* (5th ed.). SAGE.

deWinter, J., Kocurek, C. A., & Vie, S. (2017). Managing community managers: Social labor, feminized skills, and professionalization. *Communication Design Quarterly, 4*(4), 36–45. https://doi.org/10.1145/3071088.3071092

Double Fine and 2 Player Productions. (2012, February 28). Double fine adventure. *Kickstarter.* www.kickstarter.com/projects/doublefine/double-fine-adventure

Duffy, O. (2014, November 25). Board games' golden age: Sociable, brilliant and driven by the internet. *The Guardian.* www.theguardian.com/technology/2014/nov/25/board-games-internet-playstation-xbox

Edelstein, J. (2016, April 26). Meet the superbackers. They might not wear capes as they soar . . . | by Kickstarter | Kickstarter Magazine | Medium. *Medium.com.* https://medium.com/kickstarter/meet-the-superbackers-962bf714fc2e

Everything You Always Wanted to Know about Samus But Were Afraid to Ask. (1994, May). *Game Players, 7*(5), 18–20.

Eyman, D. (2015). *Digital rhetoric: Theory, method, practice.* University of Michigan Press.

Forgotten Realms. (2021). *Wikipedia.* https://en.wikipedia.org/w/index.php?title=Forgotten_Realms&oldid=1035196185

Frost, E. A., & Eble, M. F. (2015). Technical rhetorics: Making specialized persuasion apparent to public audiences—present tense. *Present Tense: A Journal of Rhetoric in Society, 4*(2). www.presenttensejournal.org/volume-4/technical-rhetorics-making-specialized-persuasion-apparent-to-public-audiences/

Gach, E. (2022, February 11). The best video game strategy guide ever can be downloaded for free. *Kotaku.* https://kotaku.com/earthbound-snes-tips-nintendo-switch-online-mother-3-gu-1848523188

Gartenberg, C. (2016, August 22). Who is this $800 Lord of the Rings and The Hobbit boxset meant for? *The Verge.* www.theverge.com/2016/8/22/12590394/lord-of-the-rings-hobbit-800-dollar-box-set

Grice, R. (2017). Experience architecture: Drawing principles from life. In L. Potts & M. J. Salvo (Eds.), *Rhetoric and experience architecture* (pp. 41–56). Parlor Press. https://parlorpress.com/products/rhetoric-and-experience-architecture

Gruwell, L. (2018). Constructing research, constructing the platform: Algorithms and the rhetoricity of social media research. *Present Tense: A Journal of Rhetoric in Society, 6*(3). www.presenttensejournal.org/volume-6/constructing-research-constructing-the-platform-algorithms-and-the-rhetoricity-of-social-media-research/

Hall, C. (2020, December 22). Games broke funding records on Kickstarter in 2020, despite the pandemic. *Polygon.* www.polygon.com/2020/12/22/22195749/kickstarter-top-10-highest-funded-campaigns-2020-video-games-board-games

Hocutt, D. L. (2018). Algorithms as information brokers: Visualizing rhetorical agency in platform activities. *Present Tense: A Journal of Rhetoric in Society, 6*(3). www.present-tensejournal.org/volume-6/algorithms-as-information-brokers-visualizing-rhetorical-agency-in-platform-activities/

Igarashi, K. (2015, May 11). Bloodstained: Ritual of the night. *Kickstarter.* www.kickstarter.com/projects/iga/bloodstained-ritual-of-the-night

inXile Entertainment. (2012, March 13). Wasteland 2. *Kickstarter.* www.kickstarter.com/projects/inxile/wasteland-2

Johnson, R. R. (1998). *User-centered technology: A rhetorical theory for computers and other mundane artifacts.* SUNY Press.

Johnson-Sheehan, R. (2008). *Writing proposals.* Pearson Longman.

Lady Tarot Cards. (2020, April 20). Lady Tarot Cards: LGBT+ and POC inclusive Tarot Deck. *Kickstarter.* www.kickstarter.com/projects/novaandmali/lady-tarot-cards-lgbt-and-poc-inclusive-tarot-deck

Larian Studios, LLC. (2013, March 27). Divinity: Original sin. *Kickstarter.* www.kickstarter.com/projects/larianstudios/divinity-original-sin

Larian Studios, LLC. (2015, August 26). Divinity: Original sin 2. *Kickstarter.* www.kickstarter.com/projects/larianstudios/divinity-original-sin-2

Larian Studios, LLC. (2019, November 20). Divinity original sin the board game. *Kickstarter.* www.kickstarter.com/projects/larianstudios/divinity-original-sin-the-board-game

Latour, B. (2007). *Reassembling the social: An introduction to actor-network-theory.* Oxford University Press.

Lundberg, C. (2009). Enjoying god's death: The passion of the Christ and the practices of an evangelical public. *Quarterly Journal of Speech, 95*(4), 387–411. https://doi.org/10.1080/00335630903296184

Monroe, R. (2019, October 9). When GoFundMe gets ugly. *The Atlantic.* www.theatlantic.com/magazine/archive/2019/11/gofundme-nation/598369/

Mueller, D. N. (2012a, January 15). Views from a distance: A nephological model of the CCCC chairs' addresses, 1977–2011. *Kairos: A Journal of Rhetoric, Technology, and Pedagogy.* https://kairos.technorhetoric.net/16.2/topoi/mueller/

Mueller, D. N. (2012b). Grasping rhetoric and composition by its long tail: What graphs can tell us about the field's changing shape. *College Composition and Communication, 64*(1), 195–223.

Palmeri, J., & McCorkle, B. (2017). *A distant view of English journal, 1912–2012.* https://kairos.technorhetoric.net/22.2/topoi/palmeri-mccorkle/methodology.html

Pope, A. R. (2017). Bloodstained, unpacking the affect of a Kickstarter success—present tense. *Present Tense: A Journal of Rhetoric in Society, 2*(6). www.presenttensejournal.org/volume-6/bloodstained-unpacking-the-affect-of-a-kickstarter-success/

Pope, A. R. (2018). Understanding the writing demands of crowdfunding campaigns with the genre-mapping report. *Business and Professional Communication Quarterly, 81*(4), 485–505. https://doi.org/10.1177/2329490618795935

Potts, L., & Salvo, M. J. (Eds.). (2017). *Rhetoric and experience architecture.* Parlor Press. https://parlorpress.com/products/rhetoric-and-experience-architecture

Purchese, R. (2019, June 6). It's true: Divinity studio Larian is making Baldur's Gate 3. *Eurogamer.* www.eurogamer.net/articles/2019-06-05-its-true-divinity-studio-larian-is-making-baldurs-gate-3

Relative Frequency Analysis (Keyness): Tutorials for Quanteda. (n.d.). Retrieved August 10, 2021, from https://tutorials.quanteda.io/statistical-analysis/keyness/

Rice, J. (2016). *Craft obsession: The social rhetorics of beer.* Southern Illinois University Press.

Ringelmann, D. (2011, April 20). President Obama's Startup America selects IndieGoGo as crowdfunding partner along side AMEX, Facebook, Google, HP, LinkedIn and Cisco. *The Indiegogo Review.* https://go.indiegogo.com/blog/2011/04/president-obamas-startup-america-selects-indiegogo-as-crowdfunding-partner-along-side-amex-facebook.html

Salvo, M. J. (2001). Ethics of engagement: User-centered design and rhetorical methodology. *Technical Communication Quarterly, 10*(3), 273–290. https://doi.org/10.1207/s15427625tcq1003_3

Spinuzzi, C., & Zachry, M. (2000). Genre ecologies: An open-system approach to understanding and constructing documentation. *ACM Journal of Computer Documentation, 24*(3), 169–181. https://doi.org/10.1145/344599.344646

Springtime in New York to be Released September 17 | The Official Bob Dylan Site. (n.d.). Retrieved August 4, 2021, from www.bobdylan.com/news/springtime-in-new-york-release/

Super Metroid: Chapter 1: Red Alarm! (1994, February). *Nintendo Power!, 67*(February), 58–69.

The STEAM Chasers: Books on Black American STEM Innovators. (n.d.). *Kickstarter.* Retrieved July 27, 2022, from www.kickstarter.com/projects/thesteamchasers/the-steam-chasers-books-on-black-american-stem-innovators

Tidyverse. (n.d.). Retrieved August 6, 2021, from www.tidyverse.org/

Tomczak, A., & Brem, A. (2013). A conceptualized investment model of crowdfunding. *Venture Capital, 15*(4), 335–359. https://doi.org/10.1080/13691066.2013.847614

Tracy, S. J. (2013). *Qualitative research methods: Collecting evidence, creating analysis, communicating impact* (1st ed.). Wiley-Blackwell.

United24—The initiative of the President of Ukraine. (n.d.). Retrieved May 11, 2022, from https://u24.gov.ua/

Walton, R., Moore, K. R., & Jones, N. N. (2019). *Technical communication after the social justice turn: Building coalitions for action.* Routledge.

Warner, M. (2002). *Publics and counterpublics.* Zone Books.

West, S., & Pope, A. R. (2021). Rubles and rhetoric: Corporate Kairos and social media's crisis of common sense—present tense. *Present Tense: A Journal of Rhetoric in Society, 9*(1). www.presenttensejournal.org/volume-9/rubles-and-rhetoric-corporate-kairos-and-social-medias-crisis-of-common-sense/

Wickham, H. (2014). Tidy data. *Journal of Statistical Software, 59*(1), Article 1. https://doi.org/10.18637/jss.v059.i10

Williams, M. E. (2015, September 4). No GoFundMe for Kim Davis: Crowdfunding puts the brakes on the disturbing bigots-get-rich-quick trend | Salon.com. *Salon.* www. salon.com/2015/09/04/no_gofundme_for_kim_davis_crowdfunding_puts_the_ brakes_on_the_disturbing_bigots_get_rich_quick_trend/

Wolff, W. I. (2015, May 15). Baby, we were born to Tweet Springsteen fans, the writing practices of in situ Tweeting, and the research possibilities for Twitter [Text]. *Kairos: A Journal of Rhetoric, Technology, and Pedagogy.* https://kairos.technorhetoric.net/19.3/ topoi/wolff/methodology.html

Yacht Club Games. (2013, March 14). Shovel knight. *Kickstarter.* www.kickstarter.com/ projects/yachtclubgames/shovel-knight

3
ASSESSING PLATFORMS

Having mapped crowdfunding campaigns as XAs in Chapter 2, we now turn to analyzing the framing power that a given crowdfunding platform provides to nascent campaigns. Choosing a platform is a necessary first step in any crowdfunding campaign due to the central role that crowdfunding platforms play in shaping and structuring a given project. While some organizations may have the skill, time, and need for using a bespoke platform for their campaigns, most crowdfunding campaigns rely on a handful of major players in the crowdfunding space due to a mix of convenience as well as findability, as we'll discuss later in this chapter. These platform choices are important because they will define what your campaign can and cannot do (quite literally in some cases) as well as the types of deliverables and engagement you can leverage.

To get started, we'll begin with an important look at the political and editorial control that platforms have (as a reminder from Chapter 1, crowdfunding platforms have a history for sporadic editorial control that often impacts marginalized communities the worst). Next, we'll transition into an analytic rundown of the various platform choices and their possibilities and positions in the marketplace. Finally, we'll circle back to choosing a platform for your future campaign.

Platforms Politics and Interface Activism

Platforms are synonymous with crowdfunding, and for good reason, but they are not simple intermediaries with no goals or stakes. Platforms provide creators with a suite of tools for publicizing their projects as well as a system for collecting funding from backers. Without these platforms, crowdfunding as it currently exists simply wouldn't exist—these platforms in many ways have created, defined, and continue to shape what exactly crowdfunding is for the majority of users. It is

DOI: 10.4324/9781003308966-3

quite hard to separate the modern conception of a crowdfunding campaign from specific platform iterations like Patreon or GoFundMe in the same way it is hard to separate the social media as it exists from platforms like TikTok, Twitter, or Instagram. Functionally, the platforms are the genre and they cocreate it through the choices they make available or remove.

As Tartleton Gillespie (2010, 2015) has argued, the very concept of a platform is a rhetorical one, designed to position the platforms on the ground favorable to them when they deal with users, advertisers, creators, and legislative bodies. When we work through platforms, we are working through actors with social, economic, cultural, and political values and goals that may or may not align the values and goals of our teams and our backing coalitions. Not treating these platforms as innocent is important, especially considering the types of behavior noted in Chapter 1 and how they have in the past treated multiply marginalized creators. The platforms will not offer us a critical view of themselves, nor will they (without the threat of legal action many times) disclose how and why they act on the content that they steward and curate for our consumption. Critical analysis of these platforms is left to creators and their backing coalitions. As Gillespie (2015) explains in broad strokes, we must remember these are businesses at the end of the day:

> Recognizing that social media platforms shape the social dynamics that depend on them allows us to draw connections between the design (technical, economic, and political) of platforms and the contours of the public discourse they host. Remembering that they are private businesses reminds us that some of their decisions will be craven, or financially motivated, or constrained in ways even they cannot recognize.
>
> *(p. 2)*

I suppose you could say, at the risk of being too cheesy, that the unexamined platform is not worth posting on.

An important facet of how platforms specifically act on our campaigns and potential coalition members is their interface, a facet of our technology that often goes under-theorized in technical communication (Bacha, 2012). Discussing interfaces, I rely on the foundational work of Cynthia L. Selfe and Richard J. Selfe Jr. (1994). As Selfe and Selfe explain, interfaces are "sites within which the ideological and material legacies of racism, sexism, and colonialism are continuously written and re-written along with more positive cultural legacies" (p. 484). An interface for any given system will, generally speaking, reflect the cultural logic and power dynamics of those who have created it. The values and choices embodied in those interfaces then serve to privilege some and alienate others whose points of view and values were not centralized in the development of the design. Simply, "the interface as an interested and partial map of our culture and as a linguistic contact zone that reveals power differentials" (p. 495).

As Bethany Monea (2020) so elegantly explains, the problem in our modern world is that

> we are surrounded by interfaces; they construct and facilitate every human-computer interaction. However, the development and design process of these interfaces is not neutral. It is embedded within and emerges from a particular cultural and historical trajectory that not everyone may share.

The problem of interface, as pressing as it was at the early stages of our computerized society in the 1990s, has grown almost endlessly as our day-to-day lives are mediated at every turn by a never-ending parade of interfaces and platforms with particular political, social, and business interests that often do not align with our own.

Interfaces then, taken together with our broad understanding of platforms as articulated by Gillespie, play a central role in crowdfunding projects by mapping a typology and categorization onto our campaigns and projects secondary to any descriptions we might provide ourselves thanks to the power of their interface taxonomies. As Grace G. Lau (2015) explains, "Although the word 'taxonomy' is often used interchangeably with tagging, building an enterprise taxonomy means more than tagging content. It's essentially a knowledge organization system, and its purpose is to enable the user to browse, find, and discover content." Certain interfaces (and the taxonomies they are built with) will bring one type of content to the forefront while preventing the visibility of another that doesn't neatly fit into the pre-formed categorization system. If a platform supports a specific identifier, such as campaigns by Black creators, then that content will rise to the forefront of the interface, but without that specific identifier, the content will simply exist as a facet of the overall sea of content on a given platform. The taxonomy of interfaces and the way they hide and expose content is powerful and should not be overlooked.

Campaigns and projects that represent multiply marginalized individuals and groups and their causes are at particular risk when confronting interfaces and platforms that fail to account for their presence. As Walton et al. (2019) put it,

> Injustices often live in the mundane choices that technical communicators make: How drop down menus look, whether a form is translated into another language, if captioning is included in a tutorial video, the default setting on a topic-based authoring system.
>
> *(p. 163)*

When choosing to work with a platform, such campaigns must ensure they are allowed to exist, and perhaps encouraged to thrive, within the platform and its interface system.

The process through which a given platform makes visible and champions multiply marginalized individuals through system-level choices in the design and terminology of their interfaces I term "interface activism." Interface activism is aligned with Jennifer Sano-Franchini's (2017) concept of culturally reflexive frameworks for design. As Sano-Franchini explains, "User experiences are shaped by culturally contingent and ideologically laden symbolic representations that are conveyed through alphabetic texts, user interfaces, and physical interactions between humans and machines" (p. 30). Interface activism focuses narrowly on the specific taxonomy choices of navigational interfaces via a combination of visibility and what Sano-Franchini terms "desire." In tackling race and desire, Sano-Franchini's heuristic asks: "Are particular races, identities, or features cast as desirable (or undesirable)?" (p. 42). By focusing specifically on interfaces, I hope to both draw attention to the power of the seemingly mundane design choices in an interface taxonomy and provide a metric for assessing how friendly a given platform is to multiply marginalized individuals. Interfaces and their associated taxonomies represent a way of seeing the world and hold within them a logic and set of values, as Selfe and Selfe (1994) remind us, and the categories that an interface leverages can create space for multiply marginalized individuals and Black, Indigenous, and people of color.

As an example from retail shopping, Target Corporation began prominently featuring at the top of their "Categories" navigation "Black-owned or founded branded at Target," (*Black-Owned or Founded Brands at Target*, n.d.) and more directly relevantly to crowdfunding, GoFundMe lists "Celebrate Black Joy" (GoFundMe, n.d.-a) at the bottom of their "Discover" menu. By choosing to prominently feature these categories, these organizations have made a system-level choice to engage in interface activism, foregrounding those who have been historically marginalized. In the terms of Sano-Franchini, the presence of these interface choices highlights the desirability of content from or products created by Black creators and Black-owned and -founded brands. These choices are fairly mundane, in that they are simply binary inclusions or exclusions from a given interface and its taxonomy, but the visibility and favorability they provide fundamentally rewrite how Black creators and brands exist on these platforms.

As I'll investigate in much more detail shortly in the practical section of this chapter, different platforms allow different sorts of campaigns by multiply marginalized individuals to show up in different ways, and those choices amount to activism that directly impacts the potential success of a given crowdfunding campaign and should be taken into account when planning a given campaign. Not all platforms provide the same visibility and promotion to all types of creators (and all types of campaigns). Critically engaging with the platforms and their choices is the first and most fundamental step in starting a sustainable crowdfunding campaign.

Platform Overview

Having already covered the history and some of the ethical issues associated with each of the major crowdfunding platform players, in this section, we will simply focus on assessing the way each platform positions itself and its users before analyzing the strengths and weaknesses of each platform via a series of heuristic questions designed to assist in analyzing the impact of a given platform on a prospective campaign:

1. How does the platform privilege or fail to privilege the campaign and/or its creators?
2. What type of campaign mechanics does the platform support?
3. What supports does the platform provide to creators?
4. What is the overall position of the platform in the crowdfunding world?

By going through these questions, we'll highlight the potential of a given platform to privilege or support particular campaigns as well as the potential for a particular campaign type to simply not mesh well or fall through the cracks of a given platform. We'll cover the major platforms before a quick overview of a few basic categories of niche platforms and their purposes/audiences.

Kickstarter

Kickstarter as a platform for crowdfunding represents itself first and foremost as being for "creators." The "creator" terminology permeates both the site itself and the various support and helps documentation portals. Concurrent with a focus on creators, Kickstarter offers only one option for crowdfunding campaigns—an all-or-nothing approach that sees a campaign earning enough funding to meet their stated goal or sees a campaign falling short with no money collected from supporters (Kickstarter, 2022f). The platform represents this as a protection for both backers and creators in that it creates a slight forcing feature that requires creators to gain enough money to meet their goals and prevents them from taking money that only partially meets their needs, preventing backers from funding a project that will fail due to explicit underfunding (though campaigns can and do still fail because of poor funding calculations or poor supply chain choices). In addition, any campaign that will be shipping a physical product is required to have a prototype available for backers to see at the start of the campaign (Kickstarter, n.d.).

How Does the Platform Privilege or Fail to Privilege the Campaign or Its Creators?

Kickstarter's direct interface activism as of this book's writing is limited to the "LGBTQIA+" listing on the "On Our Radar" section of the site's Discover menu. Using the link provides a list of all campaigns that are currently tagged "LGBTQIA+" on the platform, with the default sort being "magic," an in-house term and algorithm used by the platform.

Outside of direct advocacy via "On Our Radar," most other Kickstarter advocacy for creators comes through two channels: their use of "Projects We Love" as a quality label and selection mechanism to showcase campaigns on email and on the site front page, and the "magic" sort algorithm that promotes campaigns to the top of their selected category.

"Projects We Love," referenced without quotations from this point on for the sake of simplicity, is not curated via algorithm, but instead via a fairly opaque selection process run by staff members of Kickstarter. The attainment of a badge can be critical for campaigns, allowing them to showcase on the front page and site emails, massively increasing traffic and visibility for a project that manages to earn the badge. Kickstarter's help documents explain the selection process in general terms:

> This includes, but is not limited to, a crisp project image with no logos, badges, or text on top, a clear and detailed description that includes a thorough plan for completing your project (more guidance on that *here*), captivating images or videos, an excited community, what we think different users will be interested in, and of course, a lot of creativity.
>
> *(Kickstarter, 2022e)*

A quick read through the list of potential qualifications for the Projects We Love list shows that none of the selection criteria can be read as an objective measure of a project's content. Adjectives like "crisp," "thorough," and "excited" as well as a blanket reference to "a lot of creativity" leave the selection process almost entirely open to interpretation.

Though Kickstarter explains a general curation process by their staff, community discussions from creators on platforms like Reddit and elsewhere paint a slightly different picture of the ways to access and get featured in Projects We Love. For example, a write-up on how the developer of *Operation Outsmart* details in a post-campaign write-up on Reddit how they were able to secure a Projects We Love tag via direct communication (encouraged via YouTube help videos from Kickstarter) with the director of games at Kickstarter (Seyedhn, 2021). The project did gain the badge, but because of a lack of an existing coalition of backers, did not benefit much from the budget and failed to meet its budget. None of this is documented on the Kickstarter website.

From a technical writer's perspective, the lack of specificity is potentially frustrating if gaining access to the Projects We Love category is a campaign goal or a campaign is planning on leveraging platform-level findability via the Projects We Love designation to increase traffic and backer numbers.

In addition to the Projects We Love that is featured on the front page, most default sorting via the Discover interface leverages the "magic" mechanic. The magic sort resets regularly, and pulls from both the Projects We Love in a given category and projects that are currently popular in that same category (Kickstarter, 2021). Since the category pulls from popular projects, there is at least the potential for a campaign to generate a good deal of momentum from their backer coalition, pushing them into the "magic" sort even without a Projects We Love tag.

What Type of Campaign Mechanics Does the Platform Support?

Kickstarter only supports all-or-nothing campaigns, per their platform policy. Once a campaign is over, the donations are done and further campaign contributions can't be made through the platform. The all-or-nothing approach is something of a hallmark for the platform, setting it apart from Indiegogo as well as GoFundMe, which both allow the collection of funds without meeting a project's goal (under certain guidelines for Indiegogo).

Kickstarter allows campaigns to select from a range of potential duration options for their campaigns, with options ranging from 1 to 60 days (Kickstarter, 2022d). While 60 days is certainly an option, the platform strongly encourages creators to use campaigns that are 30 days or less, citing the perception of immediate need created by the shorter duration campaigns.

In addition, the platform allows campaigns to create prelaunch pages that can be used for sign-ups by coalition members so they will be notified after the campaign is launched, with the page itself tracking and displaying the number of folks on this list after it hits a minimum of 10 followers (Kickstarter, 2022c).

Kickstarter also supports backer referral programs, though the platform provides strict guidelines and language around the use of these programs. Backers can earn back the entirety of their pledged support via these referral programs, but they cannot earn more than they've pledged for the project. The reward can be in the form of a funding refund for referrals, or it can be an additional reward or physical good that is valued up to the amount pledged by the backer. Functionally, this means that if a backer funds a project at $50, they can either earn that money back, earn the chance to move up to a $100 reward tier, earn an additional award that is tied specifically to promoting the campaign that is valued at $50, or earn a physical good that is valued at $50. The language describing the referral program at times borders on vaguely ominous, with Kickstarter stating that aspiring projects should "Promote your referral program in a tasteful manner on your project page and updates, if you hope to be considered for features by our curation team" (*Can I Use Referral Programs on Kickstarter?*, n.d.). This vague language and association with promotion on the platform aligns with the obtuse references to subjective standards used elsewhere as in the Projects We Love badge system.

Finally, Kickstarter does allow integration of Google Analytics into existing campaign projects (Kickstarter, 2022b) at the platform level, giving some additional insight into traffic flow to and from a given project. The service, however, does not offer access to the Meta Pixel, which provides access to campaign data in building custom advertising on the Meta platforms of Facebook, Instagram, and so forth.

What Supports Does the Platform Provide to Creators?

Kickstarter provides supporters with several avenues for support during the project planning, implementation, and fulfillment phases:

> The Kickstarter Support help pages
> The *Creator Handbook*
> The Kickstarter Blog
> *Kickstarter Magazine*
> *The Creative Independent*
> The official Kickstarter YouTube channel

The cluster of help provided by Kickstarter covers a variety of channels, with substantial overlap between the various avenues for support, posing a bit of a maze for potential creators. The Support pages provide a Q&A format based on the staging that a project finds itself: prelaunch, during launch, postlaunch. *The Creator Handbook* covers some of the same materials, but is formatted around taking a project from the idea phase through to fulfillment via a series of content chunks that more or less align with a project's timeline. The Kickstarter blog is just that, a blog with a range of content that covers both platform updates and news and creators and their campaigns. *Kickstarter Magazine* focuses on case studies and vignettes on successful campaigns, with a variety of tips for creators interspersed. *The Creative Independent* is more of a general content platform for creatives in general, with some overlap with the platform. Finally, the YouTube channel provides a range of content from creator-centric tips to more generic platform-specific content.

For technical writers, overall, the Kickstarter content for creating campaigns tends to be generic and positive in tone. This is not to say the content isn't helpful for guiding new creators through the process of creating a campaign—it is helpful for that. Rather, the content focuses more on the general idea of genres, steps, and processes without leaning heavily onto metrics or targets for campaigns before, during, and after the process of a campaign. For example, the Kickstarter page on data refers readers to a blog covering data that was most recently updated in 2018, four years before this book was written in 2022.

What Is the Overall Position of the Platform in the Crowdfunding World?

As noted previously, Kickstarter presents itself as a platform for and by creators, with an all-or-nothing funding model that sets it apart from the other major platforms covered in this chapter. With Projects We Love featured prominently, the site focuses on a mix of curated project presentation as well as algorithmic and activity-based promotion for creators, with the site itself designed to help browsers find and follow campaigns within their set area of interest.

The most popular category on Kickstarter by far is Games, with a total funding amount as of this writing of US$1.94 billion, followed by Design at US$1.47 billion, Technology at US$1.26 billion, and Film & Video at US$530.26 million (Kickstarter, 2022a). As of this writing, the project categories with the highest project success rates were Comics at 64.01%, Dance at 61.44%, and Theater at 60.02%. Of the highest earners, Games have the highest success rate at 45.55%, followed by Design at 40.94%, with Technology lagging behind all other categories tracked with a success rate of just 21.98%.

Indiegogo

Indiegogo contrasts with Kickstarter by focusing more on the created objects and deliverables coming from campaigns in their main site language. The main page's footer carries the trademark quote, "Clever Things for Curious Humans," and the focus on things carries through the rest of the platform. Though the site also funds television, movies, and music, the focus of the platform is on technology and devices that can be created via funder backing on the site, creating a contrast with the creator and creatives mindset of Kickstarter. One other important platform-level difference is that Indiegogo does allow for less-than-goal funding collection of pledges, allowing backers to deliver funds to campaigns that haven't met their stated goal for a project. The service also allows the post-funding collection of pre-orders for native campaigns and campaigns from other platforms via their InDemand service. Indiegogo also prominently features Indiegogo China, a pitch that explicitly targets China-based companies looking to expand to global markets. As a final note, the service does not require hardware campaigns to have a working prototype at the start of their campaign, setting up a fairly stark contrast with Kickstarter's requirement for working prototypes (Indiegogo, n.d.-l).

How Does the Platform Privilege or Fail to Privilege the Campaign or Its Creators?

Indiegogo as a platform features no interface activism within the main Explore menu on their website. Projects are presented with three major divisions: "Tech & Innovation," "Creative Works," and "Community Projects." With that said, one week into July, the front page of the site still contained a link to projects by LGBTQIA+ creators (Indiegogo, n.d.-k), though the same link did not appear in the default Explore menu.

In contrast to Kickstarter, Indiegogo provides primarily an algorithm-based approach to surfacing campaigns that it terms "The Gogofactor" (Indiegogo, n.d.-m). According to Indiegogo, the Gogofactor "helps campaigns achieve greater visibility on Indiegogo.com" and is "influenced by several aspects, including the scope of a campaign's social engagement (such as Facebook likes and shares), and global reach." While not fully transparent in the sense of weighting and other factors being exposed, the explanation is arguably more direct and open than the vague subjectively determined factors that influence a project being selected as a Project We Love by Kickstarter.

What Type of Campaign Mechanics Does the Platform Support?

Like Kickstarter, Indiegogo supports campaigns that can extend up to 60 days. Unlike Kickstarter, the campaign duration is not set in stone—a campaign can extend its length a single time, but not past the cap of 60 days for a given campaign's length. The flexible timeline for campaigns does represent an interesting tool for campaigns that may feel that they just need a bit more time to squeeze in a successful funding benchmark, but the extension doesn't markedly change the terms of a given campaign.

Unlike Kickstarter, and more akin to GoFundMe, Indiegogo does allow projects to collect funds using models other than all-or-nothing models. Indiegogo terms this approach Flexible Funding (*Choose Your Funding Type*, n.d.) and contrasts it with their other option, Fixed Funding. Flexible Funding allows a campaign to keep any and all funds (after fees) from their campaign, regardless of the amount raised toward their goal. The description from Indiegogo cautions that campaigns should only choose this option if they will be able to fulfill all of their perks regardless of the amount of money raised.

Once a campaign has reached their goal successfully, they are able to move into a separate subset of the platform, InDemand. On InDemand, campaigns can continue to solicit and receive funds while concurrently providing updates and other information to backers of the project. Campaigns must be in good standing with the platform *and* have met funding goals to transition into InDemand (Indiegogo, n.d.-g). The platform pitches this explicit shift to the fulfillment phase complete with additional tools and supports for that process as a distinct perk versus Kickstarter.

Importantly, InDemand as a platform is not tied to the usage of Indiegogo for a campaign. Campaigns that began on Kickstarter or elsewhere are able to sign up to use InDemand if they meet the minimum of having a successfully funded project. Payments are sent out every four weeks after an initial disbursement period of around 15 days. The primary difference between Indiegogo-native and non-native campaigns is that the funding cut is lower. Campaigns that are native to Indiegogo only have a 5% base fee on payments, and non-native campaigns will pay out 8% as the base fee for using the platform (Indiegogo, n.d.-f).

Indiegogo also has a platform-native referral contest tool that allows campaigns to run contests among existing backers to recruit additional backers to the coalition. Tiers of rewards can be designed by campaigns to reward backers for different levels and metrics based on campaign strategies. There are limits to what a campaign can provide to backers who win contests, and a prohibition on raffles and gambling on the platform, but rewards can be tied to the project, project reward levels, or even simply consist of Amazon.com gift cards (Indiegogo, n.d.-d).

For campaigns that are looking simply to increase their funding for a given project, perhaps a nonprofit that is looking for additional funding for a local project like a community garden, flexible funding could be an option that allows any money raised to go toward the project's supplies like seeds or soil, while still providing perks to backers if those perks are created with an eye toward a curated experience for backers that allows them to see the results of the campaign rather than focusing on received goods. Such a campaign might offer vlogs and regular updates to the backers as their primary perk, reducing the impact of receiving lower amounts of funding.

Indiegogo also offers a prelaunch page for campaigns (*Pre-Launch Page*, n.d.), with a greater focus on testing and analytics in the presentation of the tool than offerings from Kickstarter. For example, Indiegogo's page includes the option for an A/B test, a classic tool in user experience (UX) and marketing for assessing the impact of different takes on a given product. In addition, the prelaunch page comes with an analytics feature that provides data on how visitors are interacting with the page.

In addition, Indiegogo provides campaigns with "secret perks" that are only accessible via a direct link, providing an additional way to leverage tools like email lists and existing social media channels to reward a campaign's initial backer coalition (@WaysUseSecret).

Indiegogo's focus on analytics extends to support for both Meta Pixel and Google Analytics for prospective campaigns. Both of these tools plug into the platform directly, allowing access to information on marketing success rates and conversation rates via the twin tools (Indiegogo, n.d.-a).

What Supports Does the Platform Provide to Creators?

Overall, Indiegogo provides more data and analytics-driven help documentation, with an emphasis on specific deliverables, metrics, and services that can be leveraged when building a campaign. The overall effect of this approach is that the service's help documentation feels more ready for use by entrepreneurs seeking to build a product from scratch and that is used to relying on data-driven analytics. Support can be divided between free and paid documentation and assistance via the platform itself.

Indiegogo provides two levels of supports for creators on the platform: a free tier of help articles, tips, and guides; and a paid service called Education Center Plus. Education Center Plus operates on a monthly subscription, with rates ranging from $9.99 to $29.99 monthly with different levels of extra assistance and guidance on top of the free materials provided by the platform.

Indiegogo's supports, in general, are markedly more detailed and data-oriented than the comparable tutorials and supports provided by Kickstarter and leverage language that is familiar to professionals in marketing, public relations (PR), and UX. Data analytics are emphasized, as well as the necessity of calculating a fundamental floor of support from your existing backer coalition when you launch a campaign. Indiegogo repeatedly recommends that aspiring campaigns ensure that 30% of their funding is guaranteed via initial pre-existing backer relationships in order to have a successful campaign (Indiegogo, n.d.-c), based on their own internal data.

Indiegogo's materials also heavily focus on email lists as a key to successful project completion, with the topic coming up repeatedly across the platform. Leaning on data metrics again, Indiegogo estimates that 5–10% of a given campaign's email list will be actual conversions that buy, meaning that a given campaign can know when to launch their campaign based on when 5–10% of their email list would generate the essential 30% for launching (Indiegogo, n.d.-b). The supports for campaign email lists get quite detailed, including approaches to A/B testing and other tools to fine-tune a message for a higher conversion rate ("Campaign Email Strategy," n.d.).

Reflecting the device-centered approach of the platform as a whole, Indiegogo also provides extended guidance and tutorials on the technical details of product creation. Resources cover everything from printed circuit board (PCB) manufacturing trends (Indiegogo, n.d.-n), choosing a manufacturing center (Indiegogo, n.d.-o), to the process of identifying and receiving various certifications for tech products (Indiegogo, n.d.-e).

For technical writers, the emphasis on metrics, existing marketing, and PR deliverables makes the help documentation from Indiegogo more immediately actionable. There are clear suggestions for genres, services, and benchmarks to be reached for a potential project to reach funding success. The focus on devices can be advantageous when working with those types of products and projects, but the emphasis at times makes non-device projects feel secondary to the platform's focus.

What Is the Overall Position of the Platform in the Crowdfunding World?

First and foremost, Indiegogo represents itself in the crowdfunding space as a platform that caters to and supports the design and creation of cutting-edge technologies and gadgets, giving backers a chance to become early adopters and trendsetters in the device world.

Indiegogo's "What We Do" link on the front page of the site situates the platform within the crowdfunding space as a hub for innovative product design that caters to early adopters. The platform calls on potential backers to "fund the next big thing" while supporting development from the earliest of stages through consumer release. As the page's intro brags, "Indiegogo is where *new* launches" (Indiegogo, n.d.-j).

Unlike Kickstarter, Indiegogo does not provide a transparent view into funding numbers and success rates per category at a platform level. There are vague references to success rates on the platform blog, such as a claim that campaigns in 2021 were 7% more likely to succeed than campaigns in 2020 (Indiegogo-wp, 2021), but there is no data dashboard equivalent to Kickstarter's. Online estimates of an actual rate can be found on various blogs and platforms, with virtually all estimates falling markedly below the base success rate of Kickstarter projects. The lack of data is curious, considering the platform's heavy use of metrics and analytics for successful campaigns.

From the perspective of potential campaigns, Indiegogo's primary differentiating factors are the focus on devices and manufactured products concurrent with the extensive tools that the platform provides via secret perks, InDemand, data analytics tracking, and referral contests. The platform doesn't carry the same aura of success (as in the example of the Comics category on Kickstarter), but for certain campaigns, the particular combination of features and positioning may make the platform make sense.

GoFundMe

Of the three major campaign-based platforms, GoFundMe stands apart in focusing on campaigns without a set deliverable outside of the attainment of the goal of the campaign. Charity donation campaigns to offset medical bills, to pay for funeral expenses, and to fund nonprofit and community projects are prominently featured on the platform, aligning with its ongoing status as the default channel for creating timely charitable giving campaigns on social media in reaction to news, events, and illness. Like Indiegogo, GoFundMe does not require a set goal to be met during the funding process, though they recommend setting goals that are attainable as a part of the campaign strategy. GoFundMe is also uniquely linked with an independent 501(c)(3) charity GoFundMe.org that provides a unique mechanic for a charitable donation to a variety of social causes.

How Does the Platform Privilege or Fail to Privilege the Campaign or Its Creators?

GoFundMe's interface activism primarily focuses on "Black Joy" as a category in their main navigation menu, but the platform also has a variety of causes that are supported through their "GoFundMe Causes" category in their main navigation, providing a wide variety of campaigns a substantial amount of privileging in the basic interface of the site. Of the big three platforms, GoFundMe's causes page provides the most comprehensive interface activism, with a variety of causes being featured through their novel GoFundMe Causes mechanic.

"Celebrate Black Joy" in the main Discover link provides visitors to the platform with a collection of resources and causes that are linked to Black campaigns and specifically Black Joy (GoFundMe, n.d.-a). The Black Joy page encourages visitors to find "inspiration, tips, and community" while browsing, and includes a mixture of case studies, tips for campaign creators of a variety of types, as well as a newsletter signup link and a selection of current campaigns that fit under the Black joy category. The "Invest in Black Joy" linked page has a further breakdown that calls on visitors to invest in the following categories: "Black Creatives," "Black Education," "Black Business", and "Black Communities" (GoFundMe, n.d.-c).

GoFundMe Causes represents the second interface activism feature of GoFundMe, and the Causes system provides a curated way for visitors to donate to a variety of projects under a wide umbrella of categories without having to individually pick and choose where their money is donated. Choosing between "Justice & Equality," "Basic Necessities," Environment," "Animal Rescue," "Pride," "COVID-19 Relief," "Learning and Education," and "Mental Health," the mechanic provides a platform within a platform for GoFundMe donors (GoFundMe, n.d.-b). The process is described in three steps: (1) a donor gives a tax-deductible donation to a cause of their choice, (2) GoFundMe sends money to a currently active campaign on their platform that falls under that cause rubric that has been either verified as an individual or is a charity in the area, (3) the donor receives updates on their donation's impact from those who receive the funds.

Causes funding is donated to a separate entity, GoFundMe.org, a 501(c)(3) charity that was created to issue grants to fundraisers as well as charities that meet their criteria for vetting and eligibility (GoFundMe, n.d.-b). Individuals who receive funds are analyzed via "social cures to determine reliability," and "independent research," and the platform asserts that they use tools "on part with those used at financial institutions" to assess the eligibility of all grant recipients (@ GoFundMeCausesGoFundMe). GoFundMe.org touts an unusually high 95.6% rate of efficiency in donations as GoFundMe, Inc. covers a majority of the associated costs. The platform aims to "eliminate the paradox of choice," and provide increased speed, getting money to grantees within a timeline of days after a crisis or disaster (GoFundMe.org, n.d.).

What Type of Campaign Mechanics Does the Platform Support?

GoFundMe provides campaigns that are built around fundraising for a campaign with no expectation of reward or deliverable goods in return for success. GoFundMe provides the closest analog of any of the big three crowdfunding platforms to traditional nonprofit and charity fundraising that simply shares a narrative and asks for giving in response to that narrative.

Unlike Kickstarter or Indiegogo, GoFundMe's goal structure is flexible over time. The service encourages campaign creators to pick a number that is achievable, with the assurance that it can be changed over time in reaction to events (GoFundMe, n.d.-e). GoFundMe encourages campaigns to provide a clear breakdown of where funding will go, and also encourages campaigns to plan around the removal of fees from funding totals when aligning a goal with a particular expense (GoFundMe, 2022). This flexibility is particularly useful when a project is in response to an ongoing series of events, such as a medical diagnosis or illness such as COVID-19. Funding goals are able to evolve as the situation does, providing a flexibility that other services simply don't match due to structural differences in how they approach funding.

Like other platforms, GoFundMe does allow to update posts over time, but there is no fundamental system for reward tiers. The system is simply not built around payment being tied to a particular reward, either physical or digital. While donor thank-you letters and other types of thank-you gifts are mentioned among the tips for the platform, there simply are not any mechanisms to track the fulfillment of rewards for giving.

As mentioned earlier, Causes plays a large role in the GoFundMe ecosystem when donors opt to give to a specific cause rather than a particular campaign of support. While this system does not provide a perfect overlay onto individual campaigns, for nonprofit organizations or campaigns that are squarely within the scope of a particular cause, the system can potentially be a benefit. Cause alignment is separate from the overall platform category for a given fundraiser and is indicated by including a hashtag that aligns with a given cause within the fundraiser description. So, a project targeting the Mental Health category would use "#FundMentalHealth" to apply for funding (GoFundMe, n.d.-b).

What Supports Does the Platform Provide to Creators?

GoFundMe offers a variety of tips and suggestions for potential campaigns, with topical choices linked to the type of fundraising being carried out, be it for a medical crisis, school, or other topic. In particular, the supports related to Celebrate Black Joy are fairly involved and detailed. Overall, the supports are less numerous and detailed than the documentation provided by Indiegogo or Kickstarter, though part of this difference is simply a function in the difference between the platforms' focus. Without merchandise changing hands, GoFundMe campaigns are fundamentally simpler with less moving parts.

What Is the Overall Position of the Platform in the Crowdfunding World?

GoFundMe is fairly unique in the variety of projects and campaigns supported, primarily because the platform presents itself fundamentally as fundraising (with an emphasis on charitable giving) rather than focusing on product development or creator support with associated rewards (as in the case of Indiegogo and Kickstarter).

GoFundMe also prominently focuses on their low fee structure, which ranges between 2.9% and 2.2% plus $0.30 for either individuals/businesses and charities, respectively (GoFundMe, n.d.-d). By comparison, Indiegogo and Kickstarter have set funding fees of 5% in addition to processing fees on top of the funding fee itself, which can vary considerably.

For technical writers, GoFundMe represents a compelling choice for nonprofit organizations that a writer may work with, since the platform's lack of award structure for backers and the markedly lower fees associated with giving mesh well with charitable giving in general where donors are particularly interested in things like overhead that seldom become a topic of conversation in a for-profit campaign. If a campaign is designed around not providing a deliverable for a given project, then GoFundMe should likely be a strong contender for a given campaign if there isn't a niche platform or bespoke solution that fits the situation better. For nationally visible charities, such as Rancho Relaxo from Chapter 6's case study, GoFundMe and its brand recognition and normalization on social media can be a compelling platform choice.

Patreon

Patreon, as the sole representative of subscription-based crowdfunding, aligns most closely with Kickstarter in that its main interface prompts visitors to "Find a creator" and proclaims directly on the front page "Change the way art is valued." An important note, to be elaborated on in more detail shortly, is that the option to "find a creator" is important because the platform does rely on users finding creators in a rather direct way via search. Unlike the other three covered platforms, Patreon does not feature a front end that allows browsing of all possible creators. Instead, there are limited options to see "notable" creators in each category (usually around 8) and the simple search function. Users can enter a term like "tone" or "cosplay" to get related creators, but the platform as a whole isn't created as a marketing tool that promotes the findability of campaigns on the platform, separating the Patreon platform dramatically from the three campaign-oriented platforms. The platform makes a three-prong pitch to creators citing the ability to create an ongoing income stream, break away from the foibles of platform algorithms, and forge closer relationships with their audiences and fans.

How Does the Platform Privilege or Fail to Privilege the Campaign or Its Creators?

Unlike almost any other crowdfunding platform, Patreon makes no overt push for a particular type of creator or campaign, nor does it privilege a particular type of campaign on its frontend. Instead, the front page of the site (and the attendant navigation structure) is almost entirely focused on persuading creators rather than members of a creator's potential coalition of backers.

There is a single primary search tool on the front end of the site's main page, that prompts visitors to "Search the 200,000+ creators on Patreon" and the search bar itself has the placeholder text "Find a creator you love." The navigation at the top of the page also has a search bar that has placeholder text that reads "Find a creator." Beyond these two entreaties to users, the entirety of the page focuses on pitching the service/platform of Patreon to creators.

Functionally, Patreon is not designed as a platform with inherent discovery, but instead as almost a backend to creators who will be fueling their traffic and growth via existing channels they've cultivated elsewhere.

What Type of Campaign Mechanics Does the Platform Support?

The central mechanic that Patreon provides to campaigns (and the same is also true of OnlyFans and other subscription-based crowdfunding services) is the ability to gate content behind a subscription paywall, with the nuances of the paywall tied to the tier of plan a creator leverages. This central lens helps understand how the platform works or does not work for a given creator. Creators target different types of content to different levels of support, with higher levels of support getting access to exclusive content beyond even that provided to lower-tier backers.

The service functions with three primary plans that are on offer, with each tied not to a static fee for access, but instead with a sliding scale of a percentage cut from the Patreon revenue. For example, the simplest plan takes 5% of all transactions, the middle 8%, and the top-tier takes 12% of all income earned (Patreon, n.d.-b).

In broad strokes, Patreon provides a variety of content channels for campaigns, including discussion boards, a direct messaging system, app-connections to limit content in other ecosystems to Patreon-based tiers, merchandise fulfillment, discount code distribution, and member-only livestreams. Functionally, Patreon is best seen as a way to either have bespoke versions of existing mediums (like discussion boards) that are tied to funding levels from backers or have the ability to take pieces of content that exist on other platforms and to hide them behind a Patreon paywall, with the rationale being that highly engaged members of the backer coalition will be motivated by the prospect of more content that is reachable for a nominal monthly fee.

What Supports Does the Platform Provide to Creators?

Patreon provides a wealth of support documentation, but it is worth reiterating that the platform provides functionally zero findability via the fundamental interface. Patreon is not a platform that assists backers in finding creators to support— it provides a set of tools and a protected environment for interacting with and supporting creators that a user is already aware of and actively seeking to support via information gathered somewhere other than Patreon's main page.

Patreon supports for creators are largely tied to the type of account a given creator leverages for their projects. Analytics, unlimited app integrations, and membership tiers are limited to those electing for a Pro plan that increases the cut from the service from 5% to 8%. To leverage most of the strengths of the platform, most creators will functionally want to leverage a Pro plan with an 8% cut.

The primary differentiation between the Pro and Premium tier are the inclusion of support for automating the creation and fulfillment of merchandise tied to particular backer tiers as well as dedicated partner managers. For creators that leverage merchandise heavily, the logistics support could potentially be quite important as it removes the logistics of creating, sourcing, and shipping merchandise as part of running their Patreon account. The partner manager is an interesting pitch as it provides a 1:1 contact within Patreon that offers coaching, access to the organization and its priorities and decision making, as well as data insights that have been pre-analyzed by that manager.

In addition to the tiered system of content for creators, Patreon provides a series of starter kits for their creators of particular types, as well as a resources tab. The resources tab provides a variety of links to an office blog, to the creator community Discord channel, events, an app directory page, and the generic Help Center and FAQ. The blog content primary focuses on platform-centered content and discussions on legal and policy changes and how they impact creators and the platform. The Patreon U section provides the most detailed content for creators, including content on best practices and how-to information on running campaigns on the platform. Much akin to Indiegogo, the content is fairly detailed and marketing-oriented. An entire segment of the U content covers marketing approaches, aligning the support content closer to the voicing of Indiegogo than Kickstarter or GoFundMe (Patreon, n.d.-a).

What Is the Overall Position of the Platform in the Crowdfunding World?

Patreon represents the first real mainstream subscription crowdfunding service, with its launch predating OnlyFans significantly. The service represents itself as supporting creators, but the included list also covers nonprofits, education providers, and local businesses. Rancho Relaxo, the case study for Chapter 6, leveraged Patreon alongside and during the two campaigns on GoFundMe analyzed in the chapter, and continue to leverage the platform today across multiple projects.

In 2022, Patreon provided their first platform survey results, giving some insights into the types of projects and associated organizations that rely on the platform. With that said, it is worth noting that since Patreon campaigns do not have a set funding goal that must be met for funding to be provided, the metric of success rate doesn't translate directly nor does it figure prominently in discussions.

Most Patreon creators produce video (38%), followed by writing (17%), and podcasting (14%). Creators in the survey self-reported with 56% seeing themselves as professional creators, and 44% closer to being new to creating. Eighty percent of all creators work alone on the platform, with YouTube, Twitter, DeviantArt, Discord, Facebook, podcasting networks, and personal websites representing the majority of traffic sources for creators (as in, where their fans live when not visiting them on Patreon). Around 40% of the respondents' creative income was reported as coming from their Patreon earnings (Patreon, 2022).

Turning to the motivations of backer coalitions on the platform, 70% of supporters reported subscribing to have the ability to support their subbed creators and their work. Sixty-nine percent reported that they supported due to the ability to get exclusive content, with early access to content coming in at 57%. Other content support rationales ranked below 40%. This data from backers meshes interestingly with the content provided by Patreon U, which emphasizes the exclusive nature of the content created and being able to leverage that content in ways that strategically reinforced the motivations of backers. Finally, data shows that campaigns that leverage a custom name for their supporters (something other than just patrons) had around 4–8% higher monthly retention rates, though Patreon is careful to note this is not a causal relationship.

For technical writers, Patreon represents an interesting proposition in that a Patreon campaign doesn't compete directly with a crowdfunding campaign on Kickstarter or Indiegogo or GoFundMe. In fact, as the next chapter shows, nonprofits can and do leverage subscription-based crowdfunding as well as event or need-based crowdfunding to maintain multiple income streams and cultivate a more connected set of backers. Patreon in such a scenario is the "always on" campaign that provides regular content to highly committed backers while time-limited campaigns provide special requests to the larger community tied to particular events/issues/goals.

Any tech writers looking to create a Patreon (or OnlyFans for that matter) do, however, need to keep in mind that the platform does not provide findability. Patreon is not necessarily a place to grow a community, but instead a place to monetize a pre-existing community in order to provide ongoing income to support the content that the backer coalition enjoys or wants to see in the world.

In particular, Patreon is a useful way to preserve a community in a way that isn't tied to social media platforms (though we should be quick to acknowledge that Patreon is also a platform). With shifts like Instagram's hard pivot to video (Adam Mosseri [@mosseri], 2022; Lopatto, 2022), Patreon and other crowdfunding subscription services provide at least one way to remove the chaos of algorithmic change in how content is provided to members of a backer coalition, though as we'll discuss shortly tools like static sites and email lists should also figure prominently in such calculations.

Category-Limited Crowdfunding Platforms

Having looked at the major players in the crowdfunding space, I want to close this portion of the chapter by briefly noting the options that exist outside of this segment of the crowdfunding world. I refer to these platforms as category-limited as their platforms tend to be almost entirely built around a particular approach or category of campaign, such as campus/education crowdfunding, research funding, or vertically integrated platforms that coordinate with campaigns from pitch to fulfillment.

Campus Giving Platforms

For academics and students in particular, the rise of crowdfunding on college campuses is notable and worth mentioning for certain types of projects. Crowdfunding provides avenues to academic and student groups that are less restrictive than the traditional gatekeeping that university advancement/giving programs that restrict access to high-value donors and alumni. One of the leading platforms for this type of crowdfunding is GiveCampus (GiveCampus, n.d.), a platform leveraged by schools as diverse as Yale, the University of Southern Alabama, and the University of Notre Dame. Platforms like GiveCampus provide a pre-built set of tools for giving programs to coordinate campus giving campaigns and to provide an official university-branded presence for the campaigns. For the sake of transparency, I'd note that I am running a crowdfunding campaign for an endowed scholarship in honor of a friend that passed away in 2021 using the GiveCampus platform as I write this book.

While GiveCampus holds a prominent role, other institutions leverage either bespoke solutions to crowdfunding or smaller/different vendors such as ScaleFunder, the vendor of choice at my own institution (Ruffalo Noel Levitz LLC, n.d.).

Research Platforms

For researchers seeking funding, there are research-specific crowdfunding sites that do cater to funding and distributing the results of research studies. Experiment.com is a leading example of this type of platform, offering researchers the ability to host all-or-nothing campaigns to fund their research projects (Experiment.com, n.d.-b). The platform, as of this writing, boasts a funding success rate of 47.79% and has funded 1070 projects via 52,558 backers (Experiment.com, n.d.-a). Research from the National Bureau of Economic Research on science crowdfunding found that junior researchers and women tended to have the highest success rates for projects while noting that traditional markers of funding success (prior work published, etc.) were not as relevant to crowdfunding audiences (Sauermann et al., 2018).

Crowdfunding science (and science communication online in general) is outside the scope of this project, but Ashley Mehlenbacher's (2017, 2019) research on such work is an excellent starting place for teams looking to secure such funding.

Integrated Platforms

In addition to the aforementioned platforms, there has been some movement toward integrated platforms that provide campaigns with integrated marketing services and fulfillment services in addition to hosting the actual campaigns they are running as a platform. Some of these platforms are smaller, and more focused on advocacy, such as IFundWomen. IFundWomen explicitly fines their platform via the advantages it provides to potential entrepreneurs. The platform offers coaching for potential entrepreneurs, grants from commercial donors, and provides visibility to women who seek to start businesses. IFundWomen also highlights the activist nature of the site and the ability of the platform to provide projects with access to backers who are excited to back them specifically because of their identity and the funding gap between women and men in the business community (ifw, n.d.).

In addition to advocacy-centered platforms, there are also all-in-one platforms that bundle the same types of supports IFundWomen and other similar platforms provide while serving a broader set of campaign types and goals. For example, Backerkit, a long-standing fulfillment and campaign support service, entered the world of crowdfunding platforms with a closed beta in 2022, offering campaigns act already relied on the business the opportunity to vertically integrate their entire campaign within a single relationship with Backerkit (Backerkit, n.d.; Hoffer, 2022).

Of note, some crowdfunding platforms have themselves pushed into the fulfillment and coaching space in the same way that Backerkit has pushed into the crowdfunding platform space. Indiegogo, for example, has coordinated relationships with fulfillment services (Indiegogo, n.d.-i) in addition to an experts directory (Indiegogo, n.d.-h) as well as a subscription-based support structure with help and tutorials beyond the public-facing content they provide, much akin to the services provided by Backerkit (*BackerKit | Features | Pre-Order Website*, n.d.). Patreon also offers parallel vertical integration options with their highest tier of support that includes a dedicated manager as well as merchandise fulfillment for subscriptions (Patreon, n.d.-b).

Platform-Free Crowdfunding

When choosing a platform for crowdfunding, the first question to address is likely: does the project or organization need crowdfunding at all? This may seem counterintuitive, but as noted in Chapter 1, charities and nonprofits have thrived in a world without crowdfunding platforms, and just because such platforms exist doesn't mean that they make sense for everyone.

Platforms for crowdfunding make sense when the platform itself provides something current approaches to funding don't. If a nonprofit has a steady stream of support via donations, donation drives, and social media, there may not be a compelling need for crowdfunding platform usage. With that said, platforms make sense if they will provide access to tools or mechanisms that would otherwise be burdensome to maintain or create.

From a technical writing perspective, crowdfunding platforms are effectively a shortcut to compelling XAs that reward and engage backers of a given organization for their contributions. It is entirely possible to build a bespoke equivalent complete with member-only access to forums, content, or updates that are tied to donations. However, when no such existing infrastructure exists, crowdfunding platforms provide a relatively simple solution in exchange for their overhead rate, which will range between 2.9% and 12% depending on the solution.

As an advocate for using the best tool for a given job, I often find myself tempted to create just such a solution in response to exigent needs in my own technical writing working. However, I find it useful to remember that the less ideal way can be the best way at times. If the creation and maintenance of a bespoke solution provide too great of a barrier to running crowdfunding campaigns with thoughtfully crafted user experiences, crowdfunding platforms may be a better idea. There is something to be said for approaches that reduce the time and effort expended to get a campaign off the ground.

Choosing a Platform Home

When choosing a platform, campaigns need to carefully consider the overlapping impacts of the affordances provided by each potential platform, the interface activism present on that platform, the mechanics of the platform, and the position of the platform within the crowdfunding sphere. For example, a tabletop gaming campaign would likely be seen more at home on Kickstarter than on Indiegogo based on both the available data on success rates and the association with Kickstarter with Gaming as an area of funding. On the other hand, a campaign to support a family going through an illness would make the most sense on GoFundMe and might not even meet the guidelines for placement on some of the more deliverable-driven platforms.

What Are You Doing and Where Does It Make Sense?

Choosing a platform and conceptualizing a campaign are, many times, concurrent processes and choices. The platform and the campaign cocreate each other in that your existing ideas for a campaign will influence your platform choice while your platform choice will then rewrite and reshape what is possible or not possible in your campaign. First and foremost, however, you'll need to frame your campaign and your purpose. What are you doing, and who do you hope will support you in carrying out this work? Looking back to our assessment rubric, we can leverage these same questions to analyze where a given campaign may have the best chance to thrive:

1. Which platforms privilege or highlight the type of creators behind your campaign?
2. Which platforms support campaign mechanics that your team is interested in or that align well with your existing project ideas?
3. Which platform provides the best supports to your team as currently constituted? Which meets your needs the best?
4. Which platform has a public position that aligns with the ethos of your team and the scope/aim of your project?

From these questions, you can leverage the platform analysis in this chapter alongside your own investigations to set your sights on a particular platform for further development of your campaign, something we'll cover in the next chapter in detail.

Wrapping Up

In this chapter, we've laid out a framework for critically analyzing crowdfunding platforms through the lens of platform politics and the political choices embedded in the design, curation, and presentation of various crowdfunding platforms. We've leveraged this analysis to provide a systematic approach to choosing a home for future campaigns based on the ways that a given platform caters to the needs and approach of a given creator and their prospective projects.

Discussion Questions

1. Which crowdfunding campaigns have you encountered the most frequently? How would you characterize their self-framing of purpose and intent via your encounters with them?
2. When might it make sense for a creator to place a campaign on a platform that doesn't explicitly support or highlight them as a creator or their project's typology? What makes the choice compelling in the face of this mismatch?

References

Adam Mosseri [@mosseri]. (2022, July 26). 🔐 There's a lot happening on Instagram right now. I wanted to address a few things we're working on to make Instagram a better experience. Please let me know what you think 👍 https://t.co/x1If5qrCyS [Tweet]. *Twitter*. https://twitter.com/mosseri/status/1551890839584088065

Bacha, J. A. (2012). Taxonomies, folksonomies, and semantics: Establishing functional meaning in navigational structures. *Journal of Technical Writing & Communication, 42*(3), 249–263. https://doi.org/10.2190/TW.42.3.d

Backerkit. (n.d.). *Announcing crowdfunding by BackerKit.* Retrieved September 9, 2022, from http://backerkit.com/crowdfunding?ref=announcement_twitter

BackerKit | Features | Pre-Order Website. (n.d.). *BackerKit.* Retrieved September 13, 2022, from www.backerkit.com/features/preorders

Black-owned or founded brands at Target: Target. (n.d.). Retrieved June 3, 2022, from www.target.com/c/black-owned-or-founded-brands-at-target/-/N-q8v16

Campaign Email Strategy: Turn Your List into Contributions. (n.d.). *Indiegogo Education Center.* Retrieved July 13, 2022, from https://entrepreneur.indiegogo.com/education/guide/email-strategy-crowfunding-campaign/

Can I use referral programs on Kickstarter? (n.d.). *Kickstarter support.* Retrieved July 13, 2022, from https://help.kickstarter.com/hc/en-us/articles/115005134794-Can-I-use-referral-programs-on-Kickstarter-

Choose Your Funding Type: Can I Keep My Money? (n.d.). Retrieved June 9, 2022, from https://support.indiegogo.com/hc/en-us/articles/205138007-Choose-Your-Funding-Type-Can-I-Keep-My-Money-

Experiment.com. (n.d.-a). Crowdfunding for science | frequently asked questions. *Experiment—Moving Science Forward.* Retrieved July 27, 2022, from https://experiment.com/faq

Experiment.com. (n.d.-b). Crowdfunding platform for scientific research. *Experiment—Moving Science Forward.* Retrieved July 27, 2022, from https://experiment.com/

Gillespie, T. (2010). The politics of 'platforms.' *New Media & Society, 12*(3), 347–364.

Gillespie, T. (2015). Platforms intervene. *Social Media + Society, 1*(1). https://doi.org/10.1177/2056305115580479

GiveCampus. (n.d.). Educational fundraising technology | raise money with GiveCampus. *GiveCampus.* Retrieved March 31, 2022, from https://go.givecampus.com/

GoFundMe. (2022, April 15). Choosing your goal amount. *GoFundMe Help Center.* https://support.gofundme.com/hc/en-us/articles/4405145410331-Choosing-your-goal-amount

GoFundMe. (n.d.-a). Celebrate Black joy. *GoFundMe.* Retrieved June 3, 2022, from www.gofundme.com/c/act/celebrate-black-joy

GoFundMe. (n.d.-b). Donate to GoFundMe causes you care about. *GoFundMe.* Retrieved July 21, 2022, from www.gofundme.com/c/cause

GoFundMe. (n.d.-c). Invest in Black joy. *GoFundMe.* Retrieved July 21, 2022, from www.gofundme.com/c/celebrate-black-joy/invest-in-black-joy

GoFundMe. (n.d.-d). Pricing and fees. *GoFundMe.* Retrieved July 21, 2022, from www.gofundme.com/c/pricing

GoFundMe. (n.d.-e). *Top fundraising tips.* Retrieved June 21, 2022, from www.gofundme.com/c/fundraising-tips

GoFundMe.org. (n.d.). About. *GoFundMe.org.* Retrieved July 21, 2022, from www.gofundme.org/about/

Hoffer, C. (2022, June 15). BackerKit announces new crowdfunding platform. *Gaming.* https://comicbook.com/gaming/news/backerkit-crowdfunding-kickstarter-alternative-gloomhaven-leder-games/

ifw. (n.d.). *About us: IFundWomen's mission, vision, and team.* Retrieved March 31, 2022, from https://ifundwomen.com/about-us

Indiegogo. (n.d.-a). Conversion and remarketing pixels. *Indiegogo Help Center.* Retrieved July 13, 2022, from https://support.indiegogo.com/hc/en-us/articles/205101978-Conversion-and-Remarketing-Pixels

Indiegogo. (n.d.-b). Forget the viral videos and build your email list. *Indiegogo Education Center.* Retrieved July 13, 2022, from https://entrepreneur.indiegogo.com/education/article/build-email-list-firstbuild-forget-viral-videos/

Indiegogo. (n.d.-c). How do I choose my funding goal? *Indiegogo Help Center.* Retrieved July 13, 2022, from https://support.indiegogo.com/hc/en-us/articles/204456228-How-do-I-choose-my-funding-goal-

Indiegogo. (n.d.-d). *How do I run a referral contest?* Retrieved June 9, 2022, from https://support.indiegogo.com/hc/en-us/articles/527406-How-do-I-run-a-referral-contest-

Indiegogo. (n.d.-e). *How to figure out what certifications your product needs.* Retrieved June 8, 2022, from https://entrepreneur.indiegogo.com/education/article/certifications-how-to-figure-out-what-your-product-needs/

Indiegogo. (n.d.-f). *InDemand.* Retrieved June 8, 2022, from https://entrepreneur.indiegogo.com/how-it-works/indemand/

Indiegogo. (n.d.-g). InDemand FAQ. *Indiegogo Help Center.* Retrieved July 13, 2022, from https://support.indiegogo.com/hc/en-us/articles/204092046-InDemand-FAQ

Indiegogo. (n.d.-h). Indiegogo experts directory. *Indiegogo Experts Directory.* Retrieved September 9, 2022, from https://entrepreneur.indiegogo.com/directory/

Indiegogo. (n.d.-i). Indiegogo fulfillment solutions: Powered by Easyship. *Indiegogo | Easyship.* Retrieved September 9, 2022, from https://enterprise.indiegogo.com/easyship/

Indiegogo. (n.d.-j). Learn about crowdfunding & how Indiegogo works. *Indiegogo.* Retrieved June 8, 2022, from www.indiegogo.com/about/what-we-do

Indiegogo. (n.d.-k). LGBTQIA+ creators and entrepreneurs. *Indiegogo.* Retrieved July 7, 2022, from www.indiegogo.com/campaign_collections/lgbtqia-entrepreneurs-and-creators

Indiegogo. (n.d.-l). Running a hardware campaign. *Indiegogo Help Center.* Retrieved July 21, 2022, from https://support.indiegogo.com/hc/en-us/articles/204510248-Running-a-Hardware-Campaign

Indiegogo. (n.d.-m). The Gogofactor. *Indiegogo Help Center.* Retrieved April 15, 2022, from https://support.indiegogo.com/hc/en-us/articles/527476-The-Gogofactor

Indiegogo. (n.d.-n). Understanding the latest tech in PCB manufacturing. *Indiegogo Education Center.* Retrieved July 13, 2022, from https://entrepreneur.indiegogo.com/education/article/understanding-the-latest-tech-in-pcb-manufacturing/

Indiegogo. (n.d.-o). *What you need to know when choosing a contract manufacturer.* Retrieved June 8, 2022, from https://entrepreneur.indiegogo.com/education/article/choosing-a-contract-manufacturer/

Indiegogo-wp. (2021, July 21). At the halfway point: Top trends in 2021 so far. *The Indiegogo Review.* https://go.indiegogo.com/blog/2021/07/at-the-halfway-point-top-trends-in-2021-so-far.html

Kickstarter. (2021). *How does the "magic" search filter work?* https://help.kickstarter.com/hc/en-us/articles/115005135174-How-does-the-magic-search-filter-work-

Kickstarter. (2022a, July). *Kickstarter stats—Kickstarter.* www.kickstarter.com/help/stats

Kickstarter. (2022b, October). What is Google Analytics and how do I set it up? *Kickstarter Support.* https://help.kickstarter.com/hc/en-us/articles/115005138613-What-is-Google-Analytics-and-how-do-I-set-it-up-

Kickstarter. (2022c, October 10). Setting up your project's pre-launch page. *Kickstarter Support.* https://help.kickstarter.com/hc/en-us/articles/360034769114-Setting-up-your-project-s-pre-launch-page

Kickstarter. (2022d, October 21). What is the maximum project duration? *Kickstarter Support.* https://help.kickstarter.com/hc/en-us/articles/115005128434-What-is-the-maximum-project-duration-

Kickstarter. (2022e, October 26). *How does my project become a Project We Love or get featured on the homepage?* https://help.kickstarter.com/hc/en-us/articles/115005135214-How-does-my-project-become-a-Project-We-Love-or-get-featured-on-the-homepage-

Kickstarter. (2022f, October 30). Why is funding all-or-nothing? *Kickstarter Support.* https://help.kickstarter.com/hc/en-us/articles/115005047893-Why-is-funding-all-or-nothing-

Kickstarter. (n.d.). *Project claims—Kickstarter.* Retrieved July 21, 2022, from www.kickstarter.com/honest

Lau, G. (2015, September 1). Building the business case for taxonomy. *Boxes and Arrows.* https://boxesandarrows.com/building-the-business-case-for-taxonomy/

Lopatto, E. (2022, July 26). Adam Mosseri confirms it: Instagram is over. *The Verge.* www.theverge.com/2022/7/26/23279815/instagram-feed-kardashians-criticism-fuck-it-im-out

Mehlenbacher, A. R. (2017). Crowdfunding science: Exigencies and strategies in an emerging genre of science communication. *Technical Communication Quarterly, 26*(2), 127–144. https://doi.org/10.1080/10572252.2017.1287361

Mehlenbacher, A. R. (2019). *Science communication online: Engaging experts and publics on the internet.* The Ohio State University Press. https://ohiostatepress.org/books/titles/9780814213988.html

Monea, B. (2020). *Screenreading: A gallery of (re)imagined interfaces.* https://kairos.technorhetoric.net/24.2/disputatio/monea/index.html

Patreon. (2022, May 4). The first-ever Patreon Creator Census. *Patreon Blog.* https://blog.patreon.com/the-first-ever-patreon-creator-census

Patreon. (n.d.-a). Marketing & promotion. *Patreon Blog.* Retrieved July 26, 2022, from https://blog.patreon.com/tag/marketing-promotion

Patreon. (n.d.-b). Pricing. *Patreon.* Retrieved July 26, 2022, from https://patreon.com/pricing

Pre-Launch Page: How to Go Live with Backers Already By Your Side. (n.d.). Retrieved June 8, 2022, from https://entrepreneur.indiegogo.com/education/webinar/how-to-go-live-with-backers-already-by-your-side/

Ruffalo Noel Levitz, LLC. (n.d.). Digital fundraising overview | RNL. *Ruffalo Noel Levitz.* Retrieved September 9, 2022, from www.ruffalonl.com/higher-education-fundraising-management/digital-giving-online-giving/

Sano-Franchini, J. (2017). What can Asian eyelids teach us about user experience design? A culturally reflexive framework for UX/I design. *Journal of Rhetoric, Professional Communication, and Globalization, 10*(1). https://docs.lib.purdue.edu/rpcg/vol10/iss1/3

Sauermann, H., Franzoni, C., & Shafi, K. (2018). *Crowdfunding scientific research* (Working Paper No. 24402; Working Paper Series). National Bureau of Economic Research. https://doi.org/10.3386/w24402

Selfe, C. L., & Selfe, R. J. (1994). The politics of the interface: Power and its exercise in electronic contact zones. *College Composition and Communication, 45*(4), 480–504.

Seyedhn. (2021, September 3). How I got the "Project We Love" badge on Kickstarter [Reddit Post]. *R/Gamedev.* www.reddit.com/r/gamedev/comments/phewox/how_i_got_the_project_we_love_badge_on_kickstarter/

Walton, R., Moore, K. R., & Jones, N. N. (2019). *Technical communication after the social justice turn: Building coalitions for action.* Routledge.

4

PLANNING AND RUNNING CAMPAIGNS

Having defined crowdfunding historically and theoretically in Chapters 1 and 2 and analyzed the playing field for running a campaign in Chapter 3, we now turn to mapping out the theory and practice of building a crowdfunding campaign. This chapter is broken down into two major segments, an initial theory segment followed by a discussion of the planning of a campaign, building of XA, and then the final running of the planned campaign. As a note, this content is almost entirely focused on the work of technical writers working on campaigns. This is not a one-stop solution for running a campaign but instead provides guidance to technical writers and communicators supporting the campaign's deliverables and user experience. As such, this chapter provides a series of suggestions and frameworks for making decisions and structuring your campaign, but the specifics of that work can and should be worked out contextually within a given team.

Theories to Inform the Planning and Running of Campaigns

Before we get to the practical nuts and bolts of running a crowdfunding campaign, I want to provide some brief theoretical approaches that can be useful in our day-to-day writing and planning of these campaigns. We'll look at work on content marketing, rhetorical velocity, and reach/engagement as foundational frameworks for understanding how to plan and then run our future campaigns.

Content Marketing and Building a Coalition

Projects need a coalition of backers to meet their funding goals, and subscription-based crowdfunding efforts need a critical mass of subscribers to make the content

DOI: 10.4324/9781003308966-4

curation and creation worthwhile. Therefore, a necessary part of building any crowdfunding success is building an awareness of yourself, your organization, or your cause while simultaneously building both trust and passion in the coalition of backers that you're building. To provide a theoretical lens for this part of XA, I leverage the definition of content marketing as laid out by Amanda Wall and Clay Spinuzzi (2018). Wall and Spinuzzi define content marketing as "a method of marketing a product or service by creating and distributing free informational or entertainment content, especially online," and involves storytelling across multiple genres (p. 137). For a brief example, an aspiring vendor of guitar effects pedals might begin their content marketing by creating a series of YouTube videos, discussing common questions that players have about the components within the effects devices. Over time this might expand into blog posts, Instagram, or TikTok content presenting the vendor as a trustworthy and passionate member of the guitar effects community.

Wall and Spinuzzi label this type of marketing as dialogic (p. 139), cocreating value via the shared actions of the creator and the audience. In many ways, it aligns with Michael Warner's (2002) concept of the public that comes into form by virtue of being addressed (p. 67). In our terms, this type of content marketing helps to assembler our coalition of backers by bringing them together around content that represents their values, goals, and ideals.

Wall and Spinuzzi found that professional content marketers tended to create their content in its own internalized content ecology (p. 144), with each piece being taken into the various marketing channels of a given organization after its creation. To return to the example of the aspiring guitar pedal builder, a short video that has been recorded discussing the difference between two different types of components might initially be published to YouTube, republished on the builder's Facebook page, and segmented into smaller enticing bits to feature on an Instagram or Facebook story. At the same time, the builder might document the process of filming the video via a series of photos that could then be shared on Instagram to tease or promote the content release. In this elaborate resharing and repacking (not unlike component content management, as Wall and Spinuzzi note), a single piece of content is worked into an existing system of channels the creator has built over time to attract and maintain a following.

Within these content marketing ecologies, Wall and Spinuzzi explain that "content not only proliferates into different genres but also becomes interconnected in deliberate and persuasive ways" (p 147). The goal in these messages is to build a connection with the source (often a brand) and to simply keep the audience of the message in contact with that brand and to keep the brand on their radar. As content is liked, shared, and commented on, it also increases the likelihood that the content will be exposed to other potential audiences that will be interested. Some of this exposure will be algorithmic—social media companies promote content that is highly engaging (for better or for worse); the rest of the exposure will be via the followers and friends of the readers doing the liking, sharing, and commenting (and hopefully even tagging of others).

For us, this ecology of persuasive content can be seen as the beginning of our user experience architecture. Before the campaign even launches, a steady stream of content related to the topic that a given campaign or subscription will cover. The marketing phase allows a campaign to tweak their content and to get a better understanding of who their coalition is and what they value. Simple metrics such as views, likes, click-throughs, and shares can be useful starting points for simply seeing which content has legs and which content doesn't, but because of the social nature of online platforms, there is also a chance for dialogues and feedback directly from coalition members via comments and replies (sometimes quite involved in the case of platforms like TikTok). Ideally, a campaign in this phase can supply value and learn about their backer coalition while also laying the groundwork for selling the coalition on a potential campaign or subscription crowdfunding operation.

In the words of Wall and Spinuzzi,

> This double orientation to selling and not selling is thus the defining characteristic of content marketing ecologies. When taken separately, many pieces of content marketing may seem agnostic; when taken together, the persuasive pathways within the genre ecology hold it together and expose the orientation to selling.
>
> *(p. 155)*

Content marketing is not about directly influencing someone to buy into a campaign, "selling" them on the project. That is a separate process entirely. Instead, this early content creation is designed to gently persuade the audience, assembling at least a part of a potential backer coalition, learning what they value and want to see.

Though we may go into a given campaign's infancy with a firm understanding of the coalition we aim to attract and how we aim to attract them, an early focus on that work as content marketing helps us understand and adapt to any gaps in our understanding of the key tropes and types of information that will resonate with our backer coalition (and can even help us understand if and when our coalition evolves in ways we've not planned for). Even gaps in our content (and associated community expectations) can be identified in this early content when we start to notice potential coalition members commenting and querying about deliverables and goals we may not have planned on covering in our actual campaign. These queries and interactions provide us with direct information on our proto-coalition about what they are motivated by and what they identify with in our project, giving us additional confidence in the planning and implementation of our project's launch.

Rhetorical Velocity and Corporate Kairos

Having discussed content marketing, I now want to turn briefly to two important concepts we can and should overlay onto our understanding of content creation for crowdfunding: rhetorical velocity and corporate kairos. Each of these theories provides a window into the ways that we both design and place texts into the world with the hopes that they will be mobile and they'll get shared widely with the target audience we're writing toward. A user experience isn't terribly useful if no one experiences it, so these two theories help us articulate the process and peril of getting our work out there in front of our potential backers. In short, these two theories focus on how delivery matters in online writing (and how texts can be written for better delivery).

Rhetorical Velocity

Rhetorical velocity, as originally described by Jim Ridolfo and Dànielle DeVoss (2009), pays attention to the delivery of a particular text and the ways that a text's composition can be focused on how the text will be used and shared beyond the initial publication. Ridolfo and DeVoss define rhetorical velocity as "a conscious rhetorical concern for distance, travel, speed, and time, pertaining specifically to theorizing instances of strategic appropriation by a third party". Rhetorical velocity then looks at how a text will function once it enters circulation and specifically how other authors and organizations will leverage that text and reuse it in their own writing. Ridolfo and DeVoss focus on the press release as a classic example of this process and approach, documents that are written almost entirely for the purposes of being reused in part by reporting organizations in a given industry.

Key to rhetorical velocity is understanding the ways that texts are recomposed as a method for a better composition of those same texts. As Ridolfo and DeVoss explain,

> In the inventive thinking of composing, rhetorical velocity is the strategic theorizing for how a text might be recomposed (and why it might be recomposed) by third parties, and how this recomposing may be useful or not to the short- or long-term rhetorical objectives of the rhetorician.

Rhetorical velocity is about delivery, but its understanding of delivery stretches back into and impacts composition. Instead of simply thinking about how something is placed into the ecosystem of social media for consumption and sharing and commenting, the author thinks about how and why someone might take the text and share or rework it, and then composes in ways to make the text better suited to the types of sharing that the author thinks would be best for their goals.

Functionally for crowdfunding technical and professional writers and communicators, rhetorical velocity asks us to think about what happens when we make a post and how that post then lives in the ecosystems that we've placed it in (and elsewhere). The depth and breadth of social media platforms makes this a fairly complicated task, and one that deserves more than a little thought. When writing in a given social media setting, to properly leverage rhetorical velocity, we need to actually understand how that platform works, what the tropes and genres are in our area of interest as well as the patterns of engagement and sharing (and remixing). TikTok, for example, may be a currently hot social media platform as I write this book, but that doesn't mean that a crowdfunding campaign should simply start making their content available on TikTok. Rhetorical velocity prompts us to have an understanding of how that platform works to the point we can be strategic in how, when, and why we create and share information about and leading into our campaign. It doesn't allow us to use TikTok just for the sake of having a TikTok.

As I'll discuss shortly, rhetorical velocity provides us with the insights we need to compose our texts strategically and aids us in understanding how to look at our project through the lens of shareability and engagement as we attempt to leverage our understanding of the key tropes and values of our backer coalition. We don't simply want to create a text that our coalition will find valuable—we want to compose a text that they will engage with and share with others like them, ideally building our coalition further thanks to our attention to rhetorical velocity.

Corporate Kairos

With the advent of modern social media, we have one additional angle to consider whenever we discuss delivery and the ways that delivery impacts our content's reception: the idea of targeted ad placement and the logic and systems behind that process. Targeted placement is the bread and butter of social media and web search engine companies, with all the free services that we've come to expect and reply upon on the web relying in some way form or fashion (for the most part) on their ability to monetize the information we expose about ourselves while we use these platforms. Sara West and Adam R. Pope (2018) term this corporate need for customer data to feed ad targeting as corporate kairos, which they define as "the demand of corporate members of social media platforms to circumvent the normal rules of rhetorical velocity and kairos." The idea behind corporate kairos is that by being able to specifically target an audience (or build an audience for a text based on exact parameters), authors are about to fundamentally alter the normal writing process by partially eliminating the need to leverage kairos and rhetorical velocity to create texts that are timely. Instead, authors are able to simply pick and choose when, where, and how their texts are delivered to audiences.

As West and Pope (2021) explain, corporate kairos creates a contrast in social media usage and underscores how these platforms are built for advertisers first rather than users:

> Corporate kairos is best understood when set in opposition to what is available to normal, non-corporate (or non-paying) users of social media. The average user or content creator has to first understand the demands of the platform, as well as the types of content the platform allows and/or privileges. . . For the average user, going viral intentionally is hard work and often out of reach.

Unlike normal users, paying users can simply pick and choose when and where a post should be posted, the timing of the post, and even the audience. (It should also be noted that any pages posting through the Facebook Business Suite can also choose when to post, unlike normal user accounts.)

This level of access creates a minefield of ethical problems, many of which have been reported on time after time, including scandals regarding housing ads that violate federal laws related to targeting and exclusion by race or family status, ad buys during the 2016 election by Russian Troll farms, and targeting data being created and then exposed to advertisers that targeted anti-Semitic users. If ever there was a system in need of Walton et al.' (2019) 4Rs, it would be social media targeted advertising, and most especially targeted ads on Facebook, something we'll discuss in more specific detail later in the chapter when we get into the planning of targeted content placement.

Reach and Engagement

Reach and engagement are intertwined concepts that provide a measurement of success in the analytics dashboards and datasets of social media platforms. These terms provide a window into how companies view and use platforms for their own ends while also providing organizations and individuals a window into their rhetorical velocity and impact on a given platform. In this section, I will provide both the platform-supplied definitions of the concepts of reach and the follow-through marker of engagement while also providing scholarly insights into the workings of these systems and ideas. Most of the scholarship will come from the broader world of social media studies, as the scholarship on the subject in technical communication has been somewhat limited vis-a-vis practitioner concerns in social media content marketing and placement (though that is beginning to change!). As with much of the social media platform discussions, Meta tends to dominate these discussions (and practice) of many in this space, often due to a combination of their ubiquity in the space and the ubiquity of their scandals in the space. With that said, things have been shifting and continue to shift as platforms like TikTok and Snap grow and create generational shifts in platform choice (Vogels et al., 2022).

Reach and engagement are paired terms, with one leading to the other. Reach is a hard metric that simply quantifies the number of users that a given piece of content might reach, whereas engagement moves beyond simply reaching and audience and spurs an audience into action—a step that is important when social media platforms and their payment schemes for creators is overlaid on top of the reach/engagement numbers game.

"Reach" as a term is used consistently across the major players in social media, and generally references the number of unique viewers of a given bit of content. Meta defines reach as "the number of people who saw your ads at least once," disambiguating between the concrete number of viewers versus the number of times placed content has been viewed, which Meta refers to as "impressions" (Meta, n.d.-e). TikTok leverages a similar definition, explaining that reach is "a term in advertising that refers to the number of people who saw or interacted with your ads" (TikTok, n.d.-d). Snap aligns with this definition by focusing on the number of individuals who saw a given deliverable (Snap, n.d.-e).

Reach is further disambiguated as being either "organic" or "paid" in nature. I'll cover the scholarship on the implications of these adjective choices shortly, but first want to note the general usage of the terms within platforms and their business resource pages. Organic reach tends to focus on reach that tends to happen on a platform via the nonpaid distribution systems in place. Snap tends to reference organic content indirectly, describing any and all content that isn't paid as organic (Snap, n.d.-c), and Meta makes the same payment-oriented distinction (Boland, 2014), with TikTok presenting content via the paid/unpaid binary using "organic" as the differentiator (TikTok, n.d.-b). As scholars have noted, this choice of terminology is not innocent, bringing along with it the virtuous associations of "organic" in broader discourses such as farming and food consumption (Petre et al., 2019).

The importance of algorithm in organic reach can't be overstated, but the systems and discussions around them are often at best problematic. Meta, for example, does not provide a given user with all or even most of the content from their selected friends and liked pages, instead focusing on providing access via their News Feed algorithm content that they deep as "high quality" that isn't "spam" (Boland, 2014). Content that doesn't meet these arbitrary guidelines is simply not shown to users unless they seek it out. TikTok (n.d.-e) leverages similar language around "high-quality" content, and Snap goes so far as to leverage the terms in the ad auction selection process (Snap, n.d.-d). As noted earlier, this distinction seeks to remove the role that platforms themselves play in content curation while simultaneously shaming creators that for one reason or another don't meet arbitrary quality guidelines (Petre et al., 2019).

Engagement is spoken about in terms of "reach," but moves beyond simply serving content into interaction, though almost always through the lens of paid placement when discussions emerge from social media platforms themselves. Meta, for example, quantifies engagement as "the total number of actions that people take involving your ads on Facebook," scoping the term primarily around the paid services on the platform (Meta, n.d.-d). Snap also leverages the term through the lens of paid promotions, and like many platforms allows placement targeting that specifically caters to users flagged as engaging with content from previous advertisements (Snap, n.d.-a). TikTok continues this trend with a focus on paid content engagement (TikTok, n.d.-c).

Discussions of reach, engagement, and content quality have been highlighted as problematic by scholars in social media studies as the terminologies and frameworks these discussions leverage undercut creators while promoting the fiction that platforms are somehow above the fray, simple disinterested arbiters of content on their systems. Caitlin Petre et al. (2019) lay out this case clearly in their scholarship on what they refer to as "platform paternalism."

Petre et al. highlight that the shifts in organic reach and how content is served to users has meant that creators are increasingly at the mercy of algorithmic systems for success on a given platform (p. 2). This means that communities increasingly create folk theories of how to get algorithmic success on a given platform as those platforms evolve (p. 3). Because platforms increasingly provide curated rather than chronological content (with TikTok being a leading example currently that Meta is aspiring to match with their controversial plans to shift Facebook and Instagram's feed mechanics), creators are often left scrambling when they notice shifts in their posts' engagement and metrics. For example, many creators in mid-2022 started to notice that because of that platforms push away from images (the reason it was created) to video content, their normal content was not getting traffic unless it was converted to video to match the algorithmic preference (McLachlan & Mikolajczyk, 2022). These shifts in algorithm end up constantly pushing creators to figure out whatever the algorithm is looking for to get their content seen by their followers, let alone new users and prospective followers.

While platforms push creators to constantly shift their practices to meet evolving quirks and FOMO impulses from Silicon Valley, they also leverage harsh terminology toward anyone seen as "exploiting" or "gaming" the system, which is to say those that are *too* effective at getting algorithmic attention. The line between "genuine" or "high quality" content and "spam" or other harmful content is largely arbitrary, but Petre et al. note that platforms leverage these terms and metaphors about creators to push the narrative that they are mere meritocracies and neutral hosts of content, even when the practices they sanction are the same practices they may well have suggested as "best practices" previously in educational texts for users (p. 8). At the end of the day, the line between good and bad content comes down to whether branded users are, perhaps, too effective at getting eyes on their content consistently without having to leverage paid placement. As Petre et al. note, they go beyond simply dissuading this effectiveness, they vilify it via "powerful moral framework[s]" (p. 8) that cater to their needs.

Practically speaking, the literature and theory on engagement as well as the evolving platform practices help frame our user experience architecture in generative ways by allowing us to recognize, and to the extent possible, plan for the role that algorithmic engagement metrics and content serving will play in the reach and impact of our texts. Simply having a large coalition and creating content for them is not always enough, and careful analysis of analytics and engagement metrics becomes essential as we test out the messaging and packaging we're leveraging to create and sustain authentic dialogues and discussions with our coalition of future backers while avoiding running afoul the current platform do's and don'ts.

Sketching Your Campaign

Having looked at the theories we'll need to frame our crowdfunding planning and implementation, we now turn to sketching out a campaign.

The first step to any campaign is to assess what your actual goal and narrative will be that the campaign is built around. What do you want to do with the funding you're asking for? Why are you asking for the funding in the first place? Why should someone trust your organization or personnel to carry out the work you're soliciting funding for anyways? All of these questions are central to a campaign's success and should serve as a starting point for your nascent project. We brought this up in the previous chapter, but now we want to go into much deeper detail.

First, see if you can get your goal into a single sentence. It may be fairly direct: we are seeking funding to create a new type of <insert product here>. It could be more abstract: we are seeking funding to grow our organization's capacity to <action/goal here>. We can use examples from the case study chapters later in the text to illustrate these differences. In the case of Lady Tarot Cards from Chapter 5, the goal is to get enough funding to print a run of tarot cards that are created by LGBTQ+ artists that represent that same community within the cards and their art. In the case of Ranch Relaxo in Chapter 6, the goal is to raise funding to expand the organization's infrastructure to allow for them to care for more animals. Using these examples and others that resonate with your project, draft a simple sentence-level narrative.

Once you have a narrative core, expand on that into a story. What is the backstory of your campaign? Why are you doing this work? Kickstarter suggests the following as a starting point for this narrative:

Who are you as a campaign team? What have you done in the past?
What are you going to be doing, and what will it look like?
Where did this project idea originate from? Provide an origin story.
What is your plan and schedule? How much time will be needed and what are you going to do?
Why do you care about this project and want to do it? (Kickstarter, n.d.).

Using these prompts and others, build out a more fundamental narrative that explains the nuts and bolts of your campaign while building a compelling image of who you are and what your motivations as a team are, and most crucially what the success of your project will mean for you and others.

Aligning Your Goal and Narrative With the Limits of the Platform

Once you have an idea of your goals for the campaign and the story you'll tell, think about this narrative as it will be translated across the platform of your choice. Different platforms emphasize different types of stories, and yours will likely do better if it resonates with the language and positioning of the platform. If you're on Kickstarter, the language of creators will matter more. If you're on Indiegogo, the idea of cutting-edge and get-it-here-first will need to shine through if you want to align with the existing audiences these platforms attract and sustain.

Campaign Funding Structure

Once you have a campaign narrative and goal, you need to figure out the actual numbers behind getting that work done. How much money will you need for your project to be carried out (realistically)? What price should be associated with someone backing the project's success in order to make the project successful? In some cases, the support can be calculated fairly simply, as in the production of a run of paperback books or other deliverables with regularized pricing. In other cases, as in the case of creating and funding a video game, there may be considerable unknowns that must be addressed. At the end of the day, your campaign has to pay the bills associated with reaching its goal. A large part of this will not be entirely your job as a technical writer on a larger project, but in this initial discussion, we'll cover the intersection of the budget, the funding tiers, and the eventual framing of the project for rhetorical velocity before shifting to selecting and planning funding tiers. So, work with your team to sketch out the actual costs of the project's success, and then go from there.

One you have a budget, you should also do some numbers gaming. Ideally, Indiegogo (Indiegogo, n.d.-c) recommends that you should aim to reach 30% of funding from your initial backer coalition that you've assembled *before* your campaign goes live, with that 30% of funding coming in the first 48 hours of your campaign. Others (Hewer, 2019) go even further, suggesting that hitting the funding goal in 48 hours should be a goal, allowing your campaign to move from a question of possibility to one of scale. This model of funding is seen in the third campaign in the STEAM Chasers series from Chapter 5. Obviously, not every campaign can aim for scale rather than possibility, but if you know the minimum floor of your campaign is going to be low, it might be a useful strategy.

To calculate your potential success going into a project and to get a feel of how much funding each tier should require, you'll need a conversion rate metric, an idea of just how many of your actual followers on social media, email lists, and so on will become active backers in your coalition during the launch phase and beyond. Indiegogo, the most metric-driven platform in their support documentation, recommends calculating email lists' conversion rate to plan your campaign's funding and launch strategy, based on a conversion rate of 5% (Indiegogo, n.d.-c). To game this out, you'll need to combine conversion rates with the cost of backing your project. Ideally, for hardware or creative campaigns, the backing tiers can simply reflect the cost of the deliverables provided with a profit margin built in and platform as well as payment processing fees accounted for (which can range from ~2% to ~10%). With campaigns that aren't providing a set deliverable to the backers, but instead offering perhaps information access or experiences or public thanks, you may need to think deeper on possible funding levels and leverage your quantitative and qualitative coalition research as well as research on similar projects that have succeeded and failed.

Let's dive into a brief example project's set of numbers. Let's say you are creating a nonprofit campaign to provide after-school activities for K–4 students in your community. If the project budget is $9,000, and your suggested default backing level is $50, you would need around 3,920 email list subscribers with a conversion rate of 5% to make your goal. This calculation is fairly conservative, estimating an 8% fee on all donations, which platforms like GoFundMe would reduce to 2.9% + $0.30. Tweaking the numbers of donors, the amount of the suggested donation, and your overall budget can change this, but that is the general idea of getting a project to succeed based off email conversions alone.

If we take our example project and move from total success to meeting the suggested 30% goal from Indiegogo, then our numbers change considerably. Gaining 30% of the $9,000 budget within 48 hours moves from needing 3,920 backers on the email list to needing a backer email list of around 1,180 to hit your 30% goal in the first 48 hours. And all of this is assuming you are simply getting funding from your default $50 donation. If you have higher tiers with perks and rewards that are enticing to your coalition members with greater financial resources, you may well reach that 30% goal (and your final goal) with markedly lower numbers of backers.

While the budget and conversion rate are essential to sketching out your campaign infrastructure, you should keep track of this data as you move to building an XA of engagement in the prelaunch period. These metrics and conversion rates can be vital tools in helping your campaign know when the safest time to attempt a launch will be. Again, crowdfunding platforms shouldn't be seen as the primary starting point of support for your campaign, but instead a place that you can attract additional growth and coalition members once you've demonstrated a fundamental core of support and the viability of your project.

Choosing Rewards and Tiers

Once know what your campaign's budget goals are, how will you build a structure around them that motivates your backing coalition to fund the campaign while getting the campaign's work done? Even for projects that are on platforms like GoFundMe that don't provide a discrete reward to backers, there is a need to think about what backing will get someone. In cases where an explicit reward structure doesn't exist, explicit rewards can exist by virtue of campaign commitments. For example, the Rancho Relaxo campaign from Chapter 6 doesn't provide physical rewards tied to funding levels on GoFundMe (that isn't a platform feature), but through updates to backers and the sharing of information about the campaign and its successes and milestones.

Perks and tiers of support on the campaign-oriented crowdfunding platforms are usually tied to some sort of reward, with each platform providing some guidance as to what that reward might look like. Kickstarter recommends rewards spanning from digital downloads of a work to limited content editions to custom deliverables or participation as a reward (@BuildingRewardsKickstarter), with the language and presentation linked to the creative/creator focus of the platform. Indiegogo provides a three-pronged approach to rewards, splitting them into material, personal, and experiential (Indiegogo, n.d.-f). Even GoFundMe recommends providing thanks for donors (GoFundMe, n.d.-b).

The three-pronged approach suggested by Indiegogo can be a generative starting point for your own campaigns, in addition to researching what other campaigns have done. Think about each of the three prongs: material, personal, and experiential and how they might map onto your campaign. Take a moment with your team, and brainstorm around 5–25 options under each category, just to see what you can think of and how it might play out for your campaign. Yes, that's a lot of options, but going for a larger number can help you really stretch out and think about possibilities and clusters of possibilities. As technical writers, in particular, think about ways that you can leverage the deliverables and processes of your project's production to create value for your backers. As noted by Rice (2016), those who are obsessed with a given topic thrive in basking in the details and minutiae of a given subject, as we discussed in Chapter 2, you can and should leverage the technical documentation and discussions that drive your project to involve and reward backers. What may seem to you to be a mundane workflow or discussion could be fascinating to your coalition.

Tiers can also be time and link and quantity limited on many platforms, meaning that you can leverage limited access or exclusive access to a particular tier or reward to encourage those who are able to afford such things to make the commitment to your project early. Again, there needs to be some ethical consideration in how these are pitched, but the general gist is that you can and should leverage the limited nature of these rewards to get folks excited, much in the way that subscription-based content or time-limited campaigns encourage donations during a given window. Remember, if a campaign stretches beyond a single month, the excitement tied to success or failure drops quickly. (Though, obviously this is not a 1:1 phenomenon for subscription-based services).

The tiers of potential support (or subscription) are also an important facet of rhetorical velocity—you need reward tiers that will pass the "can I afford this" check that any individual backer will likely apply to your campaign and its project, while also catering to the breadth and depth of your coalition's financial makeup. Some backers can and will support at higher levels, and some backers at lower levels. The goal is to match the offerings with backer resources without turning support tiers into a coercive tool to entice backers to over-commit to your campaign or spend resources on your campaign that they truthfully shouldn't be spending. There is an important ethical angle to all of this, as with all of crowdfunding.

You can also directly solicit your coalition for ideas and suggestions and feedback on these rewards, and leverage A/B testing and surveys to further analyze their feelings on what you're considering. Avoid falling into the trap that X and Y campaigns have this reward, so we should too (Unger, 2021). Your coalition and their coalitions may have different interests, and to be fair, their coalition may not even particularly like some of the rewards in a given tier despite backing the project at that tier overwhelmingly. We'll do our best to ask questions and listen to the responses in our next major section on building an XA.

Once you have an idea of what you goals and tiers could look like, sketch it all out in a spreadsheet. See how many backers you'll need at each tier to get across the finish line. Calculate the numbers across a variety of combinations, based off your own expectations in concert with data from exemplar campaigns that align with your own goals and team. These numbers will serve as a starting point for your planning and can and should be tested via engagement with your proto-coalition as you shift into building your XA of engagement.

A Special Note on Stretch Goals

No discussion of rewards and perks would be complete with a quick look at stretch goals, a campaign-driven concept that "stretches" the goals of a campaign beyond the basic goals of funding once the initial funding goals have been met. The idea behind stretch goals, in theory, is that more funding will allow the project to reach a greater scope, raising the floor for all backers involved. Stretch goals are not a platform creation nor are they platform supported (Indiegogo, n.d.-b; *What Are Stretch Goals?*, 2022). Instead, the concept of stretch goals arose from campaigns themselves. Stretch goals are now common across a variety of categories, and regularly feature in the top Kickstarter category of Games.

Stretch goals as a strategic tool in campaign research can be tricky to manage, but rewarding in some cases. Ideally, stretch goals will increase the quality of your project without creating ongoing expenses. A common example in video games is the inclusion of an orchestral soundtrack (Igarashi, 2015; Larian Studios, LLC,

2013). Once the game's soundtrack has been recorded by orchestral performers and that recording has been mixed and mastered, the work and expenditure is done. The performance and recording and mastering is a one-time expense rather than an ongoing one. Things become trickier with physically deliverables that are stretch goals or when stretch goals represent a per-unit cost increase for a campaign. For example, board games that create stretch goals that involve creating higher quality game pieces not only increase the price-per-unit of their games themselves but may also lead to unforeseen increases in things like shipping costs if they higher quality components increase the weight of the final shipped product into a new pricing tier (Rollins, 2020). These qualifiers shouldn't preclude stretch goals per se, but they should remind you and your team that stretch goals must be intensely researched and planned to avoid tanking a project's budget.

In addition to the risks of stretch goals complicating a project's budget, there are also risks that the promises made in the stretch goals may take vastly more time and resources than a team realizes on the front end, especially when goals are creating in the heat of a wildly successful campaign. A great example of the perils of stretch goals can be found in the work of Yacht Club Games on their game *Shovel Knight*. The Shovel Knight premise was fairly simple, a classic side-scrolling platformer in the vein of classic NES and SNES games like Zelda II, Mario, and Mega Man. The campaign, however, offered stretch goals that extended the playable characters of the game from one to four. As the development process went into gear, these stretch goals grew in scope, leading to a game development process that stretched over seven years (Schreier, 2019). Because these stretch goals were binding promises made to backers, Yacht Club ended up tied down to their Shovel Knight property and game for markedly longer than they ever intended. The follow-up content based on the stretch goals was quite successful, but the scope and length of the project were tripled.

Campaign Messaging

Once you know what you're doing, and how you're structuring the funding, you'll want to think through the campaign messaging. How can you develop your story into a pitch document, and how can you develop that pitch document's core into a pitch video that captures the spirit and excitement of the campaign and all of the details that demonstrate the campaign is worth funding?

The messaging process is an extension of the goals discussion earlier and will be tested and tweaked as you build out XA to attract your coalition to your proto-campaign. For each bullet point in your goal discussion, think about how that can be translated into a section of your pitch and then an eventual video. As you do so, think about how you can translate your existing sketch of backing tiers and deliverables into a compelling portion of that pitch. How will you talk about the funding tiers, and how will that content align with your campaign's goal and story?

The pitch video itself will depend highly on the scale and scope of your team and campaign, and as such, I'll not spend very much time on it at all. However, know that successful campaigns have been shown time and time again to be those that make use of a pitch video. There are outliers, such as Lady Tarot Cards' serial successes covered in Chapter 5, but those outliers are exceptions to the general trend.

Campaign Updates

Once you've decided the direction of your messaging, based on your team and your goals and your backing levels, you'll need to think through how you will maintain momentum through the campaign. Some campaigns will meet goals immediately (especially those designed for growth and scale), but your campaign may not. How will you create and curate updates that maintain and advance your campaign during the duration of your campaign?

First, working as a team, think about the aspects of your pitch and story that would benefit from the extended discussion. Perhaps your team members have particularly compelling narratives that make you a great choice for a given project—narratives about those members and their histories would make for a compelling update or series of an update. Are there particular components to your campaign or deliverable that you can get into the mundane details of? As noted in Chapter 2 (and illustrated across our case studies), the mundane details of a campaign are often some of the most compelling features outside the campaign's narrative and creator story. Which details would make for compelling updates? Think through the examples of what you could show and how it might impact your coalition. For example, Rancho Relaxo example in Chapter 6 features simple photos and discussions of key events in the purchasing of additional land for the animal shelter, such as shots of the keys to the property and billing breakdowns for fencing.

Once you have brainstormed out the content for potential updates with your team, think quantitatively about your update strategy. Surveying peers and aspirant peers, note how many updates they provide, the frequency and length, as well as the content. From this research, you can build a skeletal target for your own content. That content will then serve as a map for placing your brainstormed content for updates.

Working from your existing outline of an update schedule, work through different mappings of your content onto the schedule. What sort of pacing makes sense? How much work will be involved? Once you've sketched this out, you'll be in a position to test these ideas with your coalition as you build your initial XA and lay campaign groundwork.

Campaign Customer Service

Before wrapping up your top-level planning for your proto-campaign, you'll want to think about the resources you'll leverage for supporting your backers and answering their questions during and after the campaign. How often will you comment and answer questions? Will you have an email address that you funnel questions into? Will the campaign have a secondary site that supports backers and provides additional information? All of these questions are compelling and will need some discussion among your team. The handling of customer service may well be beyond your role as a technical writer, but the ways that the customer service integrates into the user experience are important, and there should be *some* sort of plan to support your backers.

Assessing the Ethics of the Proposed Project

Finally, before diving into the XA and creation any crowdfunding project, technical communicators should assess whether the associated campaign crosses any ethical boundaries in presentation or structure as the project gets rolling. Crowdfunding fraud and mismanagement is very real (Farivar, 2015; Kravets, 2017; Mullin, 2015), and any technical writer tackling a project must ensure the project accurately and ethically represents goals, means, and outcomes.

Ethics and ethics-related conversations abound in technical and professional communication, but for the purposes of this chapter, I provide a fairly truncated approach to crowdfunding ethics informed by the work of Walton et al. (2019). Crowdfunding campaigns are inherently risky because there are no strict legal guidelines on when failure moves from missing the mark on goals to wholesale fraud. Yes, there are legal actions carried out in blatant cases of fraud, but by and large, most crowdfunding platforms are very clear that success is not guaranteed nor enforced (though updates usually are). Technical communicators who wish to work with crowdfunding campaigns either as members of the sponsoring organization or as a freelancer must take care to recognize, reveal, and reject injustices in crowdfunding projects. To assess whether a given project contributes to injustices, I provide the following questions that any crowdfunding project should leverage to self-assess:

Are the goals of the project clearly articulated and illustrated to backers?
Does the project team document the extent to which they have the skills and expertise to complete the project? If expertise or skills are lacking within the team, is there a clear plan/partner who will provide those skills and expertise?
If the project will impact a multiply marginalized or historically marginalized group, have members of the group been consulted or involved in the project?
Does the project provide a nuanced and frank risk assessment to backers?
Is the proposed project or product ethical when assessed via Sano-Franchini's (2017) cultural reflexive framework?
Does the campaign work on a budget? Is it fully itemized, including any platform-specific reserves, fees, and a buffer for refunds and cost overflow? Are perks/rewards itemized, price-confirmed, and shipping price confirmed? If

applicable, is your supply chain verified and durable? Have you included pricing for events and ad-buys during and before the campaign?
Is the project timeline realistic? Are there any risks to the project tied to timelines?

While these questions are not exhaustive, they provide a starting point for assessing the ethics of a given campaign, building on the 4Rs of Walton et al. (2019) and a recognition that an important facet of ethical technical communication is actively avoiding being complicit in injustices.

Building an Experience Architecture of Engagement

Having laid a sketch of the proto-campaign, we now turn to building and then sustaining engagement with our coalition outside of any crowdfunding campaign platforms that we plan on leveraging for the project launch. This may seem counterintuitive, but as noted in the campaign sketch discussion, crowdfunding campaigns don't succeed because of a given platform's existing audience and engagement systems—they succeed because they start with an existing backing coalition that creates momentum and attracts further interest from within and without the platform of their choice. So, to start our crowdfunding campaign, we don't actually start with a campaign—we start instead with building out a presence online that can attract, build, and most importantly listen to and learn from a proto-coalition of backers that will eventually form the core of our project's funding in the crucial first 48 hours of the campaign.

To create an XA, we'll need to identify the channels we plan on leveraging for engagement and plan for sustainable engagement on those channels. As we begin this planning of our crowdfunding campaign, as technical communicators, we should resist the urge to silo deliverables or channels into discrete units—we should instead focus on creating compelling XAs that are, that cross channels and deliverables, uniting them into a single messaging/experience engine.

Practically, from start to finish, a good crowdfunding campaign (be it subscription or project-oriented) is composed of a group of channels and deliverables that work together, with a unified voice and purpose to inform, persuade, and most importantly engage with members of a potential backer coalition. In the words of Potts and Salvo (2017), we're building "ecosystems of activity" (p. 4) that will function together to attract our coalition. From start to finish, we are building an XA with moving parts that should work in unison and coordination and not against each other. A part of this is thinking through how and why the various channels should work and respond to your users, taking care to avoid what Polaine et al. (2013) refer to as experience crevasses, places where an otherwise outstanding user experience fails spectacularly, such as with a user who needs to ask a question about a product they've backed never getting a reply from a support email even though every single Twitter mention your organization has gets a response within a couple of hours at max.

Identify Channels for Engagement

First and foremost, a nascent campaign needs to find and engage with a core coalition of backers. Though crowdfunding platforms can be a way to grow your audience, crowdfunding platforms are not intrinsic drivers of success. Even the best crowdfunding platform will only foreground and share campaigns that meet metrics of success, engagement, and quality sufficient to trigger algorithmic intervention or attract attention from the platform team (in the case of Projects We Love on Kickstarter).

To build engagement, you need to have durable channels that you can leverage to get your organization or team's message out. The first step in such a process is choosing the channels that you know that you can leverage and leverage consistently to begin to attract an audience and a core coalition of backers. This often will be a social media presence of some sort, but care has to be taken that you only really choose the social media channels that you can actually maintain. Everyone loves to talk about meme-generating and constantly posting Twitter accounts for this or that brand, but not everyone has the bandwidth and skill to actually run a Twitter account with that level of energy, and your audience may not even be on Twitter.

To choose these channels, you need to research the social media platforms where hashtags, pages, and groups, whatever the grouping mechanism, demonstrate that your potential backer coalition has a presence. This research can and should look something like the research on the messaging and strategy of campaigns in your area of interest, as modeled in Chapters 5 and 6. Once you have found the areas where your campaign's backers have historically existed, you need to then begin engaging with them as a presence in that space in a sustainable way. You might have to make a Twitter account, but you don't have to vie for internet fame with all-star Twitter brands—you have to simply meet the metrics expected by your coalition members.

If you already have a social media presence, then the task becomes easier, but you need to begin the process of seeding interest and backing in your future campaign via those existing channels or your novel channels you're creating to maintain for the long haul based on the start of your engagement with your backer coalition. A part of that is building engagement, and a part of that comes in the next phase, which is creating a content marketing system that will sustain your coalition and attract interest from new members.

Engagement with a backer coalition can look different depending on the platform and the coalition, but in general, you should strive as an organization/channel/ team to create space for conversations and discussions related to your future project and plans that solicit and then respond to feedback from backers. The goal is to listen without filtering as we build our coalition and learn from them. For a product that is material in nature, this might result in soliciting ideas for colorways that will be offered (or running a survey to see which colors will make the cut).

For creative works, you might ask for scenarios or topics that members would like to see.

Depending on your channels, the level of engagement and the frequency of response can vary. If you work on a channel like Facebook that allows for live streaming, you could have some Q&A sessions with your coalition on topics related to your campaign. If you have backers on Reddit, you might host an ask me anything (AMA) thread that allows you to respond to backer questions. You might simply post on Instagram or Facebook or Twitter with a question, and then studiously reply to responses. The goal here is to find ways to create dialogue and then make those engagements sustainable.

It is worth noting that the toolset provided by a given channel matters a great deal due to how platforms tend to value content. For example, Meta will promote content that is uploaded to the platform more than content that is linked from a competitor such as YouTube (Meta, 2022). Platforms leverage content rankings and other algorithmic hooks to keep content within their systems.

As your campaign comes closer and closer to reality, engagement can and should guide the ways that you present your campaign and its associated perks and rewards (if applicable). For Kickstarter and Indiegogo campaigns, soliciting what types of perks and rewards will motivate and be meaningful to your coalition can be an important facet of meaningful engagement, especially as you can then show those same coalition members that their ideas are being not only listened to but also leveraged in your activities. Just because everyone is doing X or Y in your space doesn't mean your coalition members will find it engaging or interesting (Unger, 2021), so ask them what they want to see and why.

Engagement builds expectations for a user experience. If you host biweekly AMA sessions on a livestream, that becomes a part of your workflow for the long term. These types of engagement need to become part of your social media presence in order to sustain long-term commitment from backer coalitions. Social media moves too quickly to not have content regularly available, and backer coalitions will come to expect the level of engagement you offer. Suddenly stopping all engagement would create the equivalent of an experience crevasse where a normally stellar user experience suddenly becomes less than ideal due to a violation of the expectations previously set. The negative version of this is fairly simple: build engagement that is meaningful *and* sustainable while avoiding unsustainable levels of engagement. You can have surges in activity, but don't set expectations that are so high that you'll expend all of your team's energy on social media content and fail to actually do the work that your social media content supports.

To return to the 4Rs of Walton et al. (@rebeccawaltonTechnicalCommunicationSocial2019), sustainable engagement is an important facet of a just and equitable technical communication strategy. Too many multiply marginalized communities are all too familiar with sustained bursts of engagement from politicians, community groups, and even universities (Flower, 2008) that vanishes after whatever event precipitated the push for engagement. Faux engagement, that is, simply a means to an end, is a form of injustice that we are ethical technical communicators must reject without exception.

Content Marketing

Having discussed engagement in an authentic sense, I now turn to engagement in the more clinical, metric-based sense of the term with content marketing. As noted previously, organizations like Meta view engagement as a valuable metric, with at times controversial platform changes based on (and at times retracted because of) engagement data (Hutchinson, 2022; Newton, 2022) as with the mid-2022 push for and then step back from a Reels-centric Instagram freed. Content marketing is partially based on metrics of engagement, in that content that is tracked as being engaging will actually be served to users of a platform, whereas content that doesn't show up as engaging often will fail to be pushed to users' feeds.

In addition, content marketing creates and sustains a level of content and familiarity that supplements more nuanced engagement strategies by simply creating a level of familiarity with your audience while also building an organization's value or brand with potential backer coalition members. Social media follows are often based on interest and information, and content marketing builds on this idea of selling without selling (Wall & Spinuzzi, 2018) by focusing on demonstrating expertise and sharing knowledge or even just amusing content with users on a regular basis. While direct engagement will pay greater dividends over the long term, content marketing allows your channel to build up enough of a following for that engagement to occur.

Content marketing can help in particular when a crowdfunding project represents something new or unexpected for your team or organization. Instead of launching a campaign that seems to come from nowhere, rhetorically speaking, you can leverage content marketing by releasing posts and blogs and videos and other material that starts to demonstrate your understanding and expertise in the subject matter of your future campaign. This work is also valuable when your organization already works in a given area that a campaign will leverage—content marketing makes sure that evidence of your suitability as a team to complete the project is ample and easily accessible (and sharable).

When thinking through content marketing, as with engagement, it can be helpful to look at examples from peers and aspirational peers in crowdfunding. Successful campaigns will have already built their own content marketing networks and workflows, and simply looking over their shoulders at what they've done can be a helpful starting point. In addition, content marketing from peers and your own campaign also provides helpful metrics and insights into what has the ability to attract interest and what simply passes by without engaging audiences.

Thinking through content marketing as a strategy, teams should consider what types of content they can create that sells without selling, which is to say educational, entertaining, and interesting content that builds connections with a channel's followers. For a music-related page, it might be a regular feature where members of the team discuss their favorite records. For a technology-related team, it might be a demonstration of a prototype or a demonstration of the design process or fabrication process for a given product. For a community organization or nonprofit, it might be a tour of a facility or a walkthrough of a program. The goal is to build connections, define expertise, and generally provide something of value to your followers (and prospective followers) that exists distinct from your explicit calls to action related to campaigns, with the expectation that the familiar and relationships built from such activity will motivate your audience to become backers while building the base audience to a point that the percentage of followers that become coalition members hits your core metrics for success (as will be discussed shortly in the section on running a campaign).

Leveraging Engagement

Next, we'll look at how you can leverage your coalition and their engagement to launch strong and to continue to build your backer coalition. We'll first discuss the practical matter of email lists, a tool recommended strongly by platforms to maintain an organized way to reach your backers that is independent of algorithmic quirks and tweaks, such as the Meta Discovery Engine (Reuters, 2022). Once we've tackled mailing lists, we'll discuss old-school approaches to amplifying your rhetorical velocity via targeting media outlets, blogs, and influencers before closing the chapter with a discussion of planning (and budgeting for) corporate kairos via targeted paid advertisements.

Mailing Lists

Your project likely needs an email list. That might seem backward in the 2020s, but research from crowdfunding platforms and campaigns (Humphrey, 2020a; Indiegogo, n.d.-c) demonstrates that one of the oldest technologies on the web is still not only useful but also often vital in creating momentum in your campaign's earliest days. First, we'll cover the rationale and benefits of mailing lists before we dive into tools available for building them and best practices for building out a mailing list of coalition members and messaging them via the list.

As noted previously, email lists are one of the oldest technologies on the web, but they are vital to campaign success because they are at their heart simple tools for sharing emails directly to users without the intervention of algorithms. Modern LISTSERV technology was created in 1986 by Eric Thomas (L-Soft, n.d.), but almost 40 years later, as of this writing, the technology behind mailing lists remains incredibly useful for campaigns because it allows you to connect with your coalition in ways that bypass algorithmic judgments and build early momentum that—ironically—capitalizes on algorithmic judgment. As Gillespie

(2015) reminds us, platforms can and do continuously intervene in the ways that users of their platforms may or may not find useful. Yes, a post may quickly go viral after significant engagement from you users, catapulting you onto the feeds of users that aren't in your existing page's audience, but those same algorithms may demote your content when it doesn't meet established metrics that are algorithmically applied (Meta, n.d.-b, n.d.-c) and designed to serve the needs of the platform, not the users/creators (Petre et al., 2019).

Mailing List Benefits

Though many campaign creators think that crowdfunding platforms will provide them with organic reach via platform visibility, the scale of these platforms and the fickleness of things like "Projects We Love" badges at Kickstarter make such calculations perilous at best. Platforms tend to support projects that are already succeeding, and for that promotion, your project needs to look and be successful by their metrics (Humphrey, 2020a). As noted in the previous chapter, different platforms will measure the engagement and push your project in different ways, but that algorithmic engagement is tied to measurable metrics of success that the platform has identified. The findability of your campaign on any given platform by simply existing is not a mechanism for campaign success.

The benefits of mailing lists for crowdfunding campaigns are numerous, but the most important benefit is that they provide you with a data-driven way of planning for the campaign launch. Indiegogo explains that nominally 5–10% of an existing email list can be considered buyers, meaning that you can game out getting 30% or even 100% of your funding if you simply amass a large enough list (Indiegogo, n.d.-d). In addition, having a strong email list can let your campaign demonstrate real growth during the first 48 hours of your launch, a time period that is almost universally seen as vital for project success, with 30% put forward by Indiegogo as a target for funding during the first 48 hours (Humphrey, 2020a; Indiegogo, n.d.-c). The early success on the platform, in turn, triggers excitement in your backer coalition that things are moving briskly, while also triggering algorithms on the hosting platform of a time-limited campaign. Using the 30% and 5% numbers, you can quickly do some math on when your campaign is able to safely launch with a higher chance of success, and you can even bank on success if your email list gets high enough to allow 5% of all coalition members to get you over the funding finish line, allowing your actual campaign to serve as more of an outreach/growth event than a campaign to get initial funding.

Mailing lists also serve a practical function in that they provide an avenue for reaching your backer coalition that isn't tied to a particular crowdfunding platform, be that platform project-based or subscription-based in nature. Platforms evolve over time—sometimes for the worse—and creators and creatives that don't want their data and their connections with their coalition to be negotiated via crowdfunding platforms can leverage mailing lists as a more platform-agnostic form of communication. That way, if a major platform makes moves that unsettle your campaign (such as Kickstarter's planned shift to a carbon-negative block-chain platform (Hall, 2022), there are easy options for moving your future projects and backer coalition away from your current platform to a new one or a homegrown solution.

Building a Mailing List

Building an email mailing list can be broken down into two discrete tasks: choosing a platform for managing your email list and building the list itself. The first part of the process will depend on your team, your organizational structure, and your needs. There are certainly many free and paid mailing list services such as MailChimp, Omnisend, and Sendinblue, but the choice will largely depend on your team and parent organization's structure, contracts, and needs. Simply sending emails is often only a part of these platforms' purpose and capabilities (many offer services such as email prompts when a customer leaves items in their cart and leaves a webpage), so organizational context may lead you into an existing relationship with a mailing list vendor.

The second part of building a mailing list, the actual recruitment of list subscribers, can be approached through best practices that leverage your existing outreach and coalition building in addition to your crowdfunding project's deliverables and web footprint. First, most crowdfunding platforms will allow you to create a prelaunch page to build hype for your project, with some (as noted in the previous chapter) even allowing you to start displaying follower metrics and the like. These platforms can and should feed into your list, allowing you to start building off of interest in a discrete campaign on the platform of your choice. In addition to prelaunch pages, you can collect emails via your existing social channels, any face-to-face meetings and events you may host, as well as via subscriber outreach to their own friends and family networks (Goswami, n.d.). You can also connect with influencers that are popular in your space on social media or even collaborate with other brands that are concurrently hosting campaigns (Humphrey, 2020a).

Amplifying Your Message's Rhetorical Velocity

Having looked at the use of mailing lists as a starting point for leveraging your engagement, we now turn to strategies that specifically target increasing the rhetorical velocity of your planned campaign. Rhetorical velocity doesn't simply happen, so a good bit of planning and coordination is needed to make the most of your potential velocity when your campaign launches. Again, the first 48 hours are crucial to both perceptions of success and final success for a given campaign.

With modern crowdfunding and media practices, a good first start is simply building out a press kit for interested journalists and outlets in the same ways discussed by Ridolfo and DeVoss (2009, 2017). Such press kits usually include high-quality photos that can be used for print and online outlets, boilerplate explanations of the organization, campaign, and answers to frequently asked questions (Indiegogo, n.d.-g). A press kit ensures that even in cases where you're not soliciting journalists directly, you're still providing them the information they need to write about your campaign if they find it as part of their own work.

While national press outlets can be interesting, many platforms recommend reaching out locally first to get interest and engagement from local outlets that have a more vested interest in covering your campaign and organization (GoFundMe, n.d.-a; Indiegogo, n.d.-g).

With any press outreach, making sure that your messaging is tailored to the organization and the reporter is vital. Reporters work in different areas and beats, and messaging needs to mesh well with their expressed interests and assigned coverage. The same is also true of reporting outlets: if you have a technology-heavy project, you should like pitch it to an outlet that covers those types of subjects. If you have a community-based project, you'll want to find outlets that value that work. It is a fairly simple concept, but one to remind your team of from time to time in the rush to get as much coverage as possible.

Influencers and demo artists focus more on getting your actual product or service and using it and providing feedback on it. In theory, they provide an analysis that focuses on the positive, a different approach than the traditional review paradigm. The guitar industry, for example, makes extensive use of demo artists and influencers in their product promotion. A new product or service will often pay for product demos and tests by influencers and full-time demo artists, where the end product is a video or series of videos talking through the product, its uses, and demonstrating the functionality and underscoring the positive uses of the product. These are not reviews per se as they normally don't have a critical component, instead simply focusing on what is useful/positive about the product or service.

Niche sites, blogs, and subreddits that are specific to your area of interest can also be useful to amplify your rhetorical velocity. If your project caters to a niche or specialized set of interests, niche sites can help you target folks who may be prospective members of your coalition. Building a relationship with smaller sites and giving them access to your material exclusively for sneak peeks can give you access to additional viewers that align with your project. The same goes for blogs, as many hobbies and interests end up with central bloggers who serve as authorities on a given subject. For example, the blog/site DC Rainmaker is commonly referenced in Reddit threads on smartwatches and gadgets for running. Subreddits, subsections of the hugely popular website Reddit, can also be useful for the promotion of your project to build velocity, but Reddit's community and rule structure can make this something that shouldn't be done lightly. Reddit has a history of specifically prohibiting accounts and content that exist solely for the purposes of self-promotion (*Selfpromotion—Reddit.Com*,

2006), and that ethos continues on the site. Generally speaking, subreddits, like many groups and pages on Meta's Facebook, can be useful, but only if you're able to join that community and become an accepted, useful contributor before announcing your project.

Using Corporate Kairos With Targeted Placements

In this section, we'll cover the ethics of content placement and advertising, the strategy behind such placements, and how to perform data-driven placements that will boost your rhetorical velocity in a way that can be managed over time and analyzed for effectiveness. As a note, the majority of the discussion that gets into specifics will focus on the Meta platform as Meta's advertising and integration with their social media systems tends to put them at the center of most discussions of corporate kairos. In cases where your coalition is fundamentally not on Meta platforms, virtually all other social media platforms have equivalent placement tools.

Ethics of Content Placement

The level of detailed targeting within social media platforms as well as less mainstream data clearing houses like Experian (*Consumer Marketing Data | Experian Marketing Services*, n.d.) can be unsettling. For example, Experian provides products that allow customers to target users based on whether they are a "complacent card user" that pays off balances in full, a "reluctant revolver" that is classified as "undisciplined" (p. 3). The Experian dataset even provides categories such as "Insecure Debt Dependent" that describe those in the segment as tending to "live beyond their means" (p. 4) (Experian Information Solutions, Inc., 2018).

For ethical content placement, I suggest a few simple rules of thumb that draw on the concepts of social justice and preventing further injustice laid out by Walton et al. (2019). At the very least, our use of content placement must reject injustice, while ideally revealing those injustices in the process. While this is a subject that deserves much more scholarship and discussion than we have space for here, I will offer two simple rules that attempt to bypass some of the worst offenses of targeted placement.

Don't Target Users Based on Information That Is Highly Personal

In the past, platforms like Facebook provided targeting that could easily be seen as invasive, such as health causes, sexual orientation, as well as religious and cultural affiliations (*Removing Certain Ad Targeting Options and Expanding Our Ad Controls*, 2021; *Updates to Detailed Targeting*, n.d.).

Don't Target Users With Placements That Might Reveal Information the User Does Not Wish to Share

In many cases, platforms can and do target individuals with huge datasets that provide them with information via deduction that they might not otherwise acquire. For example, Target's marketing department allegedly tasked statistician Andrew Pole to figure out a way to use datasets to identify pregnant women as early as possible (Duhigg, 2012), a move that in a post-Roe society holds any number of ethical implications when corporate data is used without individuals' consent (Kaste, 2022). The same could be said for targeted advertisements for divorce firms, medical care, and any number of other advertisements that may provide information to casual observers of a user's device that the user is comfortable in sharing.

Though these suggestions may seem common sense, they are necessary and important in doing the work of technical communication via targeted content placement in a world where platforms simply don't prevent illegal and unethical targeting behavior while maintaining double standards in content that is placed in ways that may themselves be illegal, such as preventing women from seeing job advertisements (Hao, 2021).

Data-Driven Content Placement Strategy

When planning for content placement, funding should be considered first. Crowdfunding campaign budgets need to accommodate the projected campaign, and purchases limited to fit with existing budgets and targets.

A nuanced take on marketing strategy is beyond this text, but technical writers can and should assess the effectiveness of placed content as well as the targeting of that content on a regular basis. Simply exposing potential members of the coalition to your content will allow you to quickly note when/where/how they react to what you've presented. Some of these reactions are offered within your platform, and some require additional analysis.

When it comes to avoiding problematic targeting choices, an alternative to highly detailed targeting options can include lookalike audiences, which provide an algorithmic alternative that profiles your existing coalition members on social media and then places ads in the feeds of those that look similar to the algorithm. While this does rely on a fundamentally black-boxed system to target advertisements, it does allow categorization via interests and behaviors (Meta, n.d.-a) and fundamentally simply looks to serve ads to users of the platform that look like your audience to the system. As always, self-imposed limits are needed. For example, Meta might suggest targeting members via interest in "African-American Literature," which still has echoes of the cultural and racial affiliations that the platform has in theory removed due to abuses. Snap and TikTok also provide Lookalike services for campaigns that leverage those platforms (Snap, n.d.-b; TikTok, n.d.-a), providing the same algorithmically served targeting based on existing followers, fans, or others.

When planning advertisements, research can and should be done on peer projects and their own placements. Meta provides the most prominent tool for this work via their Ad Library that allows you to see the advertisements on the platform, their performance, budget, and generalized targeting information. Meta also provided the CrowdTangle tool that allows the tracking of links, topics, groups, and pages and their content performance in the larger ecosystem of the web, but the company has quietly moved to close access to the tool by the end of 2022 (Smalley, 2022).

Revising the Campaign Sketch for Launch

Earlier, we sketched out a campaign that made sense internally to your team as you started the crowdfunding process. This was likely based on your own internal needs and goals in addition to research you've carried out on aspirant peer campaigns. After having built an XA to support your campaign, building and listening to your proto-coalition in the process, the last step before moving on to launch is revising that campaign sketch based on the information gleaned from the work you've done. This revision will differ for each team, but as you go into the final stages of launch prep, think about the following questions:

What have you learned during the XA building about your coalition?
What types of content were the most important and motivating to your coalition?
What do you need to produce before launch to be able to have a steady stream of content without working day-to-day?
How much of a buffer do you need or want for your team during the update process??
Once you've settled these questions, you'll be in a position to transition as a team to the work of setting up and running your campaign in the sections to come.

Running a Funding Campaign

Having discussed the process of sketching a campaign and then building a robust XA and analytics system to support that campaign, we now turn to the running of the actual campaign. We'll first discuss the work and setup carried out in the prelaunch period, followed by the crucial first 48 hours of a campaign before moving into the often-present mid-campaign slump, and then finishing with the final stretch of funding. The goal in this section is not to provide you with a singular plan for creating and running your campaign, but instead to provide you with a series of markers and topics to consider as you plan your campaign based on best practices.

Prelaunch

The prelaunch period for technical writers ideally focuses on working sustainably, creating a workflow and system that does much of the heavy lifting of your campaign for you automatically, allowing you to focus on time-sensitive content and responses to your campaign in action. Since the period of the campaign is both finite and known, you can and should create, test, and revise your campaign deliverables and update content well before your actual launch window. There is no reason to chase the campaign creating content just-in-time. Much of the prelaunch period relies on the planning and analytics work you've done in the run up to your campaign, so another way to view this period is as an implementation/organization of ideas and plans you've already finalized.

You'll want to get a prelaunch page active on your platform of choice, if possible, and start the process of building hype and momentum with your core coalition members as you lead up to launch. This often takes the role of a countdown or other time-oriented messaging setup, but regardless of your approach, you want to build the energy, and excitement around your campaign will be giving those interested a concrete place to find the campaign when it launches while also hooking into your communication channels and email list in the run-up to the launch. The additional hurdle of joining the list via your prelaunch page can assist in building a strong list that maximizes your conversion rate among your coalition members (Humphrey, 2022a, 2022b).

Centralizing an Analytics Dashboard

To make decisions about the day-to-day deliverables and responses that you generate during a campaign, you will need to finalize the analytics systems that you'll be using to coordinate your campaign. This may be a combination of platforms such as the Meta tools (and perhaps Pixel or Google Analytics giving you information on traffic to and from your website) and the in-house solution provided by your crowdfunding platform. Regardless, you will want to decide which tools you'll leverage and start to track your numbers and baseline engagement and interaction figures. Watching these analytics datasets will give you a window into the effectiveness of your overall campaign as well as nuanced information on specific deliverables that you leverage as well as content placement buys.

Implementing the Experience Architecture

Having sketched your campaign, built engagement with your coalition, and crafted an analytics dashboard, your final hurdle to launching a campaign is a consistent and coordinated plan to implement your XA. The first step of this planning is simply to get everything into a single place—you need to take an inventory of your XA components and their functions, something akin to a content inventory in the work of user experience practitioners (Buley, 2013). As a starting point, you can leverage the following questions to arrange the body of your content as you create a schedule for content distribution during the campaign:

What is your narrative/story?
Where are your core backers?
What are your social media channels?
What content can go on each channel?
How many updates do you plan on having pre-created?
What types of real-time updates and content do you plan on creating?
How will you coordinate customer support and backer comment responses?
What media outlets and sites do you plan on sending press to?

Having answered these questions and corralled any extra processes and workflows into a list of content, the next step is to coordinate these systems into a schedule that will run the duration of your funding window.

Though it is a bit low-tech, I suggest you leverage an XA Grid to assist in building out your schedule. There are many solutions out there that are team-integrated and cloud-based, but a simple grid as a planning tool can go a long way. An XA Grid is a simple matrix that provides you with the ability to coordinate your schedule across your timeline, mapping overlaps and gaps in the overall XA of your project. In planning your grid, it can be helpful to build a grid tracking the distribution of content, contests, and other deliverables leveraged by peer campaigns while referencing additional resources provided by platforms themselves, such as Indiegogo's launch calendars (Indiegogo, n.d.-a) and Backerkit's checklist guidelines (Humphrey, 2020b).

The XA Grid is fairly simple, with rows for each channel or type of channel communication you plan, ideally giving you space to coordinate between planned and real-time updates, while also tracking the progress of your campaign through the three most crucial periods: the first 48 hours, the mid-campaign slump, and the final 48 hours, as seen in Figure 4.1.

Project Day	1	2	3	4	5	6	7	8	9	10	11	12	13	14	15
Kickstarter Planned Updates															
Kickstarter Real-Time Updates															
Facebook Post															
Facebook Live															
Facebook Reels															
Facebook Story															
Facebook Ad Campaigns															
Feedback															
Emails															
Bounce Rate															
Page Visits															
Funding Total															
Funding Percent															

Project Day	16	17	18	19	20	21	22	23	24	25	26	27	28	29	30
Kickstarter Planned Updates															
Kickstarter Real-Time Updates															
Facebook Post															
Facebook Live															
Facebook Reels															
Facebook Story															
Facebook Ad Campaigns															
Feedback															
Emails															
Bounce Rate															
Page Visits															
Funding Total															
Funding Percent															

FIGURE 4.1 An example XA Grid for a crowdfunding project

The XA Grid can and should serve as a living document to track your progress within the campaign. You can add or remove channels and data as needed. For example, the template tracks daily page visits, bounce rates, and funding totals as well as percentages. Consider the aforementioned a potential starting point, with changes and additions and subtractions to come both during your planning process and during the campaign itself.

In addition to structuring your XA plan, make sure to audit your content for optimal placement on platforms themselves. As a reminder, platforms can and do privilege content that is posted natively (Meta, 2022), so making sure that your videos, reels, and other content exist in a format that can be shared to various channels is essential to getting that content through any demotion algorithms on platforms.

The First 48 Hours

The first 48 hours of a campaign is widely held to be crucial in setting momentum and expectations for success. Aiming for 30% funding within 48 hours, ideally, will provide a given campaign the momentum and aura of success needed to get all the way to 100% and beyond. The first 48 hours should feature a targeted push to email lists, existing social media channels, as well as strategic content placement buys to move the needle as much as possible during the crucial early window for success.

Remember Reach

Your coalition and your followers across social media have two ways they can impact your success. They can and should engage with your campaign and back it, but they also can engage with your campaign materials, creating a flurry of likes, shares, retweets, hashtag users, and references that will create a spike in activity around your campaign that has the potential to trigger algorithmic preferential treatment.

During the first 48 hours, a campaign generally sets a trajectory and builds momentum that will either be enough or not be enough to trigger engagement-oriented algorithmic promotion (Humphrey, 2020b). With platforms that have internal promotion systems like Kickstarter, Indiegogo, and to an extent GoFundMe, this can help leverage the audience that already frequents those sites and also trigger the attention of press organizations and niche interest sites. With social media channels, engagement with deliverables and links from the campaign can provide additional organic reach by getting the content promoted within users' feeds.

In crafting your XA Grid and plan, you'll want to make sure to include as many discrete high-impact actions possible, pushing your rhetorical velocity as hard as you can during this initial phase. Ideally, your campaign will have leveraged a countdown to launch while building off and through your pre-campaign engagement. Remember that the goal is to create momentum while triggering as much earned reach as possible via algorithmic selection and simple rhetorical velocity and coalitional excitement.

The Campaign Slump/Stall

Most campaigns stall in the middle during crowdfunding, as attested by any number of practitioners and platform observers (Bowden, 2010; Bushong et al., 2018; GoFundMe, 2022; Hewer, 2014; Kickstarter, 2022). A slump is simply a slowdown in the overall funding rate of a crowdfunding campaign. You may earn 30% to 40% of your funding within 48 hours, and then only move 10% over the next 48% hours. The length and severity of the slump will be unique to a given campaign. But, you can be almost certain that it can and likely will happen in some form to your own project.

Because the slump phenomenon exists, it is worth building your campaign's XA around the expectation that you'll hit a slump. Not every campaign will hit a slump, but planning around the chances that your campaign will be an outlier puts you at a distinct disadvantage when you actually run into a slump having already burned through most of your velocity-boosting deliverables and strategies. Rhetorical velocity isn't an entirely zero-sum game, but there are certain moves that can only be pulled off effectively once in a given campaign, so carefully consider which will be needed in the early phase of your project versus in case of a slump.

When viewing your campaign's overall XA Grid and plan, plan for the slump strategically. The slump period can be an ideal time for bringing in things like a Reddit AMA, a contest (that can often be paired with an announcement about your project), major content updates on your plans/product/project, or even flash sales and secret perks (depending on platform allowances). The goals of a given campaign during slumps can vary, but you can look at the data you already have collected via analytics to help you plan your next moves.

If your campaign has succeeded and hit at least 30% during your initial 48 hours, you can and should leverage the members of your coalition that have chosen to back your project. You can leverage backer rewards (depending on the platform). For example, Kickstarter campaigns can use referral programs that can offset the cost of backer's pledge (*Can I Use Referral Programs on Kickstarter?*, n.d.), and Indiegogo campaigns can offer considerably more in terms of rewards (Indiegogo, n.d.-e).

You can and should also consider making a rather concerted effort to show how your feedback from backers and coalition members has started to come into play with your campaign and how you plan on responding (Hewer, 2014). The development of the campaign can and should continue the engagement-oriented work you started before your campaign began. These types of updates can reengage and fire up your coalition members as they both see your campaign coming to life and see their feedback shaping the campaign as it evolves. Making this part of the narrative/story of your campaign can be essential as you come into the middle of your campaign looking to continue to build on your initial 48 hours of success.

If your slump happens to coincide with reaching the halfway point, or if you manage to make it over the 50% mark, make sure to take advantage of press releases and other renewed pushes to get into the coverage of the niche your platform is within. Milestones like going over 50% can demonstrate your campaign is worth covering, and a milestone-centric approach can help you target your press release coverage to windows when your campaign is perceived as being newsworthy (Indiegogo, n.d.-g).

Regardless of your approach, know that slumps do happen, and they can be overcome with careful planning of your rhetorical resources and leveraging of your coalition and analytics.

The Final Stretch

In the final 48 hours of your campaign, focus on running up your numbers and getting to your goal (or as far beyond it as you care to push your coalition). As with the first 48 hours, the last 48 hours can be crucial in the overall funding numbers for a campaign. Research has shown that there is a noticeable effect in the amount/size of donations during the first and final days of a campaign when campaigns leverage the donations and funding amounts received, with that effect waning during the middle portions of your campaign (van Teunenbroek & Bekkers, 2020).

The closing of a campaign, much like the opening days, creates a natural sense of rhetorical velocity that can be leveraged—your campaign will move from funding to fulfillment, and usually that means that getting onboard with the project will change in some way. If a campaign offers post-campaign support options, those are usually associated with higher fees and margins from the associated platforms, so highlighting the chance to get in at a lower rate/stage can be effective. In addition, there is a meaningful distinction between someone who backs a campaign and helps it achieve funding and someone who helps after the fact. Concrete perks like a thank-you list of backers that made a campaign possible are one way to both highlight this and to provide rewards and incentives to backers, as discussed during the campaign sketching section early in this chapter.

You can begin to think about how you will transition to collecting funding (if you want to collect funding) in the post-funding environment. Many campaigns offer post-campaign funding choices such as preorders or other options. Platforms like Kickstarter don't allow for official post-campaign backing, so bespoke "Slacker Backer" support options (Parlock, 2015) or a move to platforms that allow post-campaign backing such as Indiegogo's InDemand or custom solutions like Backerkit's post-campaign preorder services.

As you close, remember to foreground again your story and the story of your coalition. The user experience architecture you're creating and maintaining will continue beyond this campaign, into the fulfillment phase where you will continue to build off of the successes and relationships you've built. Brag on your coalition and showcase what they have both done and made possible as you close. Simply taking time to thank and name supporters can build further connections and bonds while also engaging those same coalition members and encouraging those who have watched your campaign to this point without backing.

If, as you come to the final moments of a campaign, you realize you will fall short of the goal, that isn't something to totally despair over. The failed campaign itself can be a learning tool for your team and can build the groundwork needed for a successful follow-up campaign (Hewer, 2013). As can be seen in the extended analysis of Rancho Relaxo in Chapter 6, a campaign that falls short of its goal can be the impetus for a string of serial successes.

Wrapping Up

In this chapter, we've laid out a comprehensive approach to building a crowdfunding campaign from the starting point of an initial user experience to the planning and eventual rollout of your campaign, informed by research in technical communication and social media studies. Your own campaigns may not actually need the fundamental work of building an XA from the ground up, but seeding your campaign within your infrastructure is an important and integral part of success. Crowdfunding platforms help your campaign grow, but they work to supplement existing coalitions and give them additional reach and energy—your crowdfunding platform will not be the source of your backing coalition.

Discussion Questions

1. Locate a handful of crowdfunding campaigns that are currently active. Where and how can you see their platform-specific-content being amplified and supplemented by their existing social media and website infrastructure? Which of these channels and deliverables seems to be doing the best?
2. Locate a handful of recent successes on crowdfunding platforms. Look through their updates and update structure. Which of the campaigns appear to have a funding slump? How did the campaign response in the update structure?

References

Boland, B. (2014, June 5). Organic reach on Facebook: Your questions answered. *Meta for Business*. www.facebook.com/business/news/Organic-Reach-on-Facebook

Bowden, W. (2010, September 23). 9 ways to jumpstart your stalled campaign. *The Indiegogo Review*. https://go.indiegogo.com/blog/2010/09/9-ways-to-jumpstart-your-stalled-campaign.html

Buley, L. (2013). *The user experience design team of one: A research and design survival guide.* Rosenfeld Media.

Bushong, S., Cleveland, S., & Cox, C. (2018). Crowdfunding for academic libraries: Indiana Jones meets Polka. *The Journal of Academic Librarianship, 44*(2), 313–318. https://doi. org/10.1016/j.acalib.2018.02.006

Can I use referral programs on Kickstarter? (n.d.). *Kickstarter Support.* Retrieved July 13, 2022, from https://help.kickstarter.com/hc/en-us/articles/115005134794-Can-I-use-referral-programs-on-Kickstarter-

Consumer Marketing Data | Experian Marketing Services. (n.d.). Retrieved September 8, 2022, from www.experian.com/marketing-services/targeting/data-driven-marketing/consumer-view-data

Duhigg, C. (2012, February 16). How companies learn your secrets. *The New York Times.* www.nytimes.com/2012/02/19/magazine/shopping-habits.html

Experian Information Solutions, Inc. (2018). *Financial and wealth audiences: Identify your most profitable audiences and take them to the bank.* www.experian.com/content/dam/marketing/na/assets/ems/marketing-services/documents/product-sheets/financial-and-wealth-audiences.pdf

Farivar, C. (2015, November 24). Kickstarter has no clue how drone startup raised $3.4M then imploded. *Ars Technica.* https://arstechnica.com/information-technology/2015/11/kickstarter-learned-of-zano-collapse-through-a-bare-bones-project-update/

Flower, L. (2008). *Community literacy and the rhetoric of public engagement.* Southern Illinois University Press. www.siupress.com/books/978-0-8093-2852-9

Gillespie, T. (2015). Platforms intervene. *Social Media + Society, 1*(1). https://doi. org/10.1177/2056305115580479

GoFundMe. (2022, October 19). What to do when your fundraiser stalls. *GoFundMe.* www.gofundme.com/c/blog/campaign-stalls

GoFundMe. (n.d.-a). How to get local media to cover your fundraiser. *GoFundMe.* Retrieved September 1, 2022, from www.gofundme.com/c/fundraising-tips/local-media

GoFundMe. (n.d.-b). Thank your donors. *GoFundMe.* Retrieved August 11, 2022, from www.gofundme.com/c/crowdfunding-lessons/thanking-donors

Goswami, A. (n.d.). 7 surefire ways to build your email list—and your community. *Indiegogo Education Center.* Retrieved August 31, 2022, from https://entrepreneur.indie-gogo.com/education/article/7-surefire-ways-build-email-list-community/

Hall, C. (2022, August 30). Kickstarter's new director of games will fight the growing lack of trust in the platform. *Polygon.* www.polygon.com/23328798/kickstarter-new-director-of-games-interview-blockchain

Hao, K. (2021, April 9). Facebook's ad algorithms are still excluding women from seeing jobs. *MIT Technology Review.* www.technologyreview.com/2021/04/09/1022217/facebook-ad-algorithm-sex-discrimination/

Hewer, D. (2013, August 26). Kickstarter Lesson #49: To cancel or to finish. *Stonemaier Games.* https://stonemaiergames.com/kickstarter-lesson-49-to-cancel-or-to-finish/

Hewer, D. (2014, May 11). Kickstarter Lesson #95: The top 10 ways to address the mid-campaign slump. *Stonemaier Games.* https://stonemaiergames.com/kickstarter-lesson-95-the-top-10-ways-to-address-the-mid-campaign-slump/

Hewer, D. (2019, March 18). Is it now necessary to successfully fund within the first 48 hours on Kickstarter? *Stonemaier Games.* https://stonemaiergames.com/is-it-now-necessary-to-successfully-fund-within-the-first-48-hours-on-kickstarter/

Humphrey, A. (2020a, September 29). How to start a Kickstarter campaign: Hard-won lessons from a first-timer. *Crowdfunding Blog & Resources | BackerKit.* www.backerkit.com/blog/how-to-start-a-kickstarter-campaign

Humphrey, A. (2020b, October 28). Kickstarter checklist: Create a plan for crowdfunding success. *Crowdfunding Blog & Resources | BackerKit.* www.backerkit.com/blog/kickstarter-checklist

Humphrey, A. (2022a, April 4). How strong is your crowdfunding email list? *Crowdfunding Blog & Resources | BackerKit.* www.backerkit.com/blog/how-strong-is-your-crowdfunding-email-list/

Humphrey, A. (2022b, May 2). 4 reasons why you need a Kickstarter email list. *Crowdfunding Blog & Resources | BackerKit.* www.backerkit.com/blog/kickstarter-email

Hutchinson, A. (2022, July 27). Zuckerberg says that meta plans to double the amount of AI-recommended content in user feeds. *Social Media Today.* www.socialmediatoday.com/news/zuckerberg-says-that-meta-plans-to-double-the-amount-of-ai-recommended-cont/628312/

Igarashi, K. (2015, May 11). Bloodstained: Ritual of the night. *Kickstarter.* www.kickstarter.com/projects/iga/bloodstained-ritual-of-the-night

Indiegogo. (n.d.-a). *A pre-launch guide for successful campaigns + free campaign prep calendar and checklist.* Retrieved June 9, 2022, from https://entrepreneur.indiegogo.com/education/guide/pre-launch-calendar-checklist/

Indiegogo. (n.d.-b). *Building stretch goals.* Retrieved June 9, 2022, from https://support.indiegogo.com/hc/en-us/articles/205183457-Building-Stretch-Goals

Indiegogo. (n.d.-c). Campaign email strategy: Turn your list into contributions. *Indiegogo Education Center.* Retrieved July 13, 2022, from https://entrepreneur.indiegogo.com/education/guide/email-strategy-crowfunding-campaign/

Indiegogo. (n.d.-d). Forget the viral videos and build your email list. *Indiegogo Education Center.* Retrieved July 13, 2022, from https://entrepreneur.indiegogo.com/education/article/build-email-list-firstbuild-forget-viral-videos/

Indiegogo. (n.d.-e). *How do I run a referral contest?* Retrieved June 9, 2022, from https://support.indiegogo.com/hc/en-us/articles/527406-How-do-I-run-a-referral-contest-

Indiegogo. (n.d.-f). *Perks: How to use Perks to raise funds.* Retrieved June 16, 2022, from https://support.indiegogo.com/hc/en-us/articles/205157097-Perks-How-to-Use-Perks-to-Raise-Funds

Indiegogo. (n.d.-g). The power of the press: How to generate media attention for your campaign. *Indiegogo Education Center.* Retrieved September 1, 2022, from https://entrepreneur.indiegogo.com/education/article/press-strategy-how-to-get-media-attention/

Jim Ridolfo & Dànielle Nicole DeVoss. (2009). *Composing for recomposition: Rhetorical velocity and delivery.* https://kairos.technorhetoric.net/13.2/topoi/ridolfo_devoss/velocity.html

Jim Ridolfo & Dànielle Nicole DeVoss. (2017). Remixing and reconsidering rhetorical velocity. *Journal of Contemporary Rhetoric, 7*(2/3), 59–67.

Kaste, M. (2022, August 12). Nebraska cops used Facebook messages to investigate an alleged illegal abortion. *NPR.* www.npr.org/2022/08/12/1117092169/nebraska-cops-used-facebook-messages-to-investigate-an-alleged-illegal-abortion

Kickstarter. (2022, August). *My funding has stalled after a few days, what should I do?* https://help.kickstarter.com/hc/en-us/articles/115005134814-My-funding-has-stalled-after-a-few-days-what-should-I-do-

Kickstarter. (n.d.). *Telling your story—Kickstarter.* Kickstarter. Retrieved June 6, 2022, from www.kickstarter.com/help/handbook/your_story?ref=handbook_started

Kravets, D. (2017, March 29). $3.5 million crowdfunded drone campaign flops, lawsuit alleges. *Ars Technica.* https://arstechnica.com/tech-policy/2017/03/lawsuit-3-5m-indiegogo-crowdfunded-drones-are-shoddy-not-delivered/

Larian Studios, LLC. (2013, March 27). Divinity: Original sin. *Kickstarter.* www. kickstarter.com/projects/larianstudios/divinity-original-sin

L-Soft. (n.d.). History of Listserv. *L-Soft.* Retrieved August 30, 2022, from www.lsoft. com/corporate/history-listserv.asp

McLachlan, S., & Mikolajczyk, K. (2022, July 20). 2022 Instagram algorithm solved: How to get your content seen. *Social Media Marketing & Management Dashboard.* https://blog. hootsuite.com/instagram-algorithm/

Meta. (2022, August 31). *Understanding video distribution on Facebook. Understanding video distribution on Facebook | Meta for Media.* www.facebook.com/formedia/blog/ understanding-video-distribution-on-facebook

Meta. (n.d.-a). Best practices to maximize your lookalike audience. *Meta Business Help Center.* Retrieved September 8, 2022, from www.facebook.com/business/help/ 902694250080164

Meta. (n.d.-b). Guidelines for accurate, authentic content. *Meta Business Help Center.* Retrieved August 30, 2022, from www.facebook.com/business/help/538391223253327

Meta. (n.d.-c). How Facebook distributes content. *Meta Business Help Center.* Retrieved August 30, 2022, from www.facebook.com/business/help/718033381901819

Meta. (n.d.-d). Post engagement in Facebook ads. *Meta Business Help Center.* Retrieved July 28, 2022, from www.facebook.com/business/help/735720159834389

Meta. (n.d.-e). Reach. *Meta Business Help Center.* Retrieved September 14, 2022, from www.facebook.com/business/help/710746785663278

Mullin, J. (2015, June 11). Feds take first action against a failed Kickstarter with $112K judgment. *Ars Technica.* https://arstechnica.com/tech-policy/2015/06/ feds-take-first-action-against-a-failed-kickstarter-with-112k-judgment/

Newton, C. (2022, July 28). Instagram is walking back its changes for now—Adam Mosseri explains why. *The Verge.* www.theverge.com/2022/7/28/23282682/instagram-rollback-tiktok-feed-recommendations-interview-adam-mosseri

Parlock, J. (2015, September 22). Shenmue 3's "Slacker Backer" doesn't currently offer the PC version. *Destructoid.* www.destructoid.com/shenmue-3s-slacker-backer-doesnt-currently-offer-the-pc-version/

Petre, C., Duffy, B. E., & Hund, E. (2019). "Gaming the system": Platform paternalism and the politics of algorithmic visibility. *Social Media + Society, 5*(4). https://doi. org/10.1177/2056305119879995

Polaine, A., Reason, B., & Løvlie, L. (2013). *Service design: From insight to implementation.* Rosenfeld Press. https://rosenfeldmedia.com/books/service-design/

Potts, L., & Salvo, M. J. (Eds.). (2017). *Rhetoric and experience architecture.* Parlor Press. https://parlorpress.com/products/rhetoric-and-experience-architecture

Removing Certain Ad Targeting Options and Expanding Our Ad Controls. (2021, November 9). *Meta for Business.* www.facebook.com/business/news/removing-certain-ad-targeting-options-and-expanding-our-ad-controls

Reuters. (2022, July 21). Meta's Facebook revamping main feed to attract younger users. *Reuters.* www.reuters.com/technology/metas-facebook-revamping-main-feed-attract-younger-users-2022-07-21/

Rice, J. (2016). *Craft obsession: The social rhetorics of beer.* Southern Illinois University Press.

Rollins, B. (2020, September 21). How to choose realistic stretch goals for your board game Kickstarter. *Stonemaier Games.* https://stonemaiergames.com/how-to-choose-realistic-stretch-goals-for-your-board-game-kickstarter/

Sano-Franchini, J. (2017). What can Asian eyelids teach us about user experience design? A culturally reflexive framework for UX/I design. *Journal of Rhetoric, Professional*

Communication, and Globalization, 10(1). https://docs.lib.purdue.edu/rpcg/vol10/iss1/3

Schreier, J. (2019, December 13). The seven-year saga of shovel knight is finally over. *Kotaku.* https://kotaku.com/the-seven-year-saga-of-shovel-knight-is-finally-over-1840419716

selfpromotion—Reddit.com. (2006, January 17). *Reddit.* www.reddit.com/wiki/selfpromotion/

Smalley, S. (2022, August 18). Meta won't comment on its plans to abandon CrowdTangle. *Poynter.* www.poynter.org/reporting-editing/2022/meta-wont-comment-on-its-plans-to-abandon-crowdtangle/

Snap. (n.d.-a). Custom audiences overview. *Snapchat Business Help Center.* Retrieved September 15, 2022, from https://businesshelp.snapchat.com/s/article/custom-audiences?language=en_US

Snap. (n.d.-b). *Lookalike audiences.* Retrieved September 14, 2022, from https://businesshelp.snapchat.com/s/article/create-lookalike-audience?language=en_US

Snap. (n.d.-c). Promote organic content with ads. *Snapchat Business Help Center.* Retrieved September 14, 2022, from https://businesshelp.snapchat.com/s/article/organic-content-ads?language=en_US

Snap. (n.d.-d). Snap auction overview. *Snapchat Business Help Center.* Retrieved September 14, 2022, from https://businesshelp.snapchat.com/s/article/snap-auction-overview?language=en_US

Snap. (n.d.-e). *Story ad metrics glossary. Snapchat Business Help Center.* Retrieved September 14, 2022, from https://businesshelp.snapchat.com/s/article/story-ad-metrics?language=en_US

TikTok. (n.d.-a). About lookalike audience. *TikTok Business Help Center.* Retrieved September 14, 2022, from https://ads.tiktok.com/help/article?aid=9594

TikTok. (n.d.-b). How to grow your business with TikTok on PrestaShop. *TikTok: Business Help Center.* Retrieved September 14, 2022, from https://ads.tiktok.com/help/article?aid=10007790

TikTok. (n.d.-c). Measurement FAQs. *TikTok: Business Help Center.* Retrieved September 15, 2022, from https://ads.tiktok.com/help/article?aid=14127

TikTok. (n.d.-d). TikTok ads manager glossary & terms. *TikTok: Business Help Center.* Retrieved September 14, 2022, from https://ads.tiktok.com/help/article?aid=10005682

TikTok. (n.d.-e). What's the community interaction objective. *TikTok: Business Help Center.* Retrieved September 14, 2022, from https://ads.tiktok.com/help/article?aid=10008245

Unger, D. (2021, June 26). Some thoughts on Kickstarter comic campaigns [Blog]. *Indie Creator Explosion.* https://indiecreatorexplosion.com/2021/06/26/some-thoughts-on-kickstarter-comic-campaigns/

Updates to Detailed Targeting. (n.d.). *Meta Business Help Center.* Retrieved September 8, 2022, from www.facebook.com/business/help/458835214668072

van Teunenbroek, C., & Bekkers, R. (2020). Follow the crowd: Social information and crowdfunding donations in a large field experiment. *Journal of Behavioral Public Administration, 3*(1), Article 1. https://doi.org/10.30636/jbpa.31.87

Vogels, E. A., Gelles-Watnick, R., & Massarat, N. (2022, August 10). Teens, social media and technology. *Pew Research Center: Internet, Science & Tech.* www.pewresearch.org/internet/2022/08/10/teens-social-media-and-technology-2022/

Wall, A., & Spinuzzi, C. (2018). The art of selling-without-selling: Understanding the genre ecologies of content marketing. *Technical Communication Quarterly, 27*(2), 137–160. https://doi.org/10.1080/10572252.2018.1425483

Walton, R., Moore, K. R., & Jones, N. N. (2019). *Technical communication after the social justice turn: Building coalitions for action.* Routledge.

Warner, M. (2002). *Publics and counterpublics.* Zone Books.

West, S. E., & Pope, A. R. (2018). Corporate Kairos and the impossibility of the anonymous, ephemeral messaging dream. *Present Tense: A Journal of Rhetoric in Society, 6.* www.presenttensejournal.org/volume-6/corporate-kairos-and-the-impossibility-of-the-anonymous-ephemeral-messaging-dream/

West, S. E., & Pope, A. R. (2021). Rubles and rhetoric: Corporate Kairos and social media's crisis of common sense—present tense. *Present Tense: A Journal of Rhetoric in Society, 9*(1). www.presenttensejournal.org/volume-9/rubles-and-rhetoric-corporate-kairos-and-social-medias-crisis-of-common-sense/

What Are Stretch Goals? (2022, August). *Kickstarter Support.* https://help.kickstarter.com/hc/en-us/articles/115005128274-What-are-stretch-goals-

5
DISCRETE CAMPAIGNS

In this chapter, we're going to analyze a pair of campaigns that demonstrate how serial success in crowdfunding can come from the linking together of a series of discrete campaigns that draw on and build connections with the same general coalition for the same general focus and goal. In a sense, these time-limited campaigns represent the earliest tradition of crowdfunding that arose as the genre expanded across industries and into nonprofit spaces, and one-off campaigns or strings of time-limited campaigns are still very much a normal part of how many campaigns work.

As a sustainable genre, these campaigns work by primarily chaining together discrete campaigns to provide a steady stream of revenue. For some industries, such as games and comics, this approach makes particular sense because of the high set-up costs associated with work in the industries. The upfront costs of producing tabletop games, video games, and comics often prevent small, independent producers from being able to support the production of their own runs of content without considerable financial investment and risk on their part (Nuttall, 2021). The relatively steep financial risks involved historically have tended to give publishing houses and studios outsized power in these industries, and the advent of crowdfunding as a mainstream source of funding has fundamentally shifted the way these fields operate in favor of creators and their autonomy (Mollick & Nanda, 2016).

Case Study Overviews

The chapter will first introduce our case studies: Lady Tarot Cards and STEAM Chasers, both found on Kickstarter. These two campaigns serve to provide us with two different and contrasting models for

DOI: 10.4324/9781003308966-5

discrete crowdfunding campaigns that serve historically marginalized communities. Lady Tarot Cards provides us with a model for a campaign raising money to put a deliverable into production, whereas STEAM Chasers provides us with a window into campaigns that serve to amplify the release of a project rather than ensuring the project comes into existence. These two campaigns also provide contrasting scales, with STEAM Chasers' three campaigns each raising less than $6,000, and Lady Tarot Cards starting at $39, 216 and going up from there with subsequent campaigns.

Case Study Methodology Overview

We'll tackle each case by providing a brief history, followed by a quantitative analysis, and then a qualitative analysis resulting in a series of coded rhetorical moves that describe the project's approach to the pitch and updates. We'll wrap each section with a review of what the project looks like through the lens of our three-step process of listening, quantifying, and defining before shifting to a discussion of what the campaign can teach us as we aim to create sustainable crowdfunding efforts of our own.

Lady Tarot Cards

Lady Tarot Cards: LGBT+ and POC Inclusive Tarot Deck, run by two creators (Nova and Mali) under the monicker Lady Tarot Cards on Kickstarter (Lady Tarot Cards, 2020), was available for funding from April 20, 2020, through May 30, 2020, and received $39,216 in funding from 534 backers. The campaign self-describes as "a collaborative project by LGBT women and nonbinary artists for LGBT women and nonbinary people (absolutely trans-inclusive and POC inclusive!)" with the goal of printing a set of tarot cards "featuring women and non-binary people on each card." The project coordinates between 44 different artists to create the cards, with artists divided between resident and guest artists. The decks are provided with a digital booklet that contains all of the art, card info, and information on the artists behind the art. The lowest possible backing amount to get the full tarot card deck was priced at $50, and attracted 327 backers.

As a serial success, Lady Tarot Cards (referenced as LTC from this point) was the beginning of a series of projects all centered around the same thematic focus of bringing the representation of LGBT+ individuals and people of color into genres that normally did not feature them prominently. The first of these sequels was *"classics . . . but make it gay,"* a campaign that focuses on taking classical art pieces and reworking them to include and focus on "gay, trans, and POC" individuals (Lady Tarot Cards, 2021a). The campaign would be featured as a "Project We Love" on Kickstarter and earn $228,025 from 3,488 backers during 2021, hitting its initial funding goal within two hours. A second campaign was launched during late 2021, *Cover Me Queer—Romance Novels but make it gay*, a project focusing on taking cover art from romance and pulp fiction novels and making it "LGBT and POC inclusive" (Lady Tarot Cards, 2021b). *Cover Me Queer* was also featured as a "Project We Love" on Kickstarter, and would go on to earn $50,293 from 1,293 backers during late 2021.

As of 2022, the LTC creators' website (*novaandmali.com*) describes their projects as having "snowballed into independently run queer art publishing," with a sequel to the "classics . . . but make it gay" project being available for pre-order (and advertised via the existing project's updates on Kickstarter). A third book in the "classics . . . but make it gay" series is promoted as coming in 2023 (Nova and Mali, n.d.). From a single project in 2020, the creators of Lady Tarot cards earned over $300,000 in pledges over the course of the three campaigns, maintaining their existing coalitional audience while expanding the iterations of their work into different artistic directions.

Serving a historically marginalized group with their project, the LTC creators were able to create an ongoing stream of projects via a coalition on Kickstarter and to leverage that momentum into their own publishing venture and additional projects that have been funded outside of the Kickstarter ecosystem (though leveraging the connections and coalition created via Kickstarter). The project serves as a reminder of the power of coalitional action via crowdfunding and demonstrates the potential for sustainable funding via crowdfunding (and the potential for sustained crowdfunding success to continue outside of an existing platform once a backing coalition has been built and maintained over several successful campaigns (though not all serial successes choose to move away from crowdfunding as their funding vehicle as we will see in later case studies).

Campaign Funding Structure

Lady Tarot Cards campaign targeted a goal of $25,000 over the duration of their funding campaign. The project funding tiers ranged from a simple "Tip-Jar Thank You" at $5 (or more) to a single $250 pledge tier available to a single backer that included an embroidery used as the design for a campaign sticker deliverable. The campaign leveraged two early-bird tiers that were limited, one providing a discount to the first 25 backers buying a tarot deck at $40 versus the normal $50, and another providing 25 backers access to the deck and merch at $65 rather than the normal price of $75. As seen in Figure 5.1, the funding was mostly concentrated in tiers that provided a physical deliverable of some sort:

As seen earlier, most of the funding fell in the range of $50, with funding levels dropped after $75 and under $50.

Backers by Funding Tier

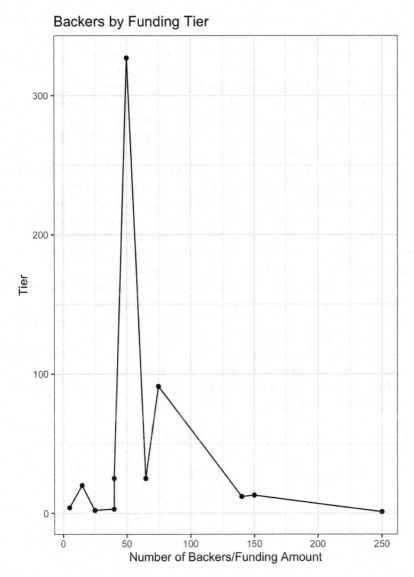

FIGURE 5.1   Chart showing the number of backers by funding tier for Lady Tarot Cards

Quantitative Analysis of Lady Tarot Cards

To frame the quantitative analysis, we'll start with a general overview of the length and number of updates and project pitch. Though this data is simply quantitative, it does provide an initial window into the writing needs represented by the Lady Tarot Cards project. The secondary review via qualitative analysis will get into the details of what types of technical writing and support texts have been created by the campaign.

Lady Tarot Cards' original crowdfunding project on Kickstarter has a total of 20 public updates (and 2 private not tracked in this data due to access barriers) in addition to the project pitch itself. Based on a simplified sample (removing redundant headings and sub-titles on images), the project pitch comes in around 750 words, with the average update on the other hand averaging 118 words. Updates range between 64 words for the shortest text and 237 words for the longest text (which is still around 1/3 of the length of the initial pitch document with all of its details and caveats). In practical terms, this all sums up to around 2,879 words in total, which is around 12 double-spaced pages of prose, with 26% of the overall writing length of the LTC project coming from the description and pitch of the project in the initial project page.

Measuring for engagement via the two primary metrics tracked by Kickstarter (likes and comments), the LTC updates received an average of 17 likes, with likes-per-update ranging from 3 to 26, and comments per update ranging from 0 to 7, with an average of 3 comments.

Lady Tarot Cards (and their subsequent campaigns) does not feature a project video. The lack of a video sets LTC as an outlier among crowdfunding successes on the platform, with the lack of video generally running counter to best practices from virtually all platforms' advice that feature and foreground videos heavily. The first LTC campaign was also the only one not featured as a "Project We Love" by Kickstarter, though it did succeed by a fairly healthy margin, raising over $39,000 to surpass the $25,000 initial goal by over $14,000 which represents additional funding that around 56% above the initial goal.

First up, we'll look in Figure 5.2 at a simple comparative word cloud of the LTC project divided by pitch, pre-funding, and post-funding usage. The *quanteda* (Benoit et al., 2018) comparison clouds provide us with a sense of the unique terms that show up across the different phases of the campaign. The ranking in

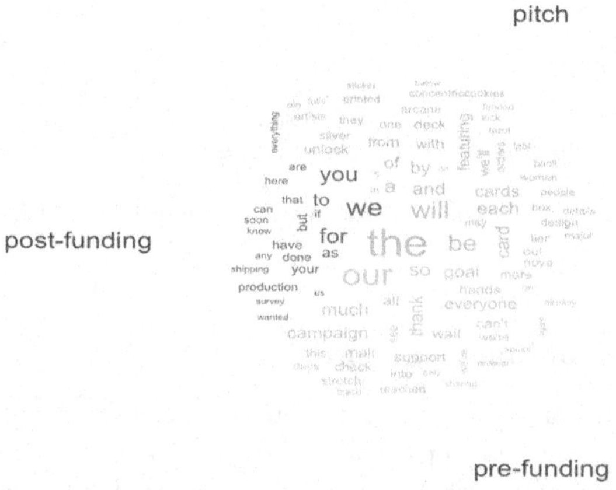

FIGURE 5.2 A comparative word cloud of the LTC project divided by pitch, pre-funding, and post-funding usage

the comparison cloud aren't a direct representation of the top words in each stage of the campaign, but instead represent the terms that are most common in each distinct section of the campaign when they are compared to each other and the whole corpus. An initial look at these terms provides a flavor to each phase of the campaign: the pitch is about what "will" happen in the project, the pre-funding period focuses on "our" as a central term, with goals and thank you and the campaign featuring, and the post-funding period foregrounds "we" and "you" as the text emphasizes the collaborative nature of the fulfillment period.

Pitch

Central to the campaign's pitch is the usage of "will," a semantically strong modal auxiliary verb (Huddleston & Pullum, n.d., p. 189). The confidence of "will" aligns with the descriptions of the deliverables of the campaign featuring prominently in the overall spread of words: "card," "cards," "featuring," "deck," and so forth. Taken together this paints a picture of a campaign pitch that focuses on the mundane details and specifics of what will be coming out of the project when it is backed.

Pre-funding

The pre-funding deadline period is dominated in the word cloud by "our," signaling an emphasis on community action and group action versus the positioning of a singular individual behind the campaign. This makes sense and aligns with the presentation of the campaign pitch as the work of a collective of artists. Beyond "our," many of the key terms centered around the campaign, its success, and invocations of the community of backers and thanks to that same community through terms like "everyone," "thank," "support," and "goal."

Post-funding

"We" and "you" together as the highest frequency terms in the post-funding window (compared to other periods) emphasize the cocreation of the project between the backing coalition and the creators of the project. As we noted in Chapter 2, there is an intense power in framing the work of a crowdfunding campaign's fulfillment as the direct result of the backing coalition, especially when that fulfillment is documented in a way that shares the mundane technical details of the coalition's project. We see evidence of those same mundane details in the word cloud differentiation given earlier, with terms like "pins," "stickers," "surveys," and "production" featuring prominently. In addition to referencing the cocreation, you also directly address the coalition members themselves, underscoring a personal relationship with the campaign and the connection of their individual actions with the campaign and its fulfillment and success. When viewed via lexical dispersion plot in Figure 5.3, we can see the usages of "we" and "you" peak after the sixth update, the final update before the funding period closed for the project.

Lexical dispersion plot

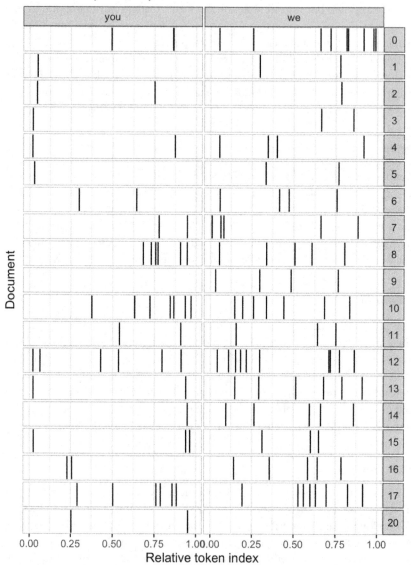

FIGURE 5.3 A lexical dispersion plot comparing the usage of "we" and "you" across the LTC project

The figure underscores the image painted by the comparative word cloud: as the project shifts toward the fulfillment phase, the texts start to more regularly reference the backing coalition members, and the communal nature of the project. The relative starkness of the plot before Update 7, the first update after the funding window, underscores this shift in language.

Seeding the Qualitative Review

Having quantitatively analyzed the structure of the Lady Tarot Card updates and pitch, we can build a general picture of what we expect to find in the qualitative analysis. Summarizing the findings from the quantitative review, the starting codebook for qualitative review has been seeded with the following moves/concepts for corpus review:

- Referencing the backing coalition
- Emphasizing communal action
- Documenting mundane details of the process

These codes are designed to serve as a halfway point between primary and secondary coding (Tracy, 2013), primarily focusing on the action being done within the text. They identify moves that appear to be happening within the primary texts via qualitative analysis, but they don't yet have a fully fleshed out explanation of how they are functioning rhetorically within the text itself. Quantitative textual analysis provides us with a window into what is being said and talked about in the text, but we are left to theorize on how these terms are working together.

Qualitative Analysis of the Lady Tarot Cards

An initial round of coding with the three seeded codes as a starting point resulted in a total of 25 discrete codes after a first pass of coding the pitch and updates. This original set of codes was then revised to streamline the codebook where redundancies had crept into the coding process. All coding was done through NVIVO. Once the initial coding was done, a second pass was made to do an initial redundancy check on the existing codes, lowering the number to 22.

The first-round coding was dominated by four codes that came in with over 25 references:

- Fulfillment Period Updates and Details
- Funding Period Updates and Details
- Deliverable Mundane Details
- Coalition or Group Reference

After this initial cluster of high-usage codes, the rest of the codes fell between 1 and 21 references, with most codes falling between 3 and 10 references in total.

Moving toward a final set of axial codes, the project's codes were next analyzed and categorized into major rhetorical moves made during the pitch and update process. This second review resulted in five broad actions carried out in the project pitch and updates, ranked below by their overall frequency:

Sharing of process updates and mundane details (146 references)
Centering the coalition of backers and their actions to create the project (54 references)
Centering the project creators and their efforts (26 references)
Requesting action on part of backing coalition (18 references)
Envisioning completion with the coalition receiving the project (8 references)

Each of these existing rhetorical moves highlights different aspects of the messaging carried out during the campaign update. The moves align with the concept of crowdfunding as an XA cocreated by backing coalitions and the creators of a given project and mediated by the platform used during the process. Next, each of these moves will be explained with contextual examples and a general overview of the rhetorical moves made and the "why" behind each.

Sharing of Process

The sharing of process via updates and mundane details represented the bulk of the overall coded references in the updates and the pitches, and sharing content was found in virtually all updates and documents. These updates and their associated details function to build and sustain the XA of the campaign from the funding period through fulfillment. Being able to see the details of the eventual end goal and see the details of the process as it unfolds reminds backers of their motivations to back the project and lets them see their funding translate into a tangible result. For example, the most highly liked updates for the entire project were specifically sharing the details of the creation process: photos of card art (Update 8), card and box proof photos (Update 13), and photos of the final cards (Update 15).

The sharing of information also functions to give backers an insider's view of the process of creating the cards and the associated merchandise. The mundane technical processes and steps that lead to the creation of the tarot cards become the heart of the content of the updates in fulfillment, with each update showing the project inching toward completion. For example, in Update 14, the LTC team shares, "Metallic prints: got the proofs and need to make some adjustments before sending off the finals," turning what is a fairly normal phase of print production (proof review and alterations based on the printed deliverable) into content for the backers.

At their core, the sharing updates are technical writing and technical communication: they document the process and procedures of making the backed campaign a reality, and that process of documentation continually reinforces the same motivations and passions that lead backers to coalesce around the project.

The updates also underscore to backers that the project is happening, with the technical details also underscoring the transparency of the creators and their competency in the creation process—something essential to sustainable crowdfunding success across multiple campaigns.

Centering the Coalition

Update content that works to center the coalition funding the creation of the Lady Tarot Cards project was the second most common rhetorical move, present in virtually all updates and documents. Centering the coalition continuously functions to remind individual members of both their impact and the power of the coalition as a force to create via crowdfunding. These references serve a parallel purpose to the sharing of process in that they remind the backers that they are part of and the reason behind a successful project, connecting the continued updates and success to both their individual action and their membership in a coalition that got things done.

A good many of the centering moves occur casually, with a simple repetition of the same invocation of "everyone," reinforcing the communal effort that created and sustained the project's success. One example would be "I wanted to email everyone," from Update 14. This centering of the backer coalition reinforces the collective nature of the project in a subtle way. The power of this approach is not in the individual usage, but instead the aggregate approach that invokes "everyone" across virtually all updates. For LTC, with its focus on providing a deliverable that is not normally inclusive of LGBTQ+ individuals and people of color, reminding "everyone" of the communal effort also centers the historically marginalized coalition that helped the project succeed.

Beyond the simple centering through repetition, particular invocations of thanks and references to the coalition support's role in the creation of the project works in coordination with the near-ubiquitous references to "everyone." Some of these references are fairly simple, such as "Thanks again for your support" from Update 12, and some are more targeted and specific such as Update 7's "we literally couldn't have done this without you:)." These specific references link the generic "everyone" usages with reminders of coalitional action and success.

The targeted centering of the coalition in these specific ways further associates the coalitional actions with the project's success in tangible ways and coordinate with the sharing of process moves. In the previous example of the reference in Update 12, the update serves to update the process's status by sharing that the card production has started with proofs being ordered. The LTC creators specifically link the thank you with this process update and fulfillment, explaining "Thanks again for your support—we're so excited that we're able to send this to production now and look forward to sharing the cards as soon as we can." The process update is happening, but it is happening because of their support, and the connection between the two moves underscores this.

Centering the Project Creators

Centering the project creators was the third most common move by a number of references, present in almost all updates, tying the coalitional centering for prevalence across updates. The centering of the project creators serves to connect the project and its success to the two specific individuals behind the LTC project (and future LTC projects), Nova and Mali. As this is the first campaign from the creators and their first presence on Kickstarter (unlike the second case study in this chapter, Lady Tarot Cards has no projects on the Kickstarter platform that they have supported), the centering of the creators serves to underscore the "who" of the project's success while also connecting that success to the actions of two individual creators that have created the coalition's project.

The creator-centering moves are often simply sign-offs at the end of updates, such as the near-constant usage of "Best, Nova and Mali" to sign off updates. In rarer cases, one member of the duo specifically attributes authorship to themselves or references the other creator as being responsible for a particular process or deliverable, such as "My (Nova) job for today is to place an order for the stickers" from Update 10. These creator-specific sign-offs move the focus from the campaign itself (and the backing creator of the same name) to these two individuals who are running the campaign and creating it. This move aligns with Grice's (2017) evolution of brands discussed in Chapter 2 where brands move from logos, to ethos, to pathos in their evolution over time (pp. 48–49). The centering of the creators by name builds a factual association with them as creators and creators specifically working with the LGBTQ+ individuals and people of color to provide representation in spaces that have marginalized them in the past.

In addition to the centering moves that serve to define the creators in a positive light and reinforce their role in the project, there are a handful of moves that specifically center the creators as independent of the Kickstarter platform, providing the campaign with a presence outside of their social media presences (to be discussed more in Requesting Action) and the campaign itself. Most of these references refer to the launch of a Storeenvy site, an e-commerce platform for hosting sales. There are a string of references to the store and its eventual launch, such as Update 11's note that "FINALLY: we are opening a storeenvy this Saturday, August 8 at noon EST." These updates are partially of necessity—unlike many crowdfunding platforms, Kickstarter does not have a built-in distribution system. With that said, the creation of the store and promotion of it serves to underscore the centering of the creators as the source of the project and projects their work beyond the end date of the original Kickstarter campaign.

Requesting Action

Requesting action was the fourth most prevalent move, and occurred only in 12 different texts, marking a step down from the previous two moves.

Requesting action leveraged the existing coalition to move the project (and its creators) forward. These requests are split between the pre-funding and post-funding windows, with most of the requests coming post funding. Importantly, these requests work to expand not only the user's experience and contributions beyond the Kickstarter pledge they made to fund the project but also their interaction with the project beyond that platform in the case of post-funding requests.

Pre-funding requests focus almost entirely on expanding the reach of the project via the efforts of the coalition. In terms of the discussion in Chapter 4, the requests serve to expand the organic reach of the campaign via the likes, shares, and traffic created by the backing coalition. These pre-funding requests are a mixture of requests to simply share the project with like-minded individuals or specific requests to share the project via social media (and to visit that social media presence). An example non-specific ask from Update 6 asks that backers "Pass the message on to anyone you think might be interested in our project." A more specific request from Update 3 reminds coalition members to "Remember to check out our twitter (@ladytarotcards)." Both serve to expand the reach of the campaign organically, with direct shares by backers contributing to the reach of the campaign and increased likes and follows on social media increasing the baseline reach of the campaign and its algorithmic organic reach.

The post-funding requests are split as well, with most of the requests relating to the project's fulfillment and a handful of requests targeting the social media presence of the campaign. The social media references work to reinforce the centering of the creators in that they all push coalition members to follow the campaign on Twitter for additional information on the project, such as Update 12's reference to project updates outside of Kickstarter: "Reminder that we are active on twitter @ladytarotcards for more info and if you wanted to scroll through the revealed artworks!" By placing key content on Twitter and nudging the coalition to make the transition to that platform for updates, the requests underscore the continuity of the campaign beyond Kickstarter and the centrality of the creators for updates (via their social media presence).

The rest of the requests for action focus on the fulfillment process and feedback on it. These requests are a mixture of entreaties to fill out the fulfillment form and requests for project feedback and questions. These requests serve both a practical function and a rhetorical one that aligns with multiple other moves highlighted (and to be highlighted). The references to fulfillment forms practically ensure the backers will receive their materials in a timely fashion, and also highlight the continued march of progress toward fulfillment. The references for feedback both attempt to ensure that issues with the user experience are met before they become persistent complaints within the coalition while also encouraging the coalition to develop a deeper and more interactive relationship with the campaign outside of having simply backed the project.

Envisioning Completion

The final set of moves made, envisioning the completion of the project, are only found in seven updates, but they serve a crucial rhetorical purpose in that they ask coalition members to imagine the impact of receiving the promised deliverables of the campaign. These moves explicitly reinforce the emotions and thought processes behind coalition members choosing to support the project while building excitement for the eventual conclusion. Most of these envisioning moves take place during the pre-funding period, with a handful more coming at the very end of the fulfillment process.

The pre-funding references use the same phrase, "get these into your hands" (or some variation of in your hands) over five different updates in the pre-funding period. These repeated references to the physical interaction with the campaign's deliverable prompt coalition members to imagine the user experience of handling and unboxing the cards, reinforcing the decision to back the cards in the first place. The repetition of the same phrasing also underscores the messaging across multiple updates during the pre-funding period. The choice to emphasize the physical interaction with the deliverables aligns with the emotional focus that Grice (2017) advocates for in user experiences while underscoring to a coalition that values seeing historically marginalized individuals foregrounded in the chosen genre of tarot cards that these cards will be physical artifacts that exist and can be used by the backers. The effect is subtle, but important in underscoring the eventual end result of the process.

The post-funding references are made to shipping, since the cards themselves have been proofed and prepped by the time the updates shift their focus (Updates 16 and 17). These same envisioning moves align with the earlier references to physically holding the cards and align with the end-phase goal of getting backers to fill out their fulfillment surveys so that cards can be shipped.

Summarizing LTC via Listening, Quantifying, and Defining

Having analyzed Lady Tarot Cards via quantitative and qualitative analysis via explanatory sequential mixed methods analysis, we now turn to the implications of the findings for building XAs of our own via the three steps of listening, quantifying, and defining.

Listening

When we go to a campaign such as Lady Tarot Cards that presents itself to a very particular subset of backers (those interested in tarot cards that feature LGBTQ+ individuals and are inclusive of people of color), we are studying the results of the action of the backing coalition. When that same coalition can be traced across multiple successful campaigns (as in the case with Lady Tarot Cards and the subsequent campaigns), that sustained success tells us a good deal about a particular coalition that exists: a coalition that is interested in print-oriented artistic deliverables that foreground LGBTQ+ individuals and people of color in genres that have historically ignored them. By then quantifying the ways these campaigns build engagement and analyzing the ways the campaigns define expectations, we can elaborate on this listening by understanding the persuasion tactics of these campaigns that attracted these coalition members while also building out an understanding of what this coalition (and those like it) may expect in future campaigns based on their experiences with Lady Tarot Cards.

Quantifying

Beyond featuring mundane information, Lady Tarot Cards provides us with a potential starting point for planning the XA beyond a simple focus on technical details by highlighting the power of centering the backing coalition, building the ethos of the project creators via a similar centering, and the leveraging of the campaign's pre-funding period to motivate backers to action to help spread the news about the project. These focuses blended with references to the completion of the project worked to get Lady Tarot Cards almost halfway to funding in 24 hours and full funding around halfway through the campaign.

The fundamental key trope or repetition in the qualitative reading, informed by the quantitative reading, is the frequent inclusion and foregrounding of the mundane process details of the campaign's creation and the mundane details of the card deliverables themselves. Lady Tarot Card's approach highlights these details the most frequently across all updates of any of the qualitative moves, underscoring the widespread presence of those same details in the quantitative analysis. For future campaigns and technical writers working on them, the prominence of those details should be useful in planning a strategic XA. It isn't enough to simply create and deliver on a campaign promise—the campaigns need to bring coalition members into the process, documenting the details and steps that the project moves through to bring the project to completion.

Of note, only three updates feature mundane information that is exclusive to Kickstarter. This choice is worth noting simply because one foundational ideal behind the backing of a crowdfunding campaign is that coalition members are then privy to updates and technical details on the campaign directly from the creators to them. Often these updates are public, though some (as in the case of a handful of LTC updates) are hidden from public view. Lady Tarot Cards chose instead to push the majority of their content through their social media channels, building on the repeated moves to center the creators of the project rather than the platform itself. This strategic choice of channels for sharing details on the project will likely be of interest to technical writers whose teams are not looking to stick to a single crowdfunding platform long-term or campaigns that are looking to continue building their coalition during the fulfillment phase in preparation for a second campaign with a larger base coalition.

One finding of note is that the total lack of references to the historically marginalized communities found in the cards. The Lady Tarot Cards pitch and campaign title both explicitly foreground the fact that this campaign focuses on "LGBT+ and POC Inclusive" deliverables, but references to the inclusion of these historically marginalized individuals doesn't happen outside of the main pitch. Instead, the updates focus on demonstrating the focus of the campaign via snippets of images from the card art and by underscoring the creation and printing the final deliverables for the backing coalition. The persuasion based on the campaign's social justice purpose exists implicitly in the update process rather than explicitly as in the pitch itself. (As a note, this pattern is also followed in the second Lady Tarot Card campaign, "classics . . . but make it gay"). For technical writers working on similar projects, the emphasis may be of interest in strategizing the XA of updates, demonstrating that similar campaigns can benefit from showing what an inclusive deliverable looks like and how it is made rather than repeatedly returning to the historically marginalized status of the subject matter of the campaign. This move highlights the joy of the community in creating its own art and deliverables rather than focusing on the historical marginalization the campaign is responding to.

Looking ahead to future campaigns and their XAs, technical writers can draw on the five major moves of Lady Tarot Cards, in addition to the quantitative findings, to help seed their own discussions and planning of user experiences based on these strategies' success in a serial crowdfunding story. Next, the data points and moves are streamlined into a series of starting points for discussion and planning of future XAs:

How can we center the backing coalition?

How can we center the project team to build trust and connection?

How can we share the process and details of the project to reconnect with backers and provide insider information?

In what ways can we help coalition members envision the future success of the project during the funding period?

How assured can we be in our pitch while maintaining an ethical stance toward the chances of our success if funding goals are met?

Though the case of Lady Tarot Cards cannot be universally applied, campaigns targeting similar coalitions or creating similar deliverables can benefit from understanding the moves and documentation behind the success of the campaign that launched two subsequent successful campaigns as well as successful projects beyond the Kickstarter platform.

Defining

As a successful project targeting a specific coalition across multiple projects, Lady Tarot Card's success provides some idea of what potential backers will expect of our own campaigns in similar areas.

In terms of sheer numbers, Lady Tarot Cards provided a pitch in addition to 20 public (and two private, not tracked in this data) updates over the span of the campaign and fulfillment process. Only six updates took place during the campaign pre-funding period, with the majority of the updates taking place in the fulfillment process, aligning with the idea of sustainable crowdfunding from Chapter 2 that builds off of a campaign's success with a sustained XA across the fulfillment period that informs the coalition while providing them with engagement via mundane details of the process and deliverables.

For technical writers planning out the workload included in updates and the pitch itself, the project updates frequently fell between 100 and 200 words, with the pre-funding updates coming in below 100 more often than not and the post-funding updates ranging markedly higher in the word count. Images, though not a primary focus of the qualitative and quantitative review process, also feature heavily in the Lady Tarot Cards updates and pitch. The campaign pitch itself has 12 separate images that are a mixture of infographics and illustrations of art, deliverables, and works by artists. The updates in general average 1.5 images per update, with images often coming in bulk drops such as 6 images in Update 8 and 7 images in Update 10 as the project fulfillment process documented the progress on card art. As noted earlier, these images were primarily featured on the campaign's social media account, and only a handful of images were exclusive to the Kickstarter campaign itself.

Regarding best practices for funding goals, Lady Tarot Cards followed the curve suggested by most platforms for success, hitting over 1/3 of their initial funding within 24 hours (the actual amount was nearly 50% of funding). The campaign then managed to reach 100% by the time the middle of the campaign window came into view, with additional growth coming through the campaign. Functionally, after the 50% marker in the campaign, all extra funding was simply growth in the coalition and growth in revenue for the campaign creators as print production costs tend to drop with scale.

Looking ahead to a second campaign, Lady Tarot Cards ended with 534 backers in total. If the campaign were to treat these backers and the existing coalition as high-quality leads for future campaigns, they would have been able to enter their second campaign with a minimum of $8,000 if all backers purchased a digital deliverable in "classics . . . but make it gay" and $16,020 if backers all purchased at least the physical tier of their second campaign. Since the campaign only received 24 of their backers from non-merchandise funding tiers in the first campaign, the second number would be a realistic ceiling if all backers transitioned to the second campaign.

STEAM Chasers

The STEAM Chasers Middle Grade Book Series, run by Dr. Doresa A. Jennings, was available for funding from June 9, 2019, until August 8, 2019, on Kickstarter (2019a). During the campaign, a total of $4,745 was raised from 50 backers, bringing over double of the baseline goal of $2,000. The campaign self-describes as "the first book in a Series introducing middle grade readers to the exciting world of STEAM." The STEAM Chasers campaign (from this point referred to periodically as the Chaser Campaign for brevity) specifically focuses on introducing children to the contrib utions made by Black Americans to everyday life while also bringing them a way to understand their place in STEAM fields. Backing levels ranged from $5 to $1,200, with the lowest backing level for a physical softcover book coming in at $25.

As a serial success, the Chasers campaign was the first in three projects, one for each book in the series focusing on a group of Black middle schoolers learning about STEAM and Black contributors to STEAM through their adventures. The project is another example of the potential of crowdfunding to support historically marginalized groups in industries that historically have not been as open to them as the series is written about Black Americans by a Black author. The second campaign, *The STEAM Chasers and the Blackness of Space*, continued the book series (Jennings, 2019b), and the third campaign, *The STEAM Chasers: Books on Black American STEM Innovators*, closed the series of three books (Jennings, 2020). The second and third campaigns were listed as "Project We Love" on Kickstarter, earning $3,955 and $5,421, respectively. These follow-up campaigns were supported by 19 and 87 backers, respectively.

The STEAM Chasers projects represent a slightly different approach to crowdfunding than the projects carried out by Lady Tarot Cards in a couple of ways. First, each of the books was already written and ready for publication when each project launched—the projects focus on building a community and excitement around the launch while building additional features into the launch (such as an audiobook in the case of the first and second project). Second, from the very beginning, the series was linked to an outside infrastructure via the author's publication site *www.doresaayanna.com* as well as the Backerkit fulfillment platform (Jennings, n.d.). Third, the STEAM Chasers represents a contained unit of projects. The three books encapsulate the whole of the series, representing a slightly different model of sustained crowdfunding as the projects start and finish a full series of books while also targeting and achieving funding that is markedly lower than any of the projects of Lady Tarot Cards, providing us with a model for smaller-scale projects on crowdfunding platforms. Finally, the author self-represents as a SuperBacker on Kickstarter (having backed 79 total projects) and foregrounds her experience as a backer of projects as an asset to the project and its trajectory (unlike Lady Tarot Cards, which solely operated on Kickstarter as a creator of three projects).

Like Lady Tarot Cards, STEAM Chasers represents a project that highlights a historically marginalized group that successfully built and maintained a coalition of backers across three projects on Kickstarter, leveraging that momentum to publicize the project and her efforts to diversify middle-age children books due to her frustration at the lack of books speaking to Black American children written by Black authors (Jennings, n.d.). In addition, Dr. Jennings highlights during the project pitch and project updates secondary goals related to social justice and diversity in children's literature. In her pitch video, she underscores that she wanted to provide content for Black children by a Black author that didn't rely on the lens of either the Civil Rights Movement or the history of slavery to ground the narrative of Black history. In addition, in her first weekly update, Dr. Jennings underscores the neurodivergent inclusivity of her series. Dr. Jennings describes herself as a severe dyslexic, a diagnosis shared by all three of her children, and highlights how she hopes dyslexic children will see the example of Terrence in the books and his use of audiobook accommodations as an inspiration to their own learning.

While the project pitch and updates are focused on the first book in the STEAM Chasers series, even in the first campaign, Dr. Jennings lays the groundwork for the sustainable nature of her usage of Kickstarter, highlighting in the project pitch video that the second book in the series will focus on the STEAM Chasers going to Space Camp.

Campaign Funding Structure

The STEAM Chasers campaign targeted a goal of $2,000 over the duration of their 60-day campaign, with tiers ranging from a simple "Shout Out!" for $5, to a "Sponsor a School!" funding tier for $1,200. The project eventually attracted 50 backers, raising over double the initial funding goal: $4,745. As seen in Figure 5.4, the funding tiers by a number of backers concentrated on the lower pledge amounts, but the higher tiers consistently gained funding as well, providing the project with a mixture of funding from large donations and smaller donations. A little over half of the project funding came from donations over $300, with the rest coming from donations of $300 or less.

The second STEAM Chasers campaign would see a drop in backers to only 19, but the final campaign would attract 87 in total. The campaigns range between $3,955 for the second campaign to $5,421 for the final campaign in the series, with the first campaign falling in between.

Quantitative Analysis of the STEAM Chasers Campaign

As with the case of Lady Tarot Cards, we'll start with an overview of the basic data on the campaign related to the length and number of updates, in the additional analysis of the project pitch. Unlike Lady Tarot Cards, the Chasers campaign features a handful of videos (most prominently a pitch video). In order to maintain parity between the campaign analyses, the pitch videos have been transcribed via NVIVO and the textual transcription has been included in both the quantitative analysis and the qualitative coding sections. As an additional note, the Chasers campaign features several more updates that have their content behind

Backers by Funding Tier

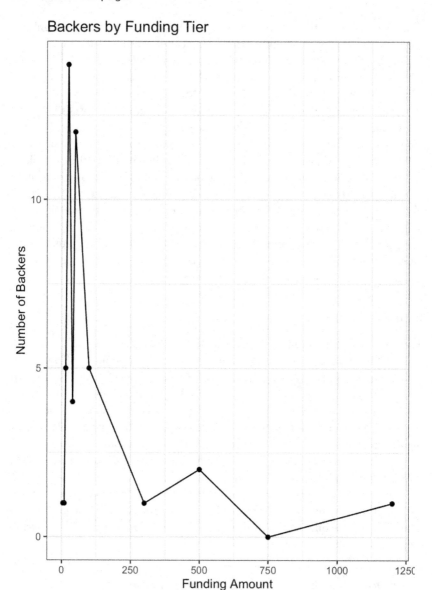

FIGURE 5.4 A comparison of the number of backers for each funding tier for the Chasers campaign

a backers-only tag, preventing analysis. In these cases, I've preserved the update titles as markers in the quantitative analysis, but these updates are not present in the overall discussion, much like the updates by the LTC campaign.

In order to highlight the unique facets of the STEAM Chasers campaign, the figures and data discussed are slightly different in format from the content in the

LTC campaign. With the focus on a pre-written book and a pre-funding heavy update pattern, the STEAM Chasers data simply doesn't work and look the same way that the LTC data does. If we're to listen without filtering to the dataset and the campaign that the backing coalition coalesced around, part of that listening involves treating each data set with an eye toward which analyses make the most sense to lay out a qualitative narrative. (Though, it must be mentioned that the act of simply starting with Lady Tarot Cards and carrying out that campaign's analysis first does alter our reading and understanding of STEAM Chasers and subsequently analyzed campaigns in this project.)

The original campaign for STEAM Chasers on Kickstarter had a total of 14 updates, of which 4 are private and not tracked in this data due to access barriers. Based on a textual word count that also includes the script of the pitch video, the project pitch comes out to 1963 words in total, almost three times more than the 750 words in the LTC campaign. The average update word count (including in that word count an update video in the third update) is 323 words, also virtually three times the length of the average updates in LTC. The updates range between 109 and 676 words in total when the video scripts are taken into account, with a maximum word count of 632 when the video word count is taken out of the equation.

The engagement measurements for the Chasers campaign are considerably lower than the metrics for LTC, with the updates and pitch only getting a total of seven likes across all content and with only four comments across all of the updates and the pitch. Considering that each of these campaigns was a serial success on Kickstarter within the scope of their own objectives and budgets, this variation would seem to indicate (though without a large enough data sample it is hard to say with certainty) that engagement metrics on Kickstarter tracked via likes and comments are not always a useful metric for gauging the strength and likelihood of success for a given campaign.

Unlike LTC, the STEAM Chasers campaign does feature a video pitch, aligning it with the best practices on the platforms covered that allow such moves. Each of the videos is a fairly simple and minimally produced from a visual effects angle: Dr. Jennings sits in front of a bookshelf full of various subject area books, and talks directly to the camera.

As with LTC, the analysis of quantitative frequency is carried out with *quanteda* (Benoit et al., 2018) as the primary tool, providing a general window into the language and choices make across the pitch, pre-funding, and post-funding periods. As with Lady Tarot Cards, some of the post-funding updates are unavailable for analysis, though the majority of all updates take place before the project was funded (8 of 14), and only 4 updates are unavailable for analysis. As noted earlier, the entire structure of the Chasers campaign differs from LTC in that the project is already written and no deliverables are being created for the original pitch. As such, the entire project and the subsequent updates are functionally sustainable crowdfunding, with this full-project focus underscored by the seeding of the second campaign in the pitch video's reference to Space Camp in book two.

As before, we'll be using quantitative analysis to see our qualitative codebook while highlighting patterns in usage that may be small enough or subtle enough to avoid notice in a qualitative reading of the texts.

In Figure 5.5, we see a simple comparative word cloud of the overall STEAM Chasers project, broken down by pitch, pre-funding, and post-funding as with the LTC project. As a reminder, these rankings are proportional to the stage of the campaign, and not a 1:1 representation of overall usage in the campaign proper. Because the updates in the post-funding period are limited in number, any patterns across the updates that are available will be highlighted based on proportional usage across the updates. For example, "have" occurs consistently across the project pitch, but proportionally speaking it is foregrounded more in the post-funding period despite less overall usage in that period.

Looking across the pitch, pre-funding, and post-funding periods, a few simple patterns emerge in the comparative word cloud. In the pitch, the terms "our" and "series" stand out at the center of the plotting. In the pre-funding update period, "we," "book," and "editor" as well as "audiobook" stand out immediately. Post-funding, "I," "chasers," "space," and "have" stand out in addition to other close matches like "your" and "copies." From the start, we see a focus on collection action and community with the use of "our" and "we"

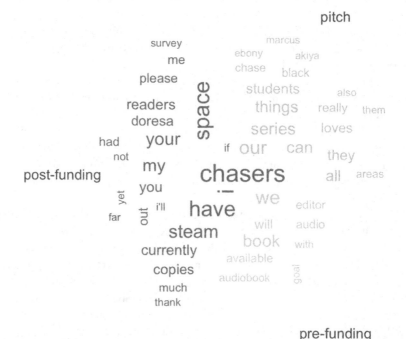

FIGURE 5.5   A comparative word cloud of the terms found in the pitch, pre-funding, and post-funding periods of the Chasers campaign

across the pitch and pre-funding updates, with references to the sustainable aims of the campaign also featuring prominently in the usage of "series" and "space" in the pitch and post-funding period. Finally, much like LTC, we see references across all three areas that underscore the mundane details of publication such as references to "editor" in the pre-funding period; "characters" and the associated names of the characters in the pitch; and "working," "soon," and "have" in the post-funding period.

Pitch

The STEAM Chasers pitch centers around the idea of "our" and "series" in the comparative plot, creating an image of the project as a communal or coalitional effort and one that is linked to a going process, not a simple one-stop deliverable or one-off campaign. Digging into the pitch-specific word counts (taking the comparative nature out of the picture), we see "you," "can," "our," and "have" as shown in Figure 5.6.

These two data points taken together suggest a campaign pitch that focuses heavily on the STEAM setting and the relationship between the author and the coalition in creating the first in a series as opposed to a discrete campaign that has no follow-up. The difference is stark when contrasted with Lady Tarot Cards where no such forecasting of an ongoing series was visible from the start. The additional repetition of the major characters and their names also provides a steady stream of mundane details about the project, details that differ slightly from the Lady Tarot Cards project since the STEAM Chasers campaign focuses on a narrative in addition to a deliverable rather than foregrounding the particulars of a specific set of deliverables (the tarot card deck).

Pre-funding

The pre-funding updates (which represent the bulk of the updates as noted previously) continue the focus on coalitional action and community, with the usage of "we" and "book" alongside "editor" in the comparative word cloud highlighting the communal action and cooperation between the author and the backers to bring the project into existence. The prominence of the references to the editor and the notes on the audiobook continue the pattern of highlighting mundane process-based details seen in Lady Tarot Cards, and align with the mundane details of the book narrative seen in the pitch and pitch video.

Post-funding

"I" in post-funding period stands out with its centering of the author and their actions in the project fulfillment, as does the usage of "chasers" and "space" and

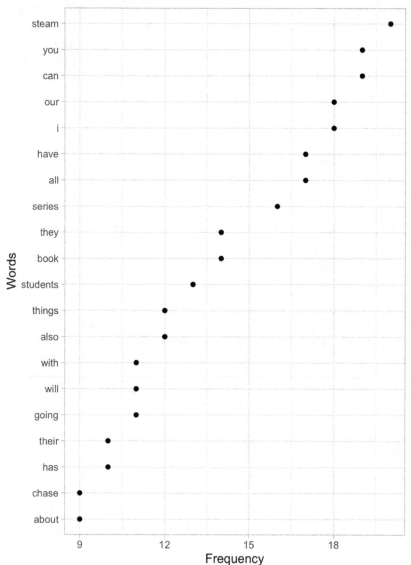

Most Used Words Across Pitch

FIGURE 5.6 Word usage chart for the Chasers campaign pitch

"have." While "I" foregrounds the author, "space" and "chasers" underscores the future of the series and the mundane details of the project, highlighting the characters themselves and the series second title. "Have," on the other hand, indicates a sense of ownership and action in the final period, mirroring the strong usage of the same term in the pitch period.

Pitch and Update Comparison

Because the STEAM Chasers campaign features a majority of updates that come before the end of the funding period (that we have access to for analysis), an analysis of the updates taken in aggregate with the overall project pitch provides us with one additional window into how the campaign functions qualitatively to build a narrative about the project. Using a keyness comparison, as illustrated in Figure 5.7, we see a fairly fundamental breakdown between the pitch and the updates for the project that mirrors some of the findings from the comparative analysis.

The pitch period is concerned with the mundane details of the project story's narrative, with introductions of the major characters taking a good deal of the term usage. The updates by comparison focus on the communal action behind the project with "we" and "you" with mundane writing process details and thanks coming into view. As with Lady Tarot Cards, "I" in the update period underscores as well the role of Dr. Jennings in creating and making the project possible, an important aspect of any serial campaign series that will rely on building a brand and identity for the creator and series.

Comparison of Term Usage in Updates versus Pitch

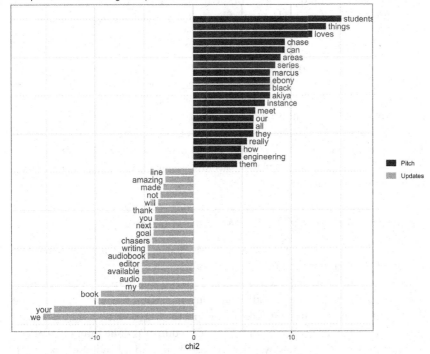

FIGURE 5.7 A comparison of relative term keyness between the pitch and updates for the Chasers campaign

Much like the LTC project, the Chasers campaign's quantitative data foregrounds coalitional action in combination with mundane details, underscoring the power of the mundane in these crowdfunding projects. These projects have attracted a coalition and are succeeding because that coalition sees something of value in the project, and the mundane details of the project coming to the foreground again and again underscore the power of the mundane in the XA of crowdfunding campaigns.

Seeding the Qualitative Review

As with Lady Tarot Cards, we'll seed the qualitative review of STEAM Chasers with findings from the quantitative analysis. Summarizing the findings from the quantitative review, the starting codebook for the qualitative review of STEAM Chasers has been seeded with the following moves and concepts for corpus review:

> Emphasizing of communal action
> Referencing the backing coalition
> Centering of the author's role in creation
> Documenting the mundane details of process
> Sharing the mundane details of the book/series narrative
> Emphasizing the serial nature of book series and campaign as starting point

These quantitative analyses of STEAM Chasers did reflect some of the same moves originally found in Lady Tarot Cards, so the codes have been aligned to use the same language for the sake of simplicity. With that said, several of the codes diverge from the LTC campaign, as we would expect with a fundamentally different campaign with a different focus. As with LTC, we'll next use these codes as a starting point to qualitatively explore the STEAM Chasers corpus, recognizing that these codes represent a tentative narrative about the campaign based entirely on numbers and frequency.

Qualitative Analysis of the STEAM Chasers Campaign

After an initial round of coding, the STEAM Chasers campaign resulted in a collection of 47 discrete codes, though many of the codes were fairly low in occurrence (29 of the codes had less than 4 occurrences in the corpus). After a revision pass to streamline the codes and reduce any redundancy in the initial coding process, the final set of starting codes (including the 6 seed codes from the quantitative review) numbered 32. As with LTC, all coding was done through NVIVO.

The first round of coding was skewed heavily toward a handful of codes that rose to the forefront with substantial reference numbers across the corpus, but the overall drop in numbers from code to code was fairly linear outside of the top four codes that each had over 25 references. These top four codes mirrored the pattern in Lady Tarot Cards, which also had four central codes in the first round that had more than 25 references. The codes were as follows:

Centering the author's role in creation
Introducing characters
Sharing the mundane detail of process and project
Referencing the editing process

After the first cluster of coding at the top of the discrete code list, all other codes fell at 17 references or less, with a very linear curve with lower user codes only dropping 1–2 references down to the lowest usage clustered among a handful of 2-reference codes.

To arrive at a final set of axial codes, the projects existing with discrete codes were then analyzed and categorized into descriptive codes that focused on the major rhetorical moves made in each type of code cluster, mirroring the process in Lady Tarot Cards and elsewhere in the book. The axial coding process resulted in a final selection of five rhetorical moves or broad classifications of action that were meaningful across the project pitch and updates. The final codes are ranked below by their overall frequency:

Explaining the book and its purpose (110 references)
Explaining publication (67 references)
Connecting with the coalition (57 references)
Centering the author as creator and person (53 references)
Sharing the mundane details of the campaign (50 references)

Though on an initial read, there may seem to be some overlap between certain codes, such as explaining publication and sharing the mundane, these moves diverge in their focus and purpose in the text. Unlike Lady Tarot Cards, there is more parity between the different major moves in terms of the number of references. As before, the next section will explain each of these coded moves with contextual examples and a general overview of the moves made and the "why" behind them.

Explaining the Book

Across the pitch and across the updates, explaining the book and its purpose represented the most common move in the STEAM Chasers campaign. Functionally, these references and moves serve to build the fundamental core of the STEAM Chasers campaign's user experience by creating and sustaining for the coalition a vision of the book, its characters, and its social justice purpose. The prevalence of these moves makes sense contextually as the STEAM Chasers series is a fundamentally novel creation of the project creator, Dr. Jennings, and without these repeated and detailed moves, the campaign's central draw would cease to exist. These explanations of the book and purpose also occur across some of the longer texts: the pitch, the pitch video, and Update 3 (and its accompanying video). Repeated underscoring of the book's narrative intersects continuously with the purpose behind the book series: increasing Black American character and author representation in middle-grade children's literature while expanding access to STEAM literacy. The narrative and the explanation of the book cannot be separated from the idea of the text as a social justice vehicle: the author, the text, and its purpose all intertwine in these explaining moves to build a consistent user experience of the project that connects the coalition's backing of the project with the mission of the series and its author.

Explaining the book revolves first and foremost around explaining the cadre of characters that make up the STEAM Chasers: Shar, Terrence, Ebony, Akiya, Marcus, and Chase. A majority of the pitch is devoted to the systematic introduction of each of these characters, their histories, and their motivations. Potential backers learn about each character in turn, with each focusing on a particular aspect of engagement with STEAM disciplines and having particular challenges and skills. For example (as seen in the pitch), Shar is interested in chemistry, a passion that ties into her baking and her living with a little brother with a nut allergy. Terrence, another STEAM Chaser is highlighted across the pitch and several updates because of his dyslexia and the author's underscoring of the importance that making visible and normalizing his neurodivergence and accommodations.

Character description work flows directly into discussions of the project's championing social justice by representation, such as in Update 3 when Dr. Jennings explains, "It would be absolutely amazing to be able to have kids that use audiobooks, learn about a character in a series that uses audio books in the same way." The character description is continuously linked to the purpose of the series and its impact. These returns to the social purpose of the text underscore the emotional impact of the project and reinforce the decision of backers to commit to funding the project.

In addition to main character links to social justice and the texts purpose, Dr. Jennings also links each character's family and associates secondary characters with expanding STEAM literacy as an act of social justice. For example, in the pitch video, Dr. Jennings highlights that the series lets students know "there's a place for them in steam right now." Later in the pitch video, she explains that the series will allow students to "get introduced and get exposure to things that maybe they haven't had an opportunity to see before seeing themselves in characters" The STEAM discussions then are defined in terms of increasing access to STEAM material while also allowing students to see themselves (through the characters) as being someone who could do that work. This sense of identifying with the main characters is eventually underscored in the second campaign via a series of "Be a STEAM Chaser" merchandise bundles available to backers.

For backing coalition members, the intertwined nature of explaining the book and its purpose explicitly aligns the backing of the project with the social justice purpose of the series and its authors. By backing the project, these coalition members are making this possible. And, as these same updates do not introduce the STEAM Chasers book as a single entry, but instead as a series, the serial nature of the crowdfunding and the potential for ongoing impact are underscored in the process.

Explaining Publication

While a good many of the updates in Chasers campaign focus on mundane details, I draw a distinction between those that focus on the creation of the book and those that center around the project process. These process-centered updates provide a central focus to the bulk of the updates in the project after the funding goal was met in the first week. These updates both provide mundane details of the process of creation behind the book, but also explain the purpose behind the moves, educating while underscoring the constant progress the project is making toward completion with the support of backers. These moves focus on two major areas: editing and preparation of the text for the publication and the production of an audiobook of the book.

Starting with Update 4, the editing moves center around both explaining the purpose of editing, the practice of editing, and the ways that this editing links up with the overall purpose/goal of the project and the quality of the project backers are supporting. For example, in Update 4, Dr. Jennings explains that editing matters in this context because "we want to ensure this book is not only entertaining and informative but also a demonstration of good writing for the middlegrade reader." Later in Update 5, she differentiates between the function of a line editor and a copyeditor in the publication process, and relates these types of editing to specific improvements in the text. She notes, "However, it can be easy to miss that you said a tie was blue on page three and mention that it is turquoise on page 104. That is why it is so important for an author to have a good, professional line editor as a part of their team." In addition to these process explanations and linking of the processes to success, Dr. Jennings underscores the background, degrees, and experience of her editor, underscoring the importance of the process as well as the quality of the project's approach. The editing discussions close in Update 7 when she explains the formatting process has been completed and an author's proof has been ordered (and the purpose of that proof).

The editing updates explaining publication work in alignment with the central focus of sharing the purpose of the book, as they don't simply provide mundane details to underscore the backing coalition's excitement in seeing the project come to life—they also underscore the ways that these mundane steps in publication support the project's goals of creating high-quality middle-grade children's litera-ture that foregrounds Black Americans. The quality-centered focus of the expla-nations also serves to advance the project to potential coalition members, as all of this takes place during the fundraising campaign before funding has been attained.

In addition to the creation of the book via traditional publication processes and editing, the explanation of publication also highlights the project's major stretch goal announced in Update 3: the recording and production of an audio-book of the STEAM Chasers book. Like the editing, these moves work to pro-vide the mundane details that excite the coalition and show progress while also linking up this work with the social justice aims of the book and underscoring the quality and impact of this stretch goal. These updates align with the attainment of the funding goal, announced in Update 6, and continue through Update 8 the last pre-funding update.

Much like the editing references, the audiobook references underscore the process itself, and the importance of rigor, while tying into the purpose of the book. In Update 3, when Dr. Jennings introduces the audiobook goal, she explains regarding dyslexic readers that "They understand the material com-pletely. They just have difficulty with eye reading, so they rely on ear reading. It absolutely opens up the world to them." This foregrounding of the audiobook as an equalizer and resource for social justice gives purpose and power to the mundane process details in Updates 6, 7, and 8 relating the auditioning of book narrators, the selection of a producer for the book, and the eventual production process with the chosen narrator.

Connecting With the Coalition

The third most common move in STEAM Chasers focuses on centering the backing coalition in various ways throughout the updates. These centering moves occur in almost all updates and also occur in the project pitch. These connection-building moves come in two primary types: connections that request action from the coalition and connections that tie the project's success to the coalition and their efforts. Each of these types of connecting with the coalition underscores the emotional ties backers already have to the project, and reinforces the choice to back the STEAM Chasers. Instead of seeing these connection-building moves as discrete messages, keep in mind that they occur alongside the centering of the project's purpose and its social justice efforts, connecting the success of the project and the social justice efforts with actions on the part of the backing community.

The requests for action by the coalition represent the smallest subset of the connection moves, but they serve as a reminder of the necessity for community action, either during the backing period or during the final stages of fulfillment and the transition to the second STEAM Chasers campaign. The connections start in the pitch, with requests for direct funding: "Now, if you are excited about this series as I am and would like to support it, please look at our various funding levels." They continue in the first and update with requests to share the project with other potential backers. Once the project reaches the initial backing goal, the requests shift slightly after funding is achieved, as seen in Update 4's appeal: "We are continuing to inform others widely as we can about this Kickstarter, and we hope you feel comfortable doing the same as well." The same more measured tone in Update 8 and beyond. Again, while these requests are but a small portion of the connections made with the coalition, they do serve as a persistent reminder that the project's continued growth is tied to new backers and existing backers sharing information on the project.

The second type of connection building is by far the most common, and this type focuses on underscoring the coalition's role in the creation of the project. These connections are present in almost all updates and deliverables, and build a consistent connection between the project's success and the existence of the coalition and their support. Each reference demonstrates the project's success while connecting that same success back to the coalition. The affective impact of this connection shouldn't be understated, as coalitions seeing the projects they've coalesced around succeeding and having that success tied to their efforts can be incredibly impactful (Pope, 2017). This language starts immediately in the first update, when Dr. Jennings tells backers, "Your amazing support has allowed us to reach 25% of our funding goal." The same direct connection making between success and the coalition continues in Update 2 when she tells backers, "We Did It!," before telling backers, "You a now an official part of the STEAM Chasers family." Dr. Jennings continues these same direct connections that position the author and the coalition as a single group in Update 3 when she tells them "we made it, we made our initial funding goal." This usage of "we" was flagged in the pre-funding updates term usage in the quantitative comparison word cloud as well as in the keyness comparison between the pitch and updates, and that numerical prevalence shines through in a qualitative reading where time and time again the same associations are made with the coalition working alongside the author to make the book project a success.

Centering the Author

The third major move made in the STEAM Chasers pitch and updates is the centering of the author, Dr. Doresa Jennings. This centering is central to the purpose of the text and the social justice efforts of the project, as Dr. Jennings identity and history are an integral part of the purpose and production of the book series. Starting in the pitch, Jennings defines herself as an educator that connects with teachers and parents, with these connections leading to her desire to write this series. Dr. Jennings own personal history also comes into play direct, when she explains in Update 3 that "audio books are just really near and dear to my heart. I'm a severe dyslexic, and all three of my kids are dyslexic as well." Her efforts to increase the representation within the text then become not only a noble effort in their own right, but connected with her own identity. This same connection-building is also seen in her web presence, *DoresaAyanna.com* where she explains her rationale for the series. She explicitly connects the importance of her identity and background to the project, explaining that "the availability of books that spoke of and spoke to Black American children was embarrassingly sparse. Even of the books that were available, only about 1/3 were written by Black American authors." As a Black author, Dr. Jennings' ability to write to these children from a perspective they recognize becomes an essential part of the narrative of the project and its success.

As the STEAM Chasers project starts and finishes on a serial funding note, the building up of the connections between the author and the project serves an important role in the future success of the project. As the project succeeds, as the various edits and other bits are carried out, all of these connections between the author and the project's success underscore that Dr. Jennings is a trustworthy and savvy crowdfunded worthy of backing. These moves to underscore her experience specifically on crowdfunding platforms begin in the project pitch, where she ties her approach to the project to her experience on Kickstarter, explaining "I am a Kickstarter Super Backer—meaning I have backed a significant number of Kickstarter campaigns and have seen what makes people successful in fulfilling pledges on time." Not only is Dr. Jennings a successful creator and skilled project manager, but also she comes from the Kickstarter community and believes in it, having supported (as she notes in Update 6) 71 projects and learned from observing the successes and failures of the platform.

Sharing the Mundane

As with Lady Tarot Cards, the STEAM Chasers campaign has a consistent stream of update references and moves that simply share the mundane bits and steps of the process, demonstrating to the backing coalition that progress is happening while underscoring their trust and choice to make this project a reality. These references are usually progress based, such as Update 3's "that's what this update is about, telling you what happens next." These updates explain the progress in the project while concurrently reinforcing the backing coalition's connection with the project and referencing their cocreation of the project.

Summarizing STEAM Chasers via Listening, Quantifying, and Defining

Having analyzed STEAM Chasers, we now turn to the implications of our findings for future campaigns that might align with the STEAM Chasers in focus or scope. The STEAM Chasers campaign, like the LTC campaign before it, provides us with a series of jumping-off points for planning and implementing our own XAs for successful serial campaigns, with STEAM Chasers providing a window specifically into smaller-scale campaigns that don't focus on or raise tens of thousands of dollars.

Listening

As with Lady Tarot Cards, reviewing the STEAM Chasers campaign and its associated deliverables is the fundamental act of listening. The campaign succeeded across three separate projects, demonstrating the durability of the sustained efforts by Dr. Jennings to bring the STEAM Chasers to the printed page. The success of STEAM Chasers shows us what a coalition-driven effort to increase representation can look like in the highly competitive world of children's literature, and the continuous stream of references and centering of the social justice dimension of the campaign demonstrates to us that there are coalitions ready and willing to make these projects come to life across multiple crowdfunding campaigns.

Quantifying

Fundamentally, the STEAM Chasers campaign demonstrates for us the power of web of moves by a campaign that all link together into a central theme, in this case, the social justice of the series and its role in bringing much-needed voices and stories to an area of children's literature. When it comes to quantifying the causes of engagement, STEAM Chasers fundamental trope and repetition is the story of the project and the purpose behind that work. The details of the story, setting, and purpose of the book repeatedly feature across the pitch and almost every update. Whereas Lady Tarot Cards focused on the mundane details without explicitly returning to the campaign's focus, STEAM Chasers repeatedly makes this move, interweaving the content of almost every update with the book's purpose and narrative. For technical writers formulating campaigns for their own teams, the STEAM Chasers campaign provides a framework for a social justice campaign that constantly centers and recenters the overarching campaign goal explicitly.

Building on the social justice of the book's narrative and purpose, the project's repeated centering of the project creator underscores the same social justice purpose and goal for the project by aligning the project's own goals with the particular person and history of the author, Dr. Jennings. Whereas Lady Tarot Cards repeatedly ties the project to Nova and Mali as creators, the references and updates in STEAM Chasers go further, diving into the history of the author, her family, and her own frustrations and goals as fuel for the project. Jennings' identity, professionalism, and history become a central pillar of the campaign, the campaign's mission, and her work managing the campaigns with minimal hiccups becomes a central point in the ongoing serial successes to follow.

Outside of the fundamental purpose and details of the narrative, the STEAM Chasers project demonstrates a useful differentiation of the mundane information provided via updates by focusing on how specific processes can serve as the bulk of entire series of updates, delving into even more minute details than simple process updates that keep backers abreast of the situation. The first major set of mundane information shifts across the publication process as the project evolves, first focusing on the editing process before shifting to audiobook creation and finally wrapping with the nuts and bolts of the final proofing and reader testing. The second major set of mundane information consistently tracks the progress of the campaign and its basic steps and timeline, demonstrating to coalition members the urgency of the timeline while documenting progress along the way.

The final trope and repetition to note with the STEAM Chasers is the repeated connection of the backing coalition to the project and its success. Yes, there are the expected requests for sharing and amplification of the project's message, but beyond the basic push for more organic reach, the project repeatedly connects the actions of the coalition to the success of the project and defines the coalition as cocreators of the project. In this repetition framework, the coalition is not only continuously reminded of their backing's impact, but also they are brought into the STEAM Chasers team explicitly, with repeated framings that situate them alongside the author in the project' creation. By positioning the backers alongside the team, backers are explicitly defined as a reason for the success of the series and its unifying purpose of social justice and increased representation in children's literature.

Looking ahead to future campaigns, especially those that focus on books or creative narrative projects, the STEAM Chasers data points provide us with a series of starting points to frame and explore our own projects:

- How can we explain the narrative and its purpose to the coalition in a way that frames the entire project?
- How can we explain the publication process to substantiate updates and show progress while tying these to the central purpose of the project?
- How can we connect the coalition and their actions with the campaign's success and the success of the project's purpose?
- How can we center the author to build a sense of trust and confidence in the project, underscoring the author's person as an integral part of the project and its purpose?
- How can we share the mundane details of the campaign in a way that demonstrate momentum and show movement while underscoring the campaign's purpose?

As with Lady Tarot Cards, the STEAM Chasers campaign can't be generalized to all possible future campaigns, but instead provides us with a vision of what success can look like for discrete campaigns, especially those that work to expand representation of historically marginalized communities while centering that task in the campaign and its updates continuously.

Defining

The Chasers campaign focuses almost entirely around the campaign's funding period, demonstrating that a campaign can be successful across multiple projects if the focus centers around publicizing the launch and process that created a fully-fleshed out project or product. The campaign begins with a finished deliverable (the book has been written, and is being edited), switching the focus from the campaign narrative toward maximizing the launch of the book rather than ensuring it exists. This shift in focus presents in a campaign that doesn't spend as much time on fulfillment and spends much more time building out content during the funding period that documents the product and its development/rationale. After Update 8 at the end of the funding period, the campaign content focuses on the logistics of getting content to the backers rather than an ongoing explication of the process as seen in LTC where the funding was needed for the process to begin.

The updates across the board in STEAM Chasers are longer than the content seen in LTC, with multiple videos bulking up the overall amount of content available to backers and potential backers. The videos, with their simple framing of the author in front of a bookshelf, demonstrate the ability for a fairly simple production setup for campaign updates for this type of project. The pitch video comes in just under seven minutes in length, and the video update for Update 3 comes in just under five minutes in length. The length of the publicly available updates drops dramatically after funding, with simple logistics taking center stage before the large final update that pushes the coalition into position to back the upcoming second project in the series. For technical writers planning campaigns, STEAM Chasers demonstrates that front-loading content can be an effective strategy for a strong backing period.

For technical writers balancing written content with non-textual content, the STEAM Chasers campaign has two videos across all public updates, one song, and nine images across these same updates. The project pitch video is simply framed, demonstrating the ability of campaigns to succeed without elaborate video setups and budgets. The lighting and background of Jennings are on par with the average Zoom background for a professional in a post-lockdown world. Most of the images are concentrated in the pitch itself (seven out of nine), with the remaining images simply serving to repeat a stylized STEAM Chasers series logo. The final deliverable of note is a short song provided by Dr. Jennings that has been produced for the STEAM Chasers series. The song represents a collaboration with the artist TXMIC, and is framed as a special reward for Kickstarter backers.

Regarding best practices for funding, the STEAM Chasers matches up fairly well with suggestions: the campaign reached 25% funding in 24 hours, and was fully funded by day 4 of the 60-day campaign. Functionally, this means that virtually all of the bulky updates and content delivery were focused in the post-funding goal space, allowing the project to focus persuasion and updates on the excitement of running up numbers for the project's distribution and expansion rather than focusing on getting the project to succeed. This early success paired with the project's finished status at the start of the campaign provides a window into leveraging Kickstarter and other crowdfunding services to boost projects that are functionally complete but benefit from the extra funding for distribution and final goals (such as an audiobook). The STEAM Chasers campaign provides a snapshot of how this approach can work for smaller campaigns that focus on social justice. For more large-scale uses of this approach see creators such as Rocketship Entertainment (2022) on Kickstarter—a comics publishing company that has 25 successful campaigns publishing comics direct via crowdfunding (interesting each with the Project We Love flag on the platform).

Because the funding of STEAM Chasers was split between high-value donations and small-value donations, the campaign's position for a second campaign is harder to predict, but still fairly good for eventual success. If the 50 existing backers went into the second campaign and funded at the lowest physical tier, the campaign would start at $1,250, more than 50% of the funding goal of $2,000.

Looking ahead to the serial successes, the STEAM Chasers interestingly performed slightly worse in the follow-up campaign, despite getting the Project We Love association on Kickstarter. The second campaign only had 19 backers and raised just $3,955. However, the third campaign would come to the platform with a markedly lower initial goal of $500 and videos from Dr. Jennings in the pitch, with one explicitly addressing the why and how of using Kickstarter to amplify the campaign (something referenced indirectly in the first campaign and minimally in the second pitch with an infographic and directly in the second campaign's second update). The final campaign would also get the Project We Love flag and would attract the highest numbers of the series with 87 backers bringing in $5,421.

Wrapping Up

Taken together, Lady Tarot Cards and the STEAM Chasers campaigns provide us with a set of perspectives on how we can format and implement our own crowdfunding campaigns that focus to create sustainable funding across a series of discrete campaigns that are linked together by either a shared set of creators or a shared project or project focus. Each of these campaigns sustained success across three different crowdfunding campaigns, demonstrating the durability of backer coalitions on these platforms and underscoring the potential of crowdfunding to support historically marginalized communities and social justice.

The two campaigns contrast in their scope and format, with LTC focusing on getting the funding needed to bring three projects into being in service of the backer coalition and STEAM Chasers focusing on the usage of crowdfunding to amplify the launch and scope of a project that has already reached completion when the campaign goes live.

Though discrete crowdfunding may not always make sense for every potential project and group, this chapter demonstrates two different cases of how serial successes can be launched via an initial successful campaign that demonstrates both the capabilities of the creators and attracts and then sustains the attention of a backing coalition willing and able to fund projects to completion.

Discussion Questions

1. Lady Tarot Cards opts to not use a pitch video across all three of their campaigns. How does the campaign make up for the lack of this pitch deliverable? What analogs that are also successful without a pitch video can you find in recent campaigns on crowdfunding platforms?
2. STEAM Chasers demonstrates a different model than LTC, focusing on the launch of a project already completed by the time the campaign goes live. What analogs to this pattern can you find in recent campaigns on crowdfunding platforms? How do they present their purpose and goals in the funding period when the project is functionally complete?

References

Benoit, K., Watanabe, K., Wang, H., Nulty, P., Obeng, A., Müller, S., & Matsuo, A. (2018). Quanteda: An R package for the quantitative analysis of textual data. *Journal of Open Source Software*, 3(30), 774. https://doi.org/10.21105/joss.00774

Grice, R. (2017). Experience architecture: Drawing principles from life. In L. Potts & M. J. Salvo (Eds.), *Rhetoric and experience architecture* (pp. 41–56). Parlor Press. https://parlorpress.com/products/rhetoric-and-experience-architecture

Huddleston, R., & Pullum, G. K. (n.d.). *The Cambridge grammar of the English language*. Retrieved July 19, 2022, from www.cambridge.org/core/books/cambridge-grammar-of-the-english-language/A78402ABF5176AD283494180BCA2046F

Jennings, D. (2019a). The STEAM chasers middle grade book series. *Kickstarter*. https://www.kickstarter.com/projects/thesteamchasers/the-steam-chasers-middle-grade-book-series

Jennings, D. (2019b, November 16). The STEAM chasers and the Blackness of space. *Kickstarter*. www.kickstarter.com/projects/thesteamchasers/the-steam-chasers-and-the-blackness-of-space

Jennings, D. (2020, June 27). The STEAM chasers: Books on Black American STEM innovators. *Kickstarter*. www.kickstarter.com/projects/thesteamchasers/the-steam-chasers-books-on-black-american-stem-innovators

Jennings, D. (n.d.). *DoresaAyanna*. Retrieved August 11, 2022, from https://doresaayanna.com

Lady Tarot Cards. (2020, April 20). Lady Tarot Cards: LGBT+ and POC inclusive Tarot Deck. *Kickstarter*. www.kickstarter.com/projects/novaandmali/lady-tarot-cards-lgbt-and-poc-inclusive-tarot-deck

Lady Tarot Cards. (2021a, April 6). Classics . . . but make it gay. *Kickstarter*. www.kickstarter.com/projects/novaandmali/classicsbut-make-it-gay

Lady Tarot Cards. (2021b, October 6). Cover Me Queer—Romance Novels but make it gay. *Kickstarter*. www.kickstarter.com/projects/novaandmali/cover-me-queer-romance-novels-but-make-it-gay

Mollick, E., & Nanda, R. (2016). Wisdom or madness? Comparing crowds with expert evaluation in funding the arts. *Management Science, 62*(6), 1533–1553. https://doi.org/10.1287/mnsc.2015.2207

Nova and Mali. (n.d.). *Nova and Mali: Make it gay. Nova and Mali*. Retrieved September 28, 2022, from www.novaandmali.com

Nuttall, A. (2021, August 18). I'll do it myself: The impact of crowdfunding on Indie comics. *Book Riot*. https://bookriot.com/impact-of-crowdfunding-on-indie-comics/

Pope, A. R. (2017). Bloodstained, unpacking the affect of a kickstarter success – present tense. *Present Tense: A Journal of Rhetoric in Society, 2*(6). https://www.presenttensejournal.org/volume-6/bloodstained-unpacking-the-affect-of-a-kickstarter-success/

Tracy, S. J. (2013). *Qualitative research methods: Collecting evidence, creating analysis, communicating impact* (1st ed.). Wiley-Blackwell.

6
INTERCONNECTED CAMPAIGNS

In this chapter, we'll be focusing on crowdfunding campaigns that don't limit their funding to discrete campaigns, but instead link discrete campaigns to ongoing funding via subscription-based crowdfunding platforms and social media presences. Interconnected campaigns will often maintain an ongoing subscription-based campaign while spinning out individual discrete campaigns for micro-goals or specific projects that would benefit from discrete funding drives that are interconnected with the existing coalition maintained via the subscription campaign and the attendant social media or web presences of the creator/organization. Nonprofits can often benefit from this model, and the model is also seen across a variety of artists and creators on platforms like Instagram such as *The Awkward Yeti* (n.d.), *Sarah's Scribbles (Andersen, n.d.)*, and Mitch Leeuwe's work (Leeuwe, n.d.).

To underscore the way that these campaigns are a web of funding that intermingles across channels and platforms, this chapter focuses on a single creator, the nonprofit animal rescue Rancho Relaxo. Instead of limiting our scope of analysis to a single campaign, we focus on Rancho Relaxo's initial campaign on GoFundMe to get funds for an expansion, a campaign that would fail in its goals during the campaign's update cycle after attaining the needed funding due to a bank's rejection of financing the purchase. The campaign, however, would be followed up by a subsequent campaign that supported the ongoing mission of expansion, a mission that would be documented during the second campaign's duration and that was supported by the funding from the first campaign. Rancho Relaxo would go on to host three further campaigns, and as of the writing of this chapter had raised over $300,000 in funding from 8,254 donations across five fundraisers on the GoFundMe platform in addition to three ongoing Patreon

DOI: 10.4324/9781003308966-6

campaigns, each with their own goals and constituents. Due to the limited nature of Patreon access, we'll be focusing on the publicly available details on these campaigns and their associated figures in a sampled window as a separate discrete analysis beyond the quantitative and qualitative review of the two linked GoFundMe campaigns.

We'll also cover, in brief, the network of social media posts and content that supports Rancho Relaxo to provide an idea of the type of content output the charity creates. These numbers matter because, as noted in previous chapters, subscription-based crowdfunding platforms like Patreon don't tend to provide any means for onboarding new coalition members on the platforms themselves. They are instead a service provider to users who already have existing coalitions or can direct those coalitions from other channels they maintain.

Case Study Methodology

We'll first cover Rancho Relaxo's two linked crowdfunding campaigns on GoFundMe with the same exploratory sequential mixed methods analysis used in Chapter 5. Once that review is complete, we'll shift our analysis to understanding the social media work that preceded the successful campaign and the ongoing subscription campaigns that preceded, accompanied, and persisted beyond the original GoFundMe project. The additional components of the Rancho Relaxo chapter support our efforts to analyze the subscription-based crowdfunding that is partially hidden from view by the Patreon paywall. To provide a balanced overview of the different strands of the Rancho Relaxo project, a final discussion on the Listening, Quantifying, and Defining work of the project will come at the end of the chapter rather than after the first analysis.

All social media research data will be taken from Meta's Crowd-Tangle tool (The CrowdTangle Team, 2022). CrowdTangle is a free service provided to certain types of accounts, in addition to researchers, that tracks public posts and data on Meta's platforms. Controversially, Meta's plans to shut down the tool emerged in 2022 (Alba, 2022), to the dismay of researchers who leverage the platform's access and tools to research and document misinformation campaigns across social media platforms run by Meta (Lawler, 2022).

Rancho Relaxo

Rancho Relaxo is a 501(3)(c) nonprofit, originally started as a rescue operation by founder Caitlin Cimini (referenced as Caitlin Stewart on GoFundMe) after her decision in 2010 to rescue a wild Mustang captured by the U.S. government that was likely destined for a slaughterhouse (Dunham, 2017). From her original rescue, Cimini would go on to purchase a farm near the Delaware border in New Jersey and in the process add an additional adoption to her workload (GoFundMe, 2018). After several years of working in animal rescue, Rancho Relaxo (a reference to *The Simpsons*) was officially filed as a nonprofit in 2015 (as noted in the second campaign's pitch). Cimini's work is often noted as being in spite of her severe allergies to animals that at times leave her in poor health (Cotroneo, 2016).

During 2016, the nonprofit would host its first fundraiser on GoFundMe to provide the funding needed for an expansion onto a ten-acre property nearby. The first campaign was successful, and brought in over $40,000, but the initial purchase was delayed beyond the scope of the campaign (Stewart, 2016a). After that delay, the property was purchased, but a second fundraiser was started on its heels as the property needed extensive work and renovations not covered by the initial funding drive (Stewart, 2016b). The campaign would go on to run several additional campaigns, five at the writing of this book. In the process, Cimini and her husband would be featured in local news coverage, *People Magazine*, and Cimini was featured as GoFundMe's Hero of the Month for April 2017 (Dunham, 2017). The GoFundMe and Patreon content continues steadily as of the writing of this book in 2022 when Rancho Relaxo tackled the takeover of a rescue they'd previously partnered that had been shuttered due to animal abuse (Stewart, 2022).

Rancho Relaxo coordinates giving across a multitude of platforms on the website (*Rancho Relaxo—Rancho Relaxo*, n.d.), with each platform framed with a different focus and goal. GoFundMe is presented as a way to donate to a specific project the rescue is involved with, PayPal donations and Venmo donations are framed as an avenue to support the purchase of general needs such as feed and supplies, with an Amazon Wishlist available to purchase specific items needed, and Patreon promoted as a way to "become a contributor and receive the inside scoop on our farm!"

For our analysis of the case study, we'll first go through the paired first campaigns that started with the raising of funding for the ten-acre land purchase in March of 2016. The first campaign continued through April when the campaign was closed after the first financing deal for the purchase fell through. The second campaign would launch shortly after in June, after closing had been completed on the same property funds were raised for in the original campaign, but with the second campaign moving beyond that initial ask to fund the renovation of the new property purchased. The second campaign would remain open indefinitely (it was still open in fall 2022), a pattern that lines up with the rest of Rancho Relaxo's campaigns—only the first campaign has ever been disabled to disallow new funding.

Rancho Relaxo, like STEAM Chasers and Lady Tarot Cards, frames the work of the charity through the lens of social justice, with the nonprofit's website listing their slogan, "We will not stop until their voices are heard." As a nonprofit, Rancho Relaxo differs from the previous campaigns in that it functions under a different set of laws, regulations, and constraints than the for-profit campaigns in Chapter 5, as the charity regularly notes by reminding donors that all donations are tax-deductible. Rancho Relaxo's distributed and interconnected fundraising linked up through their ongoing social media presences and content streams provides us with a picture of what sustainable crowdfunding can look like when adopted in the nonprofit sphere.

Campaign Funding Structure

Unlike Kickstarter or Indiegogo or Patreon, GoFundMe doesn't provide a structured donation framework or reward structure for campaigns. Instead, campaigns are allowed to set and update funding (GoFundMe, 2022). The first campaign's goal shifted over time, as Cimini adjusted the amount from a full payment to the value of a down payment for financing. The final goal isn't visible on the platform since the campaign was disabled. The second GoFundMe would go on to have a specific goal that is still visible of $100,000. As of the fall of 2022, that campaign had raised $149,880.

GoFundMe provides two metrics for tracking campaigns: the number of donations and the number of words of support. The words of support, however, are not a particularly useful metric as even a quick glance at the Ranch Relaxo follow-up campaign finds spam comments from accounts seeking to network or gain business.

Quantitative Analysis of the Rancho Relaxo Campaigns

The Rancho Relaxo campaigns combined consist of 31 updates, with 10 updates coming during the first campaign and an additional 21 updates coming during the second campaign. Across these updates (and the pitches for the various campaigns), there is an average of 146 words per update, with the maximum word count coming in at 952 words and the minimum at just 5 words. The 952-word update is something of an outlier, as it serves to launch/ introduce an additional funding campaign. The two pitches were of 958 and 563 words in total.

None of the Rancho Relaxo campaigns feature video, but video pitches are available on GoFundMe for campaigns to leverage. The first campaign uses a

campaign_two   campaign_one

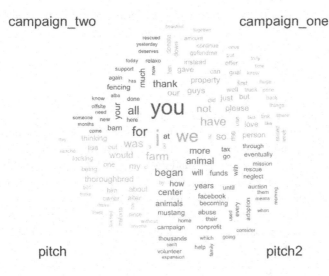

pitch   pitch2

FIGURE 6.1   Comparative word cloud of the Rancho Relaxo GoFundMe campaign pitches and updates

simple collage photo with a message about the campaign and the second campaign forgoes text in the banner photo but includes a banner photo in addition to four photos of the various animals on the farm.

First, we'll start by looking at Figure 6.1, as a comparative word cloud that outlines the two pitches for the two campaigns and the updates for those same campaigns. The four-point word cloud allows us to get a sense of the differences across the two campaigns and their subsequent updates. As before, these are relative comparisons, not absolute usage counts. The cloud foregrounds terms that are particularly prevalent in each segment of the overall corpus.

The split between the two pitches and two campaigns creates some direct patterns that differentiate the messaging in each campaign.

Pitch One

The first pitch centers on "I" as well as the past tense "was" and "farm." The first narrative's key terms taken together foreground the story of the rescue as well as the rescue's founder, Cimini. The terms align with the history of the rescue and Cimini's own narrative, foregrounding that as a basis for the pitch.

Updates Campaign One

The updates for pitch one by comparison foreground "we" and "have," shifting the narrative from the initial pitch messaging that focuses on Cimini's own narrative to a narrative that is more inclusive of the project's backers and other individuals outside of Cimini. The rest of the terms fall into a spectrum of possible uses, from thanks and requests via "please and "gave," to financing-specific terms like "property" and "price."

Pitch Two

The second pitch, instead of focusing of "I" and the narrative of Cimini, focuses on "more," "animal," and "began," in addition to other terms focused around the rescue and its purpose such as "will," "fund," and "animals." The second pitch foregrounds the needs of the animals and the needs of those animals as they relate to the rescue's mission. None of these terms dominate the count in the same way that "I" and "we" loom large above the first pitch and first campaign. Instead, the relative regularity in size among the top terms provides us with a view to the second pitch that foregrounds a collection of terms that all align with the animals and the purpose of the rescue.

Updates Campaign Two

Leading the second campaign's updates is the usage of "you" and "thank" and "you," painting a picture of this campaign as being one that focuses on the backing coalition, their actions, and thanks for their actions. There are some mundane details like "fencing" and "barn" and "rescued," but these pale in comparison in terms of the size of the first terms in the cloud. Taken together, the qualitative data gives us a picture of a campaign focused on foregrounding the work of the coalition and thanking them for that same work, which makes sense since the second campaign is a continuation of the first campaign's now-successful funding to purchase a new property.

In Figure 6.2, we see that a keyness comparison between the first and second campaigns backs up the comparative word cloud's split between a first campaign focused on the founder and a second campaign focused on the backing coalition and their work.

The first campaign focuses on terms like "I" and "me" and "my" across the board, centering the narrative on Cimini and her history. The second campaign contrasts with "thank," "for," and "you" followed by a grouping of terms that reference the mission of the rescue and mundane details such as "vet" and "offsite" and "legs."

Seeding the Qualitative Review

Having looked over the two pitches and two sets of campaign updates, we can build a general picture of the types of moves we'll expect in the qualitative analysis of the updates and the user experience that they create for the backers. As we

Comparison of Term Usage in Campaign 1 versus Campaign 2

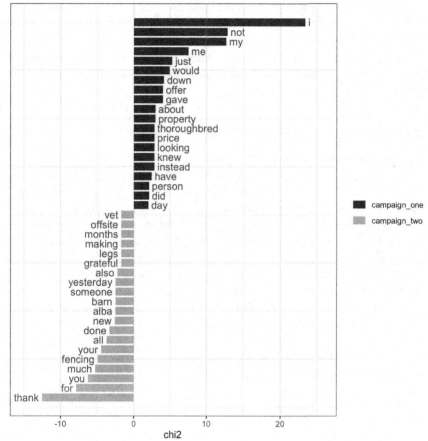

FIGURE 6.2   Keyness comparison of terms used in the first and second Rancho Relaxo GoFundMe campaigns

seed our codebook for the qualitative review, we start with the following general moves based on the quantitative analysis:

- Centering of the founder and her narrative
- Emphasizing of communal action
- Referencing the backing coalition
- Foregrounding the mission of the rescue
- Thanking the backing coalition
- Documenting mundane details of process

As with Chapter 5, I have attempted to reuse similar language when the coding process begins with sentiments that line up with previous case studies, if only to allow us to continue with a sense of a shared vocabulary across the case studies. In cases where there are meaningful differences, I've provided unique starting points for coding. For example, I have opted to not use "documenting mundane details of process" and instead leverage "foregrounding the mission of the rescue."

Qualitative Analysis of Rancho Relaxo Campaign

After the initial round of coding, the Rancho Relaxo campaigns resulted in a total of 55 discrete codes across the two campaigns, before the process of winnowing down the initial coding to remove duplicates and overlaps. After a revision pass to streamline the codes into larger bundles that allowed for a general sense of *what* was happening in the project, the resulting final list of primary codes numbered 35 in total, a sizable reduction after a grouping of single-use codes was reduced into parent codes that aggregated the general *what* of those codes.

The first round of coding had a large spread of content across the codes, which makes sense because the coding process combined two separate and discrete campaigns that are linked in purpose. Five different codes were present in the data that were leveraged at least 30 times:

- Centering of the founder and her narrative
- Documenting the mundane details of the process
- Animal narrative
- Foregrounding the mission of the rescue
- Thanking the backing coalition

Interestingly, four of the five codes that were the most prominent in the primary coding aligned with the qualitative codebook seeding from the quantitative analysis. Beyond these top-level usages, the rest of the codes were referenced 23 times or less, with regular drops in code usages coming until the final grouping of codes that were each leveraged two times. Most of the codes covered (below the top tier) were used at least four times across the corpus of the two campaigns.

Moving toward a final set of axial codes, as with the discrete case studies from Chapter 5, the project's codes were analyzed and separated into larger categories that explained the *why* of the moves identified in the primary coding cycle. The second review of the codes resulted in six codes that document the major moves and their purposes in the study. Four of these codes were used heavily, and two were used less:

- Telling the founder's story (120 references)
- Celebrating the coalition (111 references)
- Narrating the project's story and success (106 references)

- Telling animals stories (78 references)
- Calling the coalition to action (45 references)
- Telling the charity's story (35 references)

Each of these rhetorical moves highlights the *why* of the *what* from the primary coding, giving us a window into the different moves across these two campaigns that were the most common in the Rancho Relaxo messaging during pitches and updates.

The Rancho Relaxo campaign's repeated return to narrative and storytelling aligns with the findings of Campeau and Thao (2022) among medical crowd-funding campaigns, and also makes sense considering the story-centric framing of the GoFundMe platform itself. These stories and narratives also align with the pathos-centered framing that is common in charity funding letters (Myers, 2007) and follow Grice's (2017) recommendations for XAs. This focus on the story results in Rancho Relaxo breaking from the previous two case studies in that there is no major rhetorical move devoted to sharing mundane details on their own. Instead, these mundane details are found across these different stories, and are leveraged across these categories to demonstrate an evolving narrative and story. The mundane is seldom shared simply as information to excite and moti-vate backers, but instead is woven into one of the story threads being maintained across the Rancho Relaxo updates and pitches.

Next, we'll look at each of these terms in turn as in our previous two case studies, breaking down what exactly each move represents, the common permu-tations, as well as the location of these updates.

Telling the Founder's Story

The most common rhetorical move used to build the narrative and XA of the Rancho Relaxo campaigns was the telling of the story of founder Caitlin Cimini. This storytelling work was distributed across both campaigns, though the overall frequency of the storytelling was higher in the first campaign, as seen in Fig-ure 6.3. This front-loading of content makes sense, as the first campaign was the initial move onto the GoFundMe platform, and the introduction of the charity and its history to a new audience would necessitate more storytelling as the cam-paign began.

This storytelling builds an XA that introduces backers to the founder Cimini while also bringing them into her world and her experience of the work of Rancho Relaxo. The storytelling, and many of the updates across both projects, is told from Cimini's point of view. This is seen most clearly in the comparative word cloud from Figure 6.1 where "I" dominated the first pitch (which is almost entirely a narrative about Cimini and her founding of Rancho Relaxo). As we'll see, this storytelling is dominated by narratives of Cimini and the work she's done, but also interweaves Cimini's emotions and emotional labor in running

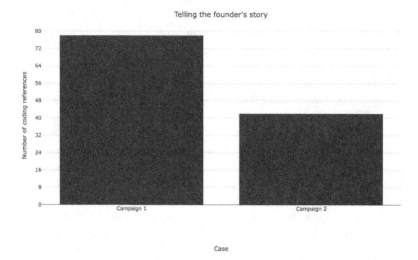

Telling the founder's story

FIGURE 6.3   Illustration of the relative occurrence of the "Telling the Founder's Story" code in the first and second GoFundMe campaigns for Rancho Relaxo

the charity and doing rescue work, building an experience that tells the story of Rancho Relaxo from a first-person perspective while also sharing the emotions and reactions to that work directly from the founder.

The narrative work of telling the founder's story and how that story connects with Rancho Relaxo is the most common of the storytelling moves about the founder. For example, in the second pitch, Cimini explains, "I started this journey on a late September morning, years ago, when I decided to rescue a mustang from the US governement [*sic*] on a whim." The narrative work builds Rancho Relaxo and its mission out of the personal history of Cimini and her work doing animal rescue. In many ways, Rancho Relaxo's story is her story, and she is the driving force and face of the charity.

The storytelling by Cimini is often deeply personal as she interweaves the narrative of the founding of Rancho Relaxo with her experience of animal suffering, as seen in examples such as this anecdote from the first campaign (repeated in the second campaign pitch):

> My mission was clear the day I drove out to a man's home who had two potbellied piglets listed on Craigslist, headed to an auction—advertised as food for exotic animals. . . I sobbed my entire ride home, just thinking about how scared they were. That was it for me. Animals needed a voice somehow—and I was going to be the one to give it to them . . . until the day I die. That was what I was going to do.

In this construction, we see Cimini both telling her own story in powerful language—her experiences with animal abuse and mistreatment are her driving force in doing the work of animal rescue—and she is compelled by this suffering to do the work she does. For backers, this narrative builds a connection with Cimini as someone who is convicted by the suffering of animals—the narrative work is factual but deeply emotional. This isn't a highly rational narrative of facts and figures, but one driven by compassion and raw emotional reactions to abuse and mistreatment.

The emotional angle noted in some of the narratives of about Cimini's founding was another major strand of storytelling about the founder of Rancho Relaxo, with many of the storytelling examples specifically centering Cimini's emotional response to the work of rescuing animals and running the campaign. This foregrounding of first-person emotional reactions builds a highly personal story that is also explicitly emotional, aligning with Grice's (2017) recommendations for pathos-driven experiences, but also underscoring the emotional nature of the work done by Rancho Relaxo as a charity focused on rescuing animals from cruel conditions and suffering. By explicitly sharing her emotional reactions, Cimini shares the emotional labor of running Relaxo while also motivating coalition members to remain engaged and supportive. For example, in the first campaign's fifth update she shares, "It has taken a toll on me physically and emotionally—on numerous occasions," and "Running a rescue is so trying and difficult." At the same time, these stories of emotional labor are intermingled with triumphant celebrations of the coalition's actions and the campaign's success as experience through Cimini, such as in the first campaign's seventh update when she shares, "My heart skips a beat when I check the campaign's status," and in the second campaign's Update 19 when she shares, "It still feels like a dream for all of us—and I'm sure the animals feel the same way!" This emotional storytelling extends the framing of Cimini as the founder and central figure of Relaxo by relaying the emotional impact and ups and downs of the animal rescue work, with the lows reminding the coalition of the stakes of the rescue's mission and the highs reinforcing their decision to follow the charity and support its mission.

These moves, as well as other lesson common moves such as relating the compulsion Cimini feels to act and the financial impact of the work of running Rancho Relaxo on Cimini and her husband, build a narrative that personalizes the work of Rancho Relaxo while building a relationship between Cimini and backers. They are working with Rancho Relaxo, but they are also working with and support her as she carries out the physical and emotional labor that supports Rancho Relaxo.

Celebrating the Coalition

The second most common move in the Rancho Relaxo campaigns focuses on celebrating the coalition and their impact on the charity, the charity's founder, and its mission. Like the first major move, these celebrations of the coalition tell the story of the charity and its founder with an often-emotional focus, but they do so by explicitly centering and celebrating the work done by the backing coalition, underscoring their choice to back the charity in the first place. Mirroring the data from the quantitative analysis, the focus on the coalition, through terms like "you" and the communal "we," is markedly more prevalent in the second campaign. The celebrations can be broken down into a few distinct celebratory moves, the most common being simply thanking and celebrating the coalition for their action, followed by narrating communal action and its impact, and finally the underscoring of the essential role the coalition plays in the charity (even to the point of aligning the coalition with the founder).

The work of thanking the coalition often comes directly from Cimini, as in the tenth update of the first campaign where she writes simply, "I love you guys," or in the second update of that campaign where she shares, "You guys are the most unbelievable human beings on the planet," and "I could not have asked for a better support system." These direct thanks from Cimini underscore the personal relationship built in the founder-centric storytelling that is most common in the updates and creates a personal user experience where coalition members are encouraged to see themselves working alongside Cimini as a friend and supporter of the charity's cause.

Messages of thanksgiving are often explicitly layered to include *all* members of the coalition, regardless of their impact, underscoring the essential nature of all support, such as in the first campaign's Update 9 where Cimini shares, "To the person who gave $5,000, to the person who gave $500, to the person who gave $1, to the person who shared the link every single day, to the person who shared the link once . . . You guys directly aided us in creating something huge," or in the second campaign's 13th update where she writes from herself and the organization, "We are so grateful for Every donation—whether it is $1 or $1,000!" These explicit references to different donation levels serve to celebrate the coalition while also directly celebrating even the smallest contributions as essential.

In addition to thanking the coalition, the celebrations often explicitly link the success and work of the rescue to communal action, as in the second campaign's 12th update where Cimini writes, "This is happening because of all of you!!!!" or the 14th update where she notes, "All because of you guys," and in the 16th update where she shares, "Rancho Relaxo is held up by all of you." These repeated connections between the success of the charity and the work being done underscore the essential nature of the coalition, celebrating their accomplishments while also providing an emotional reward to the coalition members. As they see the work of the charity's campaigns coming into existence, this progress is directly narrated as coming from them, reinforcing the emotional choice to back the charity's campaign and reminding them of why they supported (and should continue to support) the work of Rancho Relaxo.

Finally, the celebrations go so far as to align the work of the coalition with that of Cimini, taking the personal relationship built in the XA a step further. These references are spread across both campaigns, such as in the first campaign's second update where Cimini writes, "You guys are just like me—ready to dive headfirst into last minute rescues and projects," or in the ninth update where she shares, "We all have the same mission—you, me. We are all in it together." The second campaign features the same language, as in update 2 she writes, "We are changing the world—together—and we are so happy to be on the same team as you guys," and in update 21 she writes, "I sometimes get nervous that the support you all provide is suddenly going to stop but I always remind myself that you all care just as much as I do." These celebrations of the coalition as being like the founder of Relaxo further intertwine the personal and emotional labor of Cimini and the charity with the backing coalition. The backers are not only working with Cimini, they are the same sort of person with the same sort of passion and drive. As with the rest of the celebrations, these moves serve to underscore the emotional reward of working with Rancho Relaxo and counting to support the charity.

Narrating the Project's Story and Success

The third most common move in the Rancho Relaxo campaigns centers on narrating the progress of the project and the successes that arise from that progress. As with the celebrations, the second campaign is the primary location for this work, which aligns with the truncated nature of the first campaign and its ending with the rejection of the first financing application for the purchase of the expansion for the charity. Many of these updates are documentations of the mundane details of the processes behind the project, creating a narrative over time of progress and allowing the backing coalition to see the work they funded coming into existence. These narrative moves work alongside the celebrations of the coalition as they are intertwined—the story and success are because of the coalition's backing after all (and the work of the founder, Cimini).

Many of the story updates are simple progress notes, such as the first campaign's 3rd update that shared, "We put in an offer, folks," or the second campaigns' 11th update where Cimini shares, "I just sent in the deposit for the fencing." These updates on the mundane steps of buying the property and renovating the space across the second campaign create a narrative that shows progress and works alongside the celebrations of the coalition.

Several updates focus on sharing the costs of the project, showing the backers where the funding they've donated is going and how money is used by the charity. Most of the explicit references are found in the second campaign, which makes sense considering the campaign focuses on updating the property purchased thanks to the first campaign. For example in the 11th pitch of the second campaign, Cimini shares "The fencing in total is going to cost over $47,000." These specific cost references are intermingled with references to funding levels as they relate to costs, such as this note from the 19th update of the second campaign, "I also want to mention how lucky we all are that we exceeded our goal for this campaign because everything ended up being much more expensive than we initially planned." These costs are shown to be met by the work of the coalition, but also high and omnipresent in the work of animal rescue, underscoring the necessity of the funding work of the coalition.

Taken together the narration of the project's story and its successes document the results of the backers' actions and the leadership of Cimini and her team, showing the backing coalition through updates on specific deliverables coming into place intermingled with cost analysis of those same events and reminders of why the backer's support matters.

Telling the Animal's Stories

The last major move made (in terms of raw numbers) is the telling of the animals' stories, and like many of the other major moves, these are found primarily in the second campaign (though there are examples in the first campaign). The storytelling about the animals at the core of the Rancho Relaxo mission provides another avenue for backers to experience the work supported by their donations and another emotional reward/motivation for continuing to follow and back the charity's work. These narratives are broken down primarily into narratives of animal mistreatment and animal rescue, with the rest of the moves focused on underscoring the fundamental dignity of the animals (and the social justice inherent in supporting them).

Each of the animal narratives focuses on a particular animal, their name, and their story, often intermingling both a narrative of abuse and neglect before the animal came to Rancho Relaxo with the narrative of the animal overcoming this mistreatment through the aid of the charity and the backing coalition. One example is the narrative of Humphrey from the second campaign's 16th update. Humphrey comes to Rancho Relaxo in poor condition: "This poor soul looks like he is close to 30 years old—when in actuality, he is a teenager." His suffering is underscored by Cimini in explicit details as she relates that "I want you all to know that he is in excruciating pain—even with pain killers, he is uncomfortable." At the same time, the importance of Humphrey's care and treatment is underscored: "All of this on top of quarantine is just so much but it is worth it. He deserves this." The case is then leveraged directly into a plea for donations to support the work of rehabilitating Humphrey: "Please consider becoming a monthly donor, or please donate one time toward Humphrey's care, or buy merch, or share our cause! Rancho Relaxo is held up by all of you." The narrative of Humphrey personalizes the suffering of the animals cared for Rancho Relaxo, proving a name and a face to the animals in need, and connecting that need with specific and often unsettling descriptions of their suffering. This raw storytelling reminds backers of the necessity of their support, while also providing them with the assurance that progress is happening and animals are being saved.

The narratives provide an ongoing explanation during the update period of why the funding matters, and what the funding is going toward. The repeated reminders that this work is not only important but also something the animals deserve underscore the social justice of the animal rescue's mission. The animal narratives accompany the ongoing fundraising for the second pitch, which remains open as of fall 2022. The reminders are sprinkled throughout the campaigns, such as the note in both pitches that "To date, we have rescued over 300 animals—large and small, all deserving of being free of abuse and neglect." This sentiment repeats, such as in the second campaign's second update where Cimini notes, "The animals deserve this so much," and in the case of Humphrey, and in the 21st update of the second campaign (which lists a series of animal cases): "They deserve the best." Not only is the work of the campaign emotional and important, but also it is essential to social justice as these animals simply deserve the care and rescue they are receiving.

Calling the Coalition to Action

The first of the lesser used moves are explicit calls for the coalition to act. These calls exist parallel to the storytelling about the founder, the animals, and the celebrations of the coalition's actions. The emotional work done in each of these other moves becomes the impetus and rationale behind the coalition then moving to act when called to action to allow the work of the charity to continue. These calls to action are a mixture of directly addressing the audience, as in the first pitch's "This is where you all jump in"; requests for sharing as in the first campaign's 5th update, "Even if you do not donate, just read the description and share it with others"; and requests for donations as seen in the 4th update of that same campaign: "If you have $1 . . . $2 . . . $5 to spare, please do so." Taken together, these less frequent moves serve to leverage the emotional connections built in the rest of the XA.

Telling the Charity's Story

The final, and least frequent, move that the campaign makes is telling the story of the charity itself, Rancho Relaxo. Some of these references are specific and technical, such as repeated references to the charity's status as a 501(3)(c) that allows for donations to be deducted from tax filings. Other references are technical documentation of the rescue's specific properties, employees, and projects. These moves are separated from the narrative of the project and its story as they focus primarily on the breakdown of the charity's organization, operations, and capacity. They foreground the narrative work found in other places and provide a window into the larger organization being represented by the work of the founder Cimini and the project narrative and animal narratives found throughout the campaigns.

Social Media Production Analysis

Having looked at the qualitative and quantitative sides of the Rancho Relaxo campaign, we now turn to the social media output of Rancho Relaxo. The social media content created by the charity and its founder serve to bring backers to the campaigns on GoFundMe while also providing an onramp to the separate Patreon work that began during the second campaign. The main Rancho Relaxo site foregrounds the Instagram presence of founder Caitlin Cimini (@boochaces), though the rescue also has an attendant Facebook presence (with regular historical references to Patreon). Meta usually allows (and encourages) creators to cross-post between Facebook and Instagram, even bundling the two apps into the same suite of app-level tools for businesses, so we'll cover both for the sake of completeness. Instagram content can also be found on a separate charity account (@ranchorelaxoteam).

As noted earlier, Rancho Relaxo's Instagram presence pre-dates the creation of the nonprofit registration as well as the first GoFundMe drive while also serving as an onramp for Patreon backers as the Patreon campaign only gets a single mention during the two campaigns under analysis. In order to provide context for the two types of campaigns, we'll look at the content created in the year before the GoFundme launch (2015) as well as the data from the period of the two campaign's initial creation and initial update burst (2016 and 2017). Once this campaign-specific information has been documented, we'll wrap this segment with a brief survey of the last three years of Rancho Relaxo's output for a sense of how the current content creation pace and scope aligns with the historical information in the crowdfunding period, covering 2019, 2020, and 2021.

The social media data provides us with a window into the content demands that the overall charity's social media presence generated and also allows us to understand the XA and engagement structures that were behind the successes we are able to track during the two campaigns on GoFundMe and the continued success of the charity's Patreon. Because Patreon doesn't position its platform as a space to stumble upon a cause to follow and back, the social media data is necessary to understand Rancho Relaxo's interconnected campaigns.

CrowdTangle (The CrowdTangle Team, 2022) allows us to get information that can be split across monthly, weekly, or daily periods of time, and so for each period, I'll relay the information available for each period weekly. This provides a decent baseline for technical writers looking to understand the weekly commitment that a charity like Rancho Relaxo makes to social media production.

We'll cover the sheer numerical count of content created that has been tracked on CrowdTangle during each window of time, as well as the number of Interactions tracked during the same period of time. Each set of information comes from an individual Intelligence search for the time period and channel noted. Interactions should be treated carefully, as they do not track individual users that are interacting with the campaign, but instead each individual interaction that the platform sees during this period of time. So, a given pool of 50 interactions across a single month could just as easily be from 50 discrete users or from a single user who happens to like or comment on every single post a given page might create.

It is also worth noting that as of the writing of this book, Meta's slow shutdown of CrowdTangle as a service functionally means the platform can be glitchy and troublesome to use at times.

Pre-campaign Period

The pre-campaign period covers the entirety of 2015, from January 1 through December 31. There were both Facebook and Instagram posts during this content window.

During this window of time, CrowdTangle data shows that there were a total of 477 posts by Rancho Relaxo on Facebook, with an average of 9 posts per week. Of these posts, based on the CrowdTangle data, there were 215 photos and 262 Facebook Videos.

On the @boochaces Instagram account, during the same window of time, there were 3,000 posts, with an average of 57 posts per week according to CrowdTangle. There were 2,400 photos and 659 videos in this time.

There isn't any data that is available on CrowdTangle during the pre-campaign period of 2015 regarding the follower count of either the @boochaces account on Instagram or the Rancho Relaxo Facebook page.

Interactions during the pre-campaign period for the Rancho Relaxo Facebook account totaled in at 57,700 interactions, with an average number of interactions coming in at 1,100. These interactions are split between Facebook videos at 58% and photos at 41%.

The @boochaces account received 2.18 million interactions across the pre-campaign period, with an average of 41,100 interactions weekly, split between 74% for photos and 25% for videos.

Campaign Period Data

For the campaign length data, we'll focus on the content posted to Facebook and Instagram during the window of 3/16/2016 through 10/15/2017. These dates roughly align with the public time of the two campaigns, with the later date aligning with the last update provided for the second campaign.

During the campaign window, there were 1,000 posts on Facebook, with an average of 12 posts per week during that window of time. The breakdown on this content included 513 photos, 33 links, 420 Facebook videos, 34 Facebook Live videos, and 2 other videos.

For the same campaign time period, there were 3,000 posts on Instagram via the @boochaces account, which comes out to an average in the CrowdTangle data to 35 posts weekly. Out of this grouping of content, there were 66 albums, 1,900 photos, and 993 videos shared publicly.

During the campaign period, the @boochaces account went from around 36,500 followers to a peak of 137,100 followers. The Facebook data on followers isn't available on CrowdTangle for the same period of time until the very end of the selected window, when the Rancho Relaxo Facebook page ended with 23,900 followers.

Regarding interactions, there were 279,900 interactions on the Ranch Relaxo account on Facebook during the campaign window, an average of 3,300 interactions per week, with those interactions being split primarily between photos at 48% and Facebook videos at 44%. During that same period of time, the Instagram account @boochaces received 10.56 million interactions, with 125,700 weekly interactions being the average. These interactions were split primarily between photos at 60% and videos at 36%.

Recent Data

During the post-campaign sampling window of 2017–2021, the @boochaces account on Instagram posted around 1,000 posts, with an average number of weekly posts coming in at 7. In that span of time, the account posted 38 albums, 512 photos, and 488 videos.

The Facebook account for Rancho Relaxo during the same window posted around 1,100 posts, with an average of 7 posts per week. The Facebook information breaks down to 606 photos, 73 links, 7 statuses, 441 Facebook videos, 7 Facebook Live videos, 7 YouTube videos, and 5 other videos.

The data for the more recent period differentiates certain kinds of video that weren't present in the previous content, and these changes are simply based on updates in the Facebook/CrowdTangle data collection and categorization practices.

The interaction data for the same period shows the Facebook account receiving 742,800 interactions, or around 4,900 interactions per week across all content. About 58% of the interactions were on Facebook videos and 38% were on Photos. The Instagram numbers for interaction totaled 10.16 million interactions across the same period, with 66,400 interactions per week being the norm. These interactions are split primarily between photos at 52% and videos at 44%.

Social Media Patterns/Trends

Taken together, the social media data for Rancho Relaxo across the Facebook account and the Instagram account represent a steady stream of content—photos and videos. As time has gone on, the accounts have produced less content, especially the Instagram account, but the overall interaction rate for the accounts has not dropped off as the content stream has decreased.

The pacing of 57, then 35, and finally 7 posts per week on the @boochaces Instagram account during our three periods of time represents a dizzying amount of content, with content dropping as the campaign period begins and then dropping further in the most recent period of time (which includes the 2020 pandemic).

Instagram and Facebook historically have no monetization of content for creators, so the content on either platform isn't directly generating content for Rancho Relaxo in the same way that content on an ad-supported YouTube channel might. With that said, the content provides a channel that allows the charity to connect with and attracts new members to the coalition that supports Rancho Relaxo, while at the same time providing the charity with a way to direct coalition members to one of their funding channels.

Patreon Analysis

In our analysis of Patreon for Rancho Relaxo, we'll first provide an overview of the three different Patreons that the charity has active as of fall 2022 before providing an overview of the pitches and funding tiers for each Patreon. Once that analysis is complete, we'll sample update count, content, and engagement data from Rancho Relaxo Patreon presence to get a sense of how often content is posted and the types of content posted (as indicated by the previews on the Patreon page). Since Rancho Relaxo's Patreon presence is paywalled (very much the norm on the service), the depth of analysis will be limited but should provide us with a sense of the scope and scale of these contributions. In total, we'll look at a random sampling of five of the months the campaign has been active from 2016 through 2021. For each month, we'll note the number of updates, and the average number of likes and comments, and provide a summary of the types of content presented (based on update titles and the previews on Patreon).

Campaign Summary

Rancho Relaxo has three separate Patreon projects that can be backed as of fall 2022: a central Rancho Relaxo project, an animal sponsorship project, and a takeover project, which consists of the pre-existing Patreon of another animal sanctuary that Rancho Relaxo has taken over due to neglect on the part of that sanctuary's management. We'll briefly cover the rationale and presentation of these Patreon projects, as well as their funding levels, before shifting to an analysis of the content on the primary Rancho Relaxo account.

Primary Account

The primary Rancho Relaxo Patreon account has a self-description that aligns with the pitch from each of the two campaigns studied, starting with the narrative of Cimini's horse adoption and ending with her narrative about two pot-bellied pigs. After this shared content, this is a short paragraph that differentiates Patreon from other funding sources and provides a rationale for the project: the funding from Patreon allows the charity to make long-term decisions confidently, allowing them to rescue more animals and take care of the existing animals in their care ("About Rancho Relaxo" n.d.). The number of backers is not public, but the project has 1,447 posts as of fall 2022.

The available funding levels range from $1 monthly through $250 monthly, with the titles for each tier going from "Supporter" at the $1 level to "Hero" at the $250 level. There is no meaningful differentiation of funding level access to content on Patreon, but instead a note on each of the levels at and above $25 reminds backers that the more money pledged, the more the charity can do for animals.

Sponsorship Account

The Rancho Relaxo Sponsorship project has a short paragraph explaining the program: sponsors can email the organization to find an animal in need of a sponsor, and then once they start sponsorship they will get personalized certificates of sponsorship and having a chance to meet the animal they're sponsoring. The backing levels of this campaign vary wildly from $5 for a custom sponsorship and $8 for a bale of hay to $125 a month to sponsor a cow resident. Each sponsorship level is tied to a specific animal's care beyond the initial two levels. There are a total of 297 patrons for the project.

Takeover Account

The takeover account is fairly brief, noting that Patreon once belonged to a now-closed sanctuary that Rancho Relaxo has taken over, with Patreon continuing to allow Rancho Relaxo to pay the outstanding bills associated with the property. The backing levels range from $1 to $200, with no real differentiation between the levels. The content on the takeover account is sparse, with only five posts available from the takeover date in July 2022 through November 2022. Backer data is not available for the project.

Sampling of Monthly Content

To provide a random sampling of Patreon content, all months with content from 2016 through 2021 were arranged in numerical order and five were chosen via random numbers. The resulting range of content comes from November 2016, July 2017, January 2019, March 2020, and August 2020. For each month, we'll cover the amount of content created and the average number of comments and posts, with a brief summary of content types.

November 2016

The November 2016 period on Patreon is fairly sparse, with only three updates posted. Two of the updates include photos of animals, with one update featuring a blacked-out top photo. The three updates contain a greeting to the patrons, a happy holidays message, and an update about two animals Chewie and Clarabelle. Overall, the three updates received 158 likes and 36 comments, for an average of 12 comments per update and 52 likes per update.

July 2017

The July 2017 period contains five updates posted across the period. Each update features photos of either animals from the rescue or shots of the rescue property. Titles are mostly descriptive in the period, with animals named in multiple titles. The content from the period received a total of 39 comments and 364 likes, for an average of 8 comments and 73 likes per update, tracking fairly close to the previous year's update.

January 2019

The January 2019 period contains a total of 41 updates across the period, an increase of over 35 updates from the previous two sampled periods. The titles and content, as previously, are heavily weighted toward pictures of animals and posts about named animals. There are a few references to exclusivity, such as a note from January 1st noting that Patreon gets first dibs for visitor days during 2019. There are also a few updates regarding rescue cases, including a reference to involving the police in a case. Across all 41 updates, there were a total of 978 comments and 10,129 likes, for an average of 24 comments and 247 likes per update.

March 2020

The March 2020 period contains a total of 30 updates, a slight decrease from the January 2019 period, with this update period falling in the early days of the COVID-19 pandemic in the United States. As with previous periods, a good bit of the content is devoted to named animals and their photos, with additional titles documenting a roadtrip by the Rancho Relaxo team as well as the inclusion of an update full of coloring pages. Across the period, there were a total of 690 comments and 6,276 likes, with an average of 23 comments and 209 likes per update.

August 2020

In the final sampled period, there were a total of only 13 updates. The updates, as in previous samples, were a mixture of named animal updates and photos alongside updates on various animals' cases and care. There were a total of 358 comments and 2,949 likes during the period, for an average of 28 comments and 227 likes per update, putting the August 2020 period in between the previous two periods in terms of average like and comment count.

Patreon Summary

Overall, the Patreon content for Rancho Relaxo starts relatively sparse but then grows in scope and size before dropping off again in our final sampled period. Since the last two updates sampled take place during the first year of the COVID-19 pandemic, there may very well be secondary factors in the drop in content.

Regardless of content frequency and count, there is a surge in engagement numbers from the first sampled period through the remaining periods, and that engagement remains fairly steady across a series of periods with wildly differing amounts of content, demonstrating that the Patreon account was able to attract and then retain a backing coalition despite dips in the frequency of updates on the platform.

The Patreon updates align fairly closely with the updates in the second GoFundMe campaign in that they document a combination of animal abuse cases, charity updates, and named animal updates that work to remind backers of the work being done by the charity and its importance.

Listening, Quantifying, and Defining Rancho Relaxo's Interconnected Campaigns

Having looked at two GoFundMe campaigns for Rancho Relaxo, in addition to the social media output across Facebook and Instagram, as well as a brief sampling of content on the Patreon account for the rescue, we'll now turn to summarize our findings to carry out listening, quantifying, and defining of the campaigns we've covered that work together as an interconnecting body of fundraising for the charity.

Listening

Looking at the various interconnected campaigns of Rancho Relaxo through the lens of listening, we can see that charity crowdfunding can succeed across multiple platforms simultaneously with serial discrete campaigns and ongoing subscription campaigns growing in tandem with social media content streams.

This ongoing support across campaigns and platforms is an important validation of the Superbacker phenomenon from Kickstarter (Edelstein, 2016) that demonstrates that backers will not only cross between multiple campaigns but also across multiple platforms in their engagement with an organization. The substantial social media following and engagement data for the charity also gives a window into the value of that content for a wider coalition audience that follows the charity.

Quantifying

Looking across the Rancho Relaxo campaigns to quantify the causes of engagement, we see many of the same strands that motivate our two case studies on GoFundMe on the social media and Patreon channels concurrently maintained by the charity. Rancho Relaxo's content can be seen as a series of ongoing storytelling moves, with each story circling back to emphasize the emotional impact of the animal rescue's work. Rancho Relaxo's crowdfunding is a story, and the story is one that backers become part of when they back the charity.

Across the updates, we can also see a pattern of personal or personified storytelling, with ongoing narratives interweaving a cast of characters, with the founder Cimini serving as the primary face of the organization. Cimini's personal narrative and emotional reactions to the rescue work engage backers directly, and the interwoven cast of animals that are named and narrated across the crowdfunding pitches and social media content provide another ongoing strand of personalized narratives. Taken together, the stories of Rancho Relaxo are stories about individuals and individual animals, and they demonstrate to coalition members the emotional labor of animal rescue and the rewards of that same work.

For technical writers working with charity organizations, the Rancho Relaxo provides a model for regularizing the content flow and updates in a way that highlights a handful of key stories about the organization, both underscoring to backers why their support matters and allowing them to see their support doing good in the world through the organization. As each story is told through the updates, the emphasizing of coalitional action behind the work documented and done never lets the coalition forget that their contributions make the charity's work possible.

Looking hard to future campaigns and their XAs, technical writers working with nonprofit organizations can draw the major moves by Rancho Relaxo to begin planning their own strategies and approaches to content channels and updates with the following starting points for discussion:

• How can we tell our organization's story over time?
• How can we celebrate the impact of our coalition members on our work?

- How can we narrate our individual and global project and its development and success over time?
- How can we tell individual stories of those impacted by our work?
- How can we call our coalition to action alongside these regular storytelling updates?
- Across all of our storytelling, how can we share the mundane daily bits of our process and projects in a way that provides backers with an insider's perspective on our work?

As with Lady Tarot Cards and STEAM Chasers, the case of Rancho Relaxo is not universal, but it does provide us with a starting point for nonprofit and charity crowdfunding that demonstrates what has worked in the space not only across multiple campaigns but across multiple crowdfunding platforms.

Defining

Rancho Relaxo's paired campaigns, supplemented by their Patreon and social media content, sketches out a vision for a crowdfunded charity enterprise that operates via the Internet for funding purposes. We see across the GoFundMe, Patreon, and social media content of the charity a regular and at times blistering pace of updates that provide content that reinforces the central narrative storytelling of the charity while providing backers with a narrative of the work being done by the charity and the ways that their support makes that work possible.

In the sense of sheer numbers, the two campaigns on GoFundMe feature 31 updates, with 10 coming during the first and 21 coming during the second campaign. Of these updates, multiple updates in the second half of the second campaign function primarily as off-ramps from the second campaign to new funding projects the charity has begun.

Regarding images, there are regular uses of images across both campaigns on GoFundMe and almost continuous usage of images on Patreon. On GoFundMe Cimini leverages these images to illustrate process steps, such as getting the keys to the property in the second campaign or signing an offer in the first campaign. In addition, Cimini regularly leverages screenshots of emails in her updates as well as shots of invoices and other paperwork to document process updates and costs. Across the first campaign, including the pitch, there are 11 images. There are 28 across the second campaign, though not all show up correctly in the current GoFundMe update system.

The Patreon updates vary from a low of 3 to a high of 41, with content varying between individual animal narratives, narratives of animal rescues, and narratives of events and progress for the charity itself. The Patreon updates content, in general, aligns fairly closely with the moves found in the GoFundMe updates, providing some continuity between the two crowdfunding channels.

The social media production of Rancho Relaxo provides us with a window into the architecture of engagement that provides the charity with an on-ramp to its crowdfunding campaigns and projects, with content ranging from 57 posts per week before the crowdfunding project began to 7 posts per week during the most recent time period sampled, with the majority of content provided via the @boochaces Instagram account.

Technical writers looking to build XAs for nonprofit organizations can view the whole of the interconnected campaigns as a part of a singular XA of sustainable crowdfunding, with the social media content feeding into the discrete and ongoing subscription campaigns by maintaining the connections with the backing coalition outside of crowdfunding while attracting new members to the coalition at the same time. While the pace and scope of content creation during the busier periods of time for the Rancho Relaxo channels may be intimidating, the relative growth over time of Patreon and social media engagement and followers demonstrates that output doesn't correlate directly to engagement. Once a durable backing coalition has been attracted by a rapid early release of content, the Rancho Relaxo case suggests that content production can be scaled back over time without losing coalition members.

Though we only briefly mentioned them earlier, it is also worth noting that all of the content produced across our sampled funding drives is in addition to the Amazon Wishlist, merchandise shop, and direct Venmo and PayPal donations that are offered to coalition members on the organization's website and social media presences, with the inclusion of Venmo an interesting example of the charity leveraging peer-to-peer payment services to supplement their funding through discrete crowdfunding channels.

Looking ahead from our sampled GoFundMe projects, Rancho Relaxo would go on to receive over $100,000 in funding across three different ongoing GoFundMe drives, with the most recent campaign receiving $12,000 in a single day (Stewart, 2022). For some context, the 2018 and 2019 tax filings for the charity record a total of $1,110,065 and $11,170,010 in contributions and grants, with crowdfunding platforms making up an unspecified amount of that total due to the lack of public numbers for Patreon and direct donations. The growth of the gifts noted on the most recent tax return from 2019 aligns with the overall engagement data and success of the crowdfunding campaigns, with the initial 2016 filing period documenting $244,852 in contributions, followed by $667,234 in 2017, and then $1,110,065 in 2018 (The Internal Revenue Service, 2020). The growth in funding is exponential during the first several years, and then regularizes to an extent for the past two years.

Wrapping Up

In this chapter, we've attempted to paint a picture of the interconnected work of concurrent discrete and subscription crowdfunding campaigns for a single nonprofit, Rancho Relaxo, with additional data from social media supplementing the picture of what exactly the work of maintaining the interconnected projects looks like for technical writers and communicators. Rancho Relaxo maintains a steady stream of engagement and interest across the various channels over time, with engagement growing in general or maintaining despite a drop in the overall frequency of content.

Though the scope of the content is substantial, Rancho Relaxo's success and growth during the period studied, with multiple campaigns across each channel bringing in funds to the organization, provides a model for what distributed and interconnecting ongoing crowdfunding can look like for a nonprofit looking to embrace crowdfunding as a driver of ongoing funding. The narrative-driven structure of this content meshes with the overall framing of the GoFundMe platform that the campaigns live on, with personalized narratives providing coalition members with ongoing touch points to trace the progress and impact of the charity over time.

Discussion Questions

1. Rancho Relaxo's campaigns on GoFundMe are ongoing, outside of the original campaign. To what extent do you see this approach mirrored among other charities that currently operate on GoFundMe?
2. Rancho Relaxo's social presence contains a regular stream of updates that bring coalition members into the world of the charity, allowing them to see the progress of the work done while learning the story of the animals rescued and work done through the person of the found, Cimini. To what extent do you see similarities and differences among other nonprofits that leverage subscription-based crowdfunding in addition to social media presence?

References

Alba, D. (2022, June 23). Meta pulls support for tool used to keep misinformation in check. *Bloomberg.com*. www.bloomberg.com/news/articles/2022-06-23/meta-pulls-support-for-tool-used-to-keep-misinformation-in-check

Andersen, S. (n.d.). Tumblr. *Sarah's Scribbles*. Retrieved November 1, 2022, from https://assets.tumblr.com/analytics.html?_v=9f5febfd57a8a649c598d888f2d9e062#https://sarahcandersen.com

Campeau, K., & Thao, Y. (2022). "It makes everything just another story": A mixed methods study of medical storytelling on GoFundMe. *Technical Communication Quarterly*, *32*(1), 33–49. https://doi.org/10.1080/10572252.2022.2047792

Cotroneo, C. (2016, January 14). Woman severely allergic to animals has saved hundreds of them. *The Dodo*. www.thedodo.com/allergic-to-animals-sanctuary-1553719037.html

Dunham, N. (2017, April 27). How a woman with severe pet allergies has saved hundreds of animals—and counting [Magazine]. *People Magazine*. https://people.com/pets/how-a-woman-with-severe-pet-allergies-has-saved-hundreds-of-animals-and-counting/

Edelstein, J. (2016, April 26). Meet the superbackers. They might not wear capes as they soar | by Kickstarter | Kickstarter Magazine | Medium. *Medium.Com*. https://medium.com/kickstarter/meet-the-superbackers-962bf714fc2e

GoFundMe. (2018, December 13). Meet Caitlin. *GoFundMe Stories*. https://medium.com/gofundme-stories/meet-caitlin-4cf1749e31d0

GoFundMe. (2022, April 15). Choosing your goal amount. *GoFundMe Help Center*. https://support.gofundme.com/hc/en-us/articles/4405145410331-Choosing-your-goal-amount

Grice, R. (2017). Experience architecture: Drawing principles from life. In L. Potts & M. J. Salvo (Eds.), *Rhetoric and experience architecture* (pp. 41–56). Parlor Press. https://parlorpress.com/products/rhetoric-and-experience-architecture

Lawler, R. (2022, June 23). Meta reportedly plans to shut down CrowdTangle, its tool that tracks popular social media posts. *The Verge*. www.theverge.com/2022/6/23/23180357/meta-crowdtangle-shut-down-facebook-misinformation-viral-news-tracker

Leeuwe, M. (n.d.). *Mitch Leeuwe*. Retrieved November 1, 2022, from https://mitch-leeuwe.gumroad.com/

Myers, M. (2007). The use of pathos in charity letters: Some notes toward a theory and analysis. *Journal of Technical Writing and Communication, 37*(1), 3–16. https://doi.org/10.2190/2M77-0724-4110-1413

Rancho Relaxo is creating a safer world for animals to live in. (n.d.). Patreon. Retrieved October 31, 2022, from https://www.patreon.com/boochaces

Rancho Relaxo—Rancho Relaxo. (n.d.). Retrieved November 1, 2022, from https://www.ranchorelaxonj.org/

Stewart, C. (2016a, March 16). Help Rancho relaxo expand & rescue, organized by Caitlin Stewart. *Gofundme.com*. www.gofundme.com/f/ranchorelaxo

Stewart, C. (2016b, June 22). Support Rancho Relaxo's expansion. *Gofundme.com*. www.gofundme.com/f/ranchorelaxobarn

Stewart, C. (2022, August 3). Rancho Relaxo needs your help, organized by Caitlin Stewart. *Gofundme.com*. www.gofundme.com/f/zy4cv-rancho-relaxo-needs-your-help

The CrowdTangle Team. (2022). *CrowdTangle*. Facebook. https://apps.crowdtangle.com

The Internal Revenue Service. (2020). *Form 990*. https://apps.irs.gov/pub/epostcard/cor/475164730_201912_990_2021030117773223.pdf

7
SUSTAINING CROWDFUNDING

In our final chapter, we turn to what happens after a given crowdfunding campaign has been successful—what happens next and how does one success translate into serial success in the genre? In answering these questions, we'll relay our case studies from Chapters 5 and 6 as well as our understanding of crowdfunding campaigns as coalitionally powered XAs.

First, we'll cover the fulfillment period and the ways that fulfillment can be leveraged to continue building the connections forged during the funding period of a given campaign before shifting to a discussion of what comes next after a successful campaign. That might be a second campaign on the same platform, a new campaign on a second platform, or a transition out of crowdfunding platforms in general. As part of this discussion, we'll cover the framing and structure of subscription-based crowdfunding, informed by our work in Chapter 6 as well as a few clustered examples in the podcasting space.

Finally, we'll close the chapter and the book by making the case that sustainable crowdfunding projects should be seen and operated as ongoing technical communicator endeavors that leverage a myriad of skills and speak to the past and current challenges of the field, allowing technical writers to build and then maintain relationships with backing coalitions that allow organizations to build sustainable funding streams outside of traditional funding structures.

Fulfilling Fulfillment

The project funding deadline has come and gone, or the funding goal has been met. Now what? Once a project has met all of the stated goals during funding, the campaign then shifts fundraising to fulfillment, with an attendant shift in the frequency and content of updates in many cases. In this section, we'll discuss what

DOI: 10.4324/9781003308966-7

this shift looks like from both a platform-mandated level of content and as an XA while concurrently looking at the options provided to campaigns to carry out this work within their existing platforms and beyond.

Once a campaign has reached its conclusion, the initial question for many teams is how to coordinate the work of fulfillment while providing updates to backers along the way. At purely the platform level, there are often some constraints and expectations for what this process looks like. Kickstarter states that campaigns are expected to provide updates on a monthly basis at the minimum once funding is finished (*What Should I Post an Update about and How Often?*, n.d.), and Indiegogo mirrors that same requirement (*Campaign Updates Best Practices FAQ*, n.d.). Depending on the scope, scale, and timeline for a project, this could mean a handful of updates, or it could be years of updates in the case of extremely long-legged campaigns with ongoing development timelines. The example of Yacht Club Games from Chapter 3 codes to mind, with their multi-year saga of updates for the title *Shovel Knight* that was tied to the fairly ambitious stretch goals they offered for their campaigns.

When it comes to the XA of the campaign and the fulfillment period, technical writers and campaigns can learn from the examples of our case studies in Chapters 5 and 6 as far as the types of content and length of content that updates contain, but those case studies should not be the only place they look. Any crowdfunding campaign exists in alignment with others in a genre ecology (Spinuzzi & Zachry, 2000) consisting of their campaign and others like it across a given platform. When approaching a campaign's fulfillment, looking to what peers have offered, and the frequency of those offerings is essential to understanding expectations from your coalition. For a project like Lady Tarot Cards, that may mean regular updates on art and production as milestones are met, with discussions on the why, when, and how of those processes rewarding backers with mundane details and information on the project's coming to life. As seen in Lady Tarot Cards, STEAM Chasers, and Rancho Relaxo, these updates function best when they connect to the ongoing narrative for a given campaign set up by the initial funding period.

In addition to looking at peers, another simple step that campaigns and their technical writers should consider is simply looking at the processes and steps needed to go from funding to reality. What are the individual bits of information that can be shared, documented, and discussed along the way? Rancho Relaxo's campaigns provide a window into how a mundane process of bidding and then closing on a real estate purchase can be translated into blow-by-blow updates on submissions and decisions, supplemented with imagery and descriptions of the emotions and reactions to those involved. In doing so, campaigns should heed Grice's (2017) advice to focus on the emotional, underscoring those strands that motivated the backing coalition to fund the campaign in the first place. Crowdfunding can be seen through the lens of affect, with both the funding process and fulfillment serving as emotionally fulfilling and engaging experiences for backers (Pope, 2017).

When providing fulfillment updates, there is the concurrent question of access and exclusivity. Some campaigns, such as Lady Tarot Cards, provided a handful of updates that were exclusive to Kickstarter with the majority of their art updates coming via the @Nova_Mali Twitter feed. Other campaigns foreground the exclusivity of their updates, with platforms like Patreon underscoring that exclusivity via paywalls and tiers of access to content.

In addition to simply making content exclusive to the crowdfunding platform, campaigns can also opt to make content exclusive to backers on certain platforms such as Kickstarter and Patreon. For example, Nick Seluk (*The Awkward Yeti*, n.d.), an openly diagnosed attention deficit/hyperactivity disorder (ADHD) comics creator and artist (Peter, 2020), has raised upward of $1 million across nine successful Kickstarter campaigns, but virtually all of the campaigns and their associated updates are flagged "Backers only" on Kickstarter, creating an exclusivity of process and information that underscores the necessity of backing the campaign to gain access to the mundane information on the process as a given deliverable goes from planning to production. This type of backer-only access can increase the desire of coalition members to back a given campaign, but campaigns must weigh the tradeoffs in terms of the overall XA of the campaign writ large on various channels that they maintain.

In addition to platform-specific content, the example of Rancho Relaxo from Chapter 6 demonstrates the necessity of maintaining an architecture of engagement with a coalition of backers and potential backers outside of a given crowdfunding campaign's updates and emails. The overall coalition that has been attracted to a given creator or campaign may not fully engage with any one campaign. As noted in Chapter 4, the general conversion rate of a high-quality mailing list is often only 2.5–5%. As Walton et al. (2019) remind us, coalitions are no monolithic, but instead coalesce around a given cause despite differences (p. 55). Just because your coalition has found your organization doesn't mean that they'll be motivated equally to back every project and campaign that you pitch. In addition to their financial situations that will change over time, they simply may not all be interested in the same types of projects and campaigns. With that said, maintaining a connection with your larger potential backing coalition across social media allows you to leverage their likes, comments, shares, and general interest in your campaign to further your organic reach. As noted by Rancho Relaxo in several updates, even those that share a link or campaign contribute to the overall mission, and in the case of social media algorithms, contribute to the visibility of a given campaign.

Beyond the work of documenting fulfillment, writers and teams must negotiate the logistics of fulfillment when backers are signed up for physical or electronic deliverables (or even experiential ones). InDemand from Indiegogo offers one solution to campaigns, with Backerkit featuring regularly across the campaigns of Lady Tarot Cards and STEAM Chasers from Chapter 5, and Patreon offering fulfillment-level services at the highest level of creator account (as noted in Chapter 3). Though the logistics of fulfillment are beyond the scope of this text, technical writers should be aware that fulfillment services and systems provide yet another channel to both leverage and manage in maintaining an ongoing experience for backers and coalition members.

The Post-campaign Transition

Once a campaign reaches the end of its fulfillment, the question arises: where to go from here? As in the case from Chapters 5 and 6, the option to continue with a subsequent campaign is always available. As noted in Chapter 1, research attests that follow-up campaigns have markedly better rates of success than first campaigns thanks to the social capital and demonstrable success the first campaign provides to a given backing coalition (Butticè et al., 2017). With that said, not all campaigns are as successful as those that precede them: STEAM Chasers' second campaign had less backers than the first campaign before numbers rebounded in the first campaign, and the third Lady Tarot Cards campaign came in markedly below the high bar set by the second campaign in the series. Caveats aside, each of these campaigns was successful, and the coalition continued to show up and provide support across these campaigns. And, these campaigns are not alone in their serial success. Creators like Monte Cook Games have raised millions of dollars over 20+ campaigns on Kickstarter and Backerkit while relying on the same general format and formula (*Homepage*, n.d.). A follow-up campaign is often a great follow-through (Gallagher & Salfen, 2015), but if too much time passes between the first campaign and subsequent campaigns, the serial campaign effect can disappear (Butticè et al., 2017).

In addition, however, to a follow-through campaign, there is the option to provide an off-ramp from crowdfunding to a bespoke platform, as in the case of Lady Tarot Card's hosting preorders for multiple follow-up volume to their "classics . . . but make it gay" campaign via their Nova and Mali website (Nova and Mali, n.d.). While this move to a custom platform may not always make sense, once a durable coalition has been gained around a given organization, it can make sense to move away from the platform-specific processing fees associated with crowdfunding that come in addition to payment processing fees that all creators have to deal with across payment platforms.

Shifting from External to Internal Data

While looking ahead to a new campaign, one important shift can and should happen is a turn from looking solely at competitors and peers in the genre ecology. Once a campaign has gained funding, and especially once it is well into the fulfillment process, the success of the campaign and its deliverables becomes a primary source of data for planning and crafting future projects and updates. Looking to peers helps calibrate an initial effort, but once you're getting feedback from your coalition via the rate of comments, likes, and visits to subsequent content you produce, you can and should start to document the specific deliverables and messages that your campaign has created and maintained that are the most engaging to your backing coalition. This collection will often start before launch during the creation of your architecture of engagement, but once you're well into the fulfillment process and planning a secondary campaign, you can leverage the data from your own project with confidence, knowing that the project resulted in a successful campaign on its own.

One final option to consider when looking at switching from one campaign to another is the move to another platform or to another type of crowdfunding, such as moving from a discrete campaign to a subscription campaign (as in the case of Rancho Relaxo). Shifts in platform should be approached with caution, especially when a given platform's interface activism is particularly favorable to your organization or campaigns. For example, Backerkit began pitching itself as an all-inclusive destination for crowdfunding campaigns by offering campaign fundraising and fulfillment in 2022. Of the case studies mentioned briefly in this text, both *Coyote & Crow* and Monte Cooke Games made the transition to the Backerkit space during that timeframe, and each campaign's subsequent earnings were markedly lower on the new platform when compared to Kickstarter. *Coyote & Crow* went from over $1 million in funding from over 16,000 backers on Kickstarter (Alexander, 2021) to pulling in just over $172,000 from 2,417 backers in their first Backerkit campaign (Coyote & Crow Games, n.d.). Monte Cooke Games' last Kickstarter campaign, *Old Gods of Appalachia Roleplaying Game*, brought in over $2 million from over 15,000 backers (Monte Cook Games, 2022), and their first Backerkit campaign, *The Weird*, brought in just over $400,000 from just over 4,000 backers (Monte Cook Games, n.d.). As of this writing, the sample size of campaigns that have transitioned to Backerkit is fairly small, and the platform is relatively new to hosting funding campaigns, but the stark drop across each campaign does speak to the potential for less organic reach from a platform and its interface activism when making a switch from one crowdfunding site to another.

Shifting to Subscription

Having flagged the potential risks of a platform switch, I'd like to take a moment to discuss the strategy behind switching to subscription-based fundraising or supplementing existing fundraising campaigns with a discrete ongoing subscription campaign. Examples like Rancho Relaxo's Patreon campaign are common across several different types of creators and organizations, with the ongoing Patreon funding providing a steady revenue of funding while punctuated campaigns target specific projects that necessitate separate funding. For example, Nick Seluk, mentioned earlier in the chapter, also manages a Patreon campaign with 568 patrons as of this writing, bringing in $3,022 per month according to the publicly available information on the Patreon page for the creator (Seluk, n.d.). Seluk's use of Patreon is not unique among artists and creators, with countless webcomics following the same strategy to provide ongoing revenue.

When making the leap to subscription-based crowdfunding, a central question becomes what exactly can be leveraged to motivate your coalition members to follow you into an ongoing subscription-based funding relationship. With a discrete campaign, there is a singular purpose and specific scope and scale to funding, but with subscription-based content, the expectation is perpetual content for paying coalition members. How this question is addressed can vary among creators and genres. As with the larger crowdfunding landscape, understanding the genre ecology created by peers is an important first step to placing your own offerings within the general landscape. For our purposes, I'd like to share a couple of examples from a relatively small niche of creators: guitar and effects pedal podcasts to demonstrate how creators provide a range of content that often has a healthy amount of overlap in a given niche.

Subscription Example: Guitar and Effects Pedal Podcasting & YouTube Channels

The guitar and effects pedal podcast and YouTube channel world is a relatively specific niche that hosts a wide variety of content and creators. Shows range from the British-based *Guitar Nerds* to long-running company-affiliated shows like the *Chasing Tone Podcast (Wampler, et al., n.d.)* associated with Wampler Pedals, to shows associated with content creators such as *Tone Mob (Wyland, n.d.)*, *Get Offset (Harris & Rinard, n.d.)*, *60 Cycle Hum (Burke & Rowe, n.d.)*, and *Working Class Music (Mays et al., n.d.)*. Though the music industry has a reputation for being a boy's club (Snapes, 2020), the guitar podcast and YouTube channel space on Patreon hosts a variety of creators, including women-lead shows like *Get Offset* and shows and channels with creators from historically marginalized backgrounds, such as *Working Classic Music, 60 Cycle Hum*, and *Chasing Tone*. Within this narrow slice of content creators on Patreon, we can get a sense of the variety and scope of paywall-linked offerings and what they provide to subscribers.

The guitar and effects podcasts and channels range from 198 to 33 subscribers across their Patreon accounts, with earnings ranging from $1,006 to $140 on the three shows that make their earnings public on the platform. The different shows offer a range of content that is exclusive to Patreon subscribers, in addition to the backer-only updates and conversations that are available via that platform. Virtually all shows provide backers with an on-the-air shout-out for an initial backing of Patreon, with higher tiers of backing ("executive producer" and other monikers) coming with personalized shout-outs on every episode of the main show. A single show, *60 Cycle Hum*, goes so far as to offer a backers-only private Facebook group backers at the Inner Circle level. Virtually all Patreon campaigns also offer additional content in their middle-range tiers, with some offering the primary show without advertisements to patrons, and some shows offering behind-the-scenes content or the chance to help share the direction of a given episode. Finally, several shows provide merchandise access and random merchandise gifts to backers who provide funding beyond the basic funding tiers.

In the case of the guitar and effects shows, we see a continuation of some of the same patterns found in the case studies in Chapters 5 and 6. Backers are enticed with access to additional content, exclusive content, and additional mundane information and updates beyond what is publicly available. Much like social media content creation (outside YouTube and paying platforms), podcasts are generally not monetized for creators historically, so Patreon, merchandise, and advertising placements are a primary driver of revenue for the shows (in addition to any content marketing role a given show may play, as in the case of the company-sponsored *Chasing Tone Podcast*). As of fall 2022, YouTube has expanded into paid ad placement on podcasts (in addition to show-specific advertisements and placements) (Dang, 2022), but outside of subscription-based revenue, the podcast industry does not receive compensation from hosting services that they provide content to such as Apple Podcasts, though YouTube-based video offerings can monetize their content.

Using the example of the guitar and effects shows, we can recognize that genre exceptions create a thorough line of extra content and bonus episodes, with shows differentiating from each other by offering additional perks that align with the brand and content of a given creative team.

XAs in these spaces are particularly important in regard to sustainability from the content creation team, as these subscription-based content streams have no discrete ending period. When a given organization or creator opts to create a subscription-based crowdfunding offering, the tiers and content have to be understood as being something more than the burst of content and curated updates that might come with a discrete campaign. The subscription-based content has to be calibrated as a part of an overall ongoing content workflow if it is to be maintained.

Technical writers that take part in these types of campaigns should be aware of this persistent commitment and make sure that their organizations are prepared for the time and effort that will be needed to make the subscription-based content a regular part of the organization. In some cases like Rancho Relaxo's Patreon from Chapter 5, the content may simply be a slice of additional content that might otherwise show up on another channel like Instagram or Facebook. In the case of the guitar and effects shows mentioned in this chapter, it might be additional episodic content or behind-the-scenes footage. Some of these asks are greater than others. Additional photographs and narratives are not the same commitment as filming and editing additional hour-long episodes of a show, and much like the dangers of stretch goals, subscription-based content needs to be understood through the lens of risk versus reward for a given creator or organization.

Finally, as noted in several chapters, subscription-based crowdfunding campaign platforms tend to not heavily feature any sort of findability mechanic, and there is relatively little to no interface activism that allows creators to be found on the platform by new users. Instead, a subscription-based crowdfunding campaign is entirely reliant on the architecture of engagement a given campaign has created through their various content-creation channels and social media channels. In the case of Rancho Relaxo, there may be some crossover where a discrete campaign can be leveraged to mention the ongoing subscription-based campaign, but outside of those cases, a subscription-based campaign must rely on an existing coalition and existing communication channels that motivate coalition members to sign up for additional access or the chance to offer additional support.

Sustainable Crowdfunding as Technical Communication

I'd like to close our discussions in this book by framing crowdfunding, and specifically sustainable crowdfunding, as fundamentally operating as ongoing technical communication projects that leverage the breadth and depth of skills that a technical communicator to build compelling user experiences.

In many ways, crowdfunding sits at a nexus of sites and skills that technical communicators and technical writers thrive at, as these campaigns involve the coordination of social media content, website content, written documentation and process workflows, editing, and XA while providing practitioners in the field with an avenue to carry out the work of social justice by bringing funding and attention to organizations and creators that have been historically marginalized by traditional funding structures.

As we've seen across our array of crowdfunding case studies, crowdfunding campaigns at their core involve a lot of writing, design, and production, and much of that content creation does the work of technical writing. Lady Tarot Cards, the STEAM Chasers, and Rancho Relaxo all leverage their pitches as well as their updates of their campaigns to share the mundane details of the process as well as the specific technical details of the fulfillment and creation of a given campaign. Editing, document layout, proof production, and review, all of these processes feature heavily in the work of our discrete cases, and each of these processes happens to be areas of strength in technical and professional writing programs. As Clegg et al., 2021 note in their survey of programmatic outcomes in technical and professional communication programs, rhetoric, writing, design, editing, project management, all feature regularly in the outcomes of technical and professional communication programs, and these same skill sets align with the scope and breadth of crowdfunding, especially sustainable crowdfunding work.

As research in technical and professional communication on crowdfunding can also attest, the breadth and scope of crowdfunding and research on it also hold a great deal of potential for further exploration by the field. As Vealey and Gerding (2016) and Gerding and Vealey (2017) note in their work on crowdfunding, the genre can and should be seen as a site of civic entrepreneurship and engagement, allowing technical communicators to work toward solving wicked problems while engaging with communities in that same process. Ashley Rose Mehlenbacher (2017, 2019) also demonstrates the parallels that crowdfunding has with traditional technical communication genres like a proposal and grant writing, with a particular window into how crowdfunding can support science communication in online spaces. Stephen Carradini and Carolin Fleischmann (2022) demonstrate how crowdfunding can be seen as a stand-alone genre itself, with opportunities to explore the ways that multi-modality and differential presentations of a given pitch impact success, and Campeau and Thao (2022)'s work allows us to see crowdfunding as citizen-created technical writing with important ethical implications for society. The scope and breadth of this research, and its alignment with traditional areas of strength and new horizons in technical communication, show us the breadth and scope of potential engagements between crowdfunding and the wider field of technical and professional communication.

Finally, and most importantly, with the ever-growing emphasis on social justice as the new ethic of technical communication (Haas, 2019), sustainable crowdfunding provides us with a crucial genre that arose historically in response to and at times in rejection of traditional funding mechanisms and structures. Campaigns like the STEAM Chasers demonstrate for us how crowdfunding can be used as vehicles for the type of cultural empowerment among historically marginalized populations found in Natasha Jone's (2017) work with black entrepreneurs.

Working through the framework of Walton et al.' (2019) 4 R's of recognize, reveal, reject, and replace, crowdfunding provides us a platform to go about this work by building and then engaging with coalitions of backers along the way. Crowdfunding's selection process allows us a way to facilitate the type of consultation with others and humbling of our own ideas that Walton, Moore, and Jones (p. 143) advocate for, as campaigns exist in service to and in concert with their backing coalition.

Looking ahead to the future of crowdfunding and technical communication and writing, much work remains to be done as the genre continues to evolve over time with the increased presence of subscription-based crowdfunding and even the supplemental work of tip-jar-style crowdfunding. In a world of social media production and content creation with very little tangible benefits for creators, nonprofits, and organizations, crowdfunding provides alternative sources of funding and models for content curation. In many ways, sustainable crowdfunding stands alongside other methods of production covered by recent scholarship, including open game development (Thominet, 2020), with Larian Studios from Chapter 2 transitioning from crowdfunding to open development after the success of their third crowdfunding campaign.

Crowdfunding platform and approaches come with their own ethical challenges and issues, but the fundamental rejection of the traditional gatekeeping mechanisms for charity and start-up funding hold incredible potential for breaking down historical barriers across industries. While this book has attempted to map out what best practices look like across discrete and interconnected campaigns, the crowdfunding genre is vast, and the diversity of sites and campaigns, as well as evolving practices and sub-genres, mean that work on the subject is still only beginning within the field.

Wrapping Up

In this chapter, and this book, we've covered the practice of sustainable crowdfunding. In this final chapter, we've turned specifically to look at the work that happens after a campaign comes to the end of the funding process, building off the findings of our selected case studies while also exploring the work of subscription-based crowdfunding as a supplement or alternative to discrete campaigns.

As we've discussed in the closing paragraphs of this chapter, crowdfunding, and especially sustainable crowdfunding, can and should be seen as a technical writing genre and project, with crowdfunding requiring the coordination of multiple specialties and skill sets among technical communicators, while offering a chance to socially just projects that reject the historical marginalization of many groups and cultures.

Though not a perfect genre, crowdfunding is an exciting and continuously developing genre that can and should be a focus of technical and professional practice and research for years to come.

Discussion Questions

1. What role does fulfillment play in the pitch of currently active campaigns on crowdfunding platforms? How do the campaigns talk about what comes next and what backers will be able to learn during that process?
2. Choose a niche of your choice, and research subscription-based crowdfunding offerings in that niche. What are the overlapping offerings among creators in the area? How do creators differentiate themselves from each other in that same space?

References

Alexander, C. (2021, March 2). Coyote & Crow the role playing game. *Kickstarter*. www.kickstarter.com/projects/connoralexander/coyote-and-crow

Burke, R., & Rowe, S. (n.d.). 60 cycle hum is creating a podcast. *Patreon*. Retrieved November 1, 2022, from www.patreon.com/60CycleHumCast

Butticè, V., Colombo, M. G., & Wright, M. (2017). Serial crowdfunding, social capital, and project success. *Entrepreneurship Theory and Practice*, *41*(2), 183–207. https://doi.org/10.1111/etap.12271

Campaign Updates Best Practices FAQ. (n.d.). *Indiegogo Help Center*. Retrieved October 31, 2022, from https://support.indiegogo.com/hc/en-us/articles/115010524888-Campaign-Updates-Best-Practices-FAQ

Campeau, K., & Thao, Y. (2022). "It makes everything just another story": A mixed methods study of medical storytelling on GoFundMe. *Technical Communication Quarterly*, *32*(1), 33–49. https://doi.org/10.1080/10572252.2022.2047792

Carradini, S., & Fleischmann, C. (2022). The effects of multimodal elements on success in Kickstarter crowdfunding campaigns. *Journal of Business and Technical Communication*, *37*(10), 1–27. https://doi.org/10.1177/10506519221121699

Clegg, G., Lauer, J., Phelps, J., & Melonçon, L. (2021). Programmatic outcomes in undergraduate technical and professional communication programs. *Technical Communication Quarterly*, *30*(1), 19–33. https://doi.org/10.1080/10572252.2020.1774662

Coyote & Crow Games. (n.d.). Coyote & Crow: Stories of the free lands. *BackerKit*. Retrieved November 1, 2022, from www.backerkit.com/c/connor-alexander/coyote-and-crow-stories-of-the-free-lands

Dang, S. (2022, October 17). YouTube expands audio and podcast advertising for brands. *Reuters*. www.reuters.com/technology/youtube-expands-audio-podcast-advertising-brands-2022-10-17/

Gallagher, D., & Salfen, J. (2015, March 24). By the numbers: When creators return to Kickstarter. *Kickstarter News Archive*. www.kickstarter.com/blog/by-the-numbers-when-creators-return-to-kickstarter

Gerding, J. M., & Vealey, K. P. (2017). When is a solution not a solution? Wicked problems, hybrid solutions, and the rhetoric of civic entrepreneurship. *Journal of Business and Technical Communication*, *31*(3), 290–318. https://doi.org/10.1177/1050651917695538

Grice, R. (2017). Experience architecture: Drawing principles from life. In L. Potts & M. J. Salvo (Eds.), *Rhetoric and experience architecture* (pp. 41–56). Parlor Press. https://parlorpress.com/products/rhetoric-and-experience-architecture

Haas, A. M. (2019). When apathy is unacceptable and empathy is not enough: Social justice is the new ethic for TPC. In *Technical communication after the social justice turn*. Routledge.

Harris, E., & Rinard, A. (n.d.). Get offset is creating a podcast. *Patreon*. Retrieved November 1, 2022, from www.patreon.com/getoffset

Homepage. (n.d.). *Monte Cook Games*. Retrieved November 1, 2022, from www.montecookgames.com/

Jones, N. (2017). Rhetorical narratives of Black entrepreneurs: The business of race, agency, and cultural empowerment. *Journal of Business and Technical Communication*, *31*(3), 319–349. https://journals.sagepub.com/doi/full/10.1177/1050651917695540

Mays, J., Bailey, T., Cook, X., & Crawford, N. (n.d.). Working class music is creating music gear review/comparison videos on guitars, pedals, & more! *Patreon*. Retrieved November 1, 2022, from www.patreon.com/WCMshow

Mehlenbacher, A. R. (2017). Crowdfunding science: Exigencies and strategies in an emerging genre of science communication. *Technical Communication Quarterly*, *26*(2), 127–144. https://doi.org/10.1080/10572252.2017.1287361

Mehlenbacher, A. R. (2019). *Science communication online: Engaging experts and publics on the internet*. The Ohio State University Press. https://ohiostatepress.org/books/titles/9780814213988.html

Monte Cook Games. (2022, April 12). Old gods of appalachia roleplaying game. *Kickstarter*. www.kickstarter.com/projects/montecookgames/old-gods-of-appalachia-roleplaying-game

Monte Cook Games. (n.d.). The weird. *BackerKit*. Retrieved November 1, 2022, from www.backerkit.com/c/monte-cook-games/the-weird

Nova and Mali. (n.d.). Nova and Mali: Make it gay. *Nova and Mali*. Retrieved September 28, 2022, from www.novaandmali.com

Peter. (2020, September 9). Finding your funny w/ comic creator Nick Seluk. *Faster Than Normal*. www.fasterthannormal.com/finding-your-funny-w-comic-creator-nick-seluk/

Pope, A. R. (2017). Bloodstained, unpacking the affect of a Kickstarter success—present tense. *Present Tense: A Journal of Rhetoric in Society*, 2(6). www.presenttensejournal.org/volume-6/bloodstained-unpacking-the-affect-of-a-kickstarter-success/

Seluk, N. (n.d.). The Awkward Yeti is creating comics and games. *Patreon*. Retrieved October 21, 2022, from www.patreon.com/theawkwardyeti

Snapes, L. (2020, January 23). Still a boys' club: Don't fall for the hype that the music industry has changed. *The Guardian*. www.theguardian.com/music/2020/jan/23/boys-club-2020s-music-awards-superficial-change-grammys

Spinuzzi, C., & Zachry, M. (2000). Genre ecologies: An open-system approach to understanding and constructing documentation. *ACM Journal of Computer Documentation*, 24(3), 169–181. https://doi.org/10.1145/344599.344646

The Awkward Yeti. (n.d.). Retrieved October 31, 2022, from https://theawkwardyeti.com/

Thominet, L. (2020). Open video game development and participatory design. *Technical Communication Quarterly*, 30(4), 359–374. https://doi.org/10.1080/10572252.2020.1866679

Vealey, K. P., & Gerding, J. M. (2016). Rhetorical work in crowd-based entrepreneurship: Lessons learned from teaching crowdfunding as an emerging site of professional and technical communication. *IEEE Transactions on Professional Communication*, 59(4), 407–427. https://doi.org/10.1109/TPC.2016.2614742

Walton, R., Moore, K. R., & Jones, N. N. (2019). *Technical communication after the social justice turn: Building coalitions for action*. Routledge.

Wampler, B., Wyland, B., & Oliver, R. (n.d.). Chasing tone podcast is creating exclusive content for dedicated chasing tone podcast fans. *Patreon*. Retrieved November 1, 2022, from https://www.patreon.com/chasingtonepodcast

What Should I Post an Update about and How Often? (n.d.). *Kickstarter Support*. Retrieved October 31, 2022, from https://help.kickstarter.com/hc/en-us/articles/360013134673-What-should-I-post-an-update-about-and-how-often-

Wyland, B. (n.d.). The tone mob podcast is creating podcasts, community, nonsense, videos, pizza cravings. *Patreon*. Retrieved November 1, 2022, from https://www.patreon.com/tonemob

INDEX

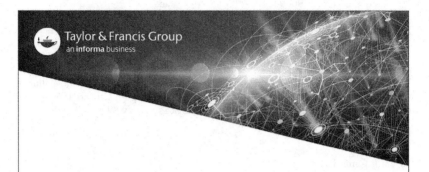

Taylor & Francis Group
an **informa** business

Taylor & Francis eBooks

www.taylorfrancis.com

A single destination for eBooks from Taylor & Francis
with increased functionality and an improved user
experience to meet the needs of our customers.

90,000+ eBooks of award-winning academic content in
Humanities, Social Science, Science, Technology, Engineering,
and Medical written by a global network of editors and authors.

TAYLOR & FRANCIS EBOOKS OFFERS:

A streamlined
experience for
our library
customers

A single point
of discovery
for all of our
eBook content

Improved
search and
discovery of
content at both
book and
chapter level

REQUEST A FREE TRIAL
support@taylorfrancis.com

Printed in the United States
by Baker & Taylor Publisher Services